J. M. SYNGE

1871–1909

THE MACMILLAN COMPANY
NEW YORK · CHICAGO
DALLAS · ATLANTA · SAN FRANCISCO
LONDON · MANILA
IN CANADA
BRETT-MACMILLAN LTD.
GALT, ONTARIO

J.M.SYNGE

❧ 1871–1909 ❧

By DAVID H. GREENE
AND
EDWARD M. STEPHENS

THE MACMILLAN COMPANY
NEW YORK 1959

First Printing

Library of Congress catalog card number: 59-7443

The Macmillan Company, New York
Brett-Macmillan Ltd., Galt, Ontario

Printed in the United States of America

ACKNOWLEDGMENTS

Permission to quote copyrighted material is acknowledged to publishers and authors as follows: George Allen & Unwin, Ltd.—*The Aran Islands* by J. M. Synge, *Plays by John M. Synge, In Wicklow, West Kerry and Connemara* by J. M. Synge; Appleton-Century-Crofts, Inc.—*Hail and Farewell* by George Moore, copyright, 1911, 1912, 1925, by D. Appleton and Company; Beacon Press Inc.—*Dialogues of Alfred North Whitehead, as Recorded by Lucien Price*; William Collins Sons & Co. Ltd.—*Cities and Sea-Coasts and Islands* by Arthur Symons (1918); Harcourt, Brace and Company—*The Fays of the Abbey Theatre* by W. G. Fay and Catherine Carswell, copyright, 1935, by Harcourt, Brace and Company; Rupert Hart-Davis Limited—*The Letters of W. B. Yeats* edited by Allan Wade (1955); Macmillan & Co. Ltd.—*Essays* by W. B. Yeats (1924), *Dramatis Personae* by W. B. Yeats (1936); The Macmillan Company—*The Letters of W. B. Yeats* edited by Allan Wade, copyright, 1953, 1954, by Anne Butler Yeats, *Essays* by W. B. Yeats, copyright, 1912, 1918, by The Macmillan Company; *Dramatis Personae* by W. B. Yeats, copyright, 1936, by The Macmillan Company; Putnam & Company, Ltd.—*Our Irish Theatre* by Lady Gregory (1913); Random House Inc.—*The Complete Works of John M. Synge*, copyright, 1904, 1905, 1907, by J. M. Synge, 1909 by John Quinn, 1910, 1936, by Edward Synge and Francis Edmund Stephens, 1911 by L. F. Bassett, copyright, 1935, by The Modern Library Inc.; Rich and Cowan—*The Fays of the Abbey Theatre* by W. G. Fay and Catherine Carswell (1935); The Talbot Press Limited—*Prose, Poems and Parodies of Percy French* (1935).

Introduction

Not the least lamentable aspect of Synge's career of frustration, belated achievement and early death is the fact that unlike his fellow Irishmen George Moore, W. B. Yeats and James Joyce he has had to wait for nearly half a century for his biography to be written. At his death in 1909 all his papers passed into the possession of his brother Edward Synge and were not made available to anyone wishing to write about him. Maurice Bourgeois' *John Millington Synge and the Irish Theatre*, published in 1913, was thus written under difficulties few biographers would willingly contend with and has perforce been a unique if meager source of information.

In 1939 custodianship of Synge's papers passed to a nephew, Edward M. Stephens. Edward Stephens had grown up literally under the same roof as Synge and had been influenced by his quiet iconoclasm. He and his cousin Edward Hutchinson Synge were in college at the time of J. M. Synge's death and to them he left his estate. From 1930, Edward Stephens had been collecting material and writing his recollections of his uncle. After he acquired the vital documents he started work on a biography of Synge which occupied whatever time a busy career as barrister and civil servant allowed him.

When my wife and I met the Stephenses in Dublin in 1939, I was writing a Harvard doctoral dissertation on Synge. Edward Stephens and his brother Frank had vivid memories of their uncle and shared them with me. Edward and I discussed each other's work. I subsequently sent him copies of articles on Synge which I had written, transcripts of some of Synge's letters which had passed into American collections, and other information. He sent me copies of three articles on Synge which he had published and kept me informed about the progress of his biography.

In 1953, after several publishers had read his manuscript, Edward asked me if I would be willing to collaborate with him. He had known Synge personally, his memories were profound, and he was an excellent narrator. But I suspect he felt too keenly his obligations as a member of one of Ireland's historic families, for his manuscript swelled to nearly three quarters of a million words and, in places at least, the story of J. M. Synge tended to be obscured by that of the Synge family. Because he had lived so long with the material and was himself a part of it I feared that it would be difficult for him to accept the kind of compromises necessary for effective collaboration.

In March of 1955 Edward Stephens died suddenly of a heart attack. His wife Lilo Stephens then suggested that I write a biography of Synge, arranged for my having access to Synge's papers, and gave me permission to use her husband's manuscript and materials, stipulating only that he receive credit of co-authorship. I agreed to this on the understanding that I would have complete freedom in writing the book. Through the help of a generous grant from the Rockefeller Foundation and a sabbatical leave from New York University I went to Ireland in September of 1955.

The collection of documents which Synge himself had saved is sizeable when one considers that his career was relatively short. In addition to his diaries, correspondence, and the manuscripts of his published work, there are unpublished works, various papers relating to the management of the Abbey Theatre, and more than forty notebooks, most of them of a size which he could carry in his pocket. In addition to these primary sources I have made use of Edward Stephens' manuscript, his many notes, and the materials he assembled over the years, such as the valuable collection of Synge's letters to Molly Allgood (Marie O'Neill), excerpts from the diaries and correspondence of Synge's mother and brothers and other family records. I have also depended on Edward's descriptions of places in Dublin and Wicklow which he knew intimately and remembered as they were in Synge's lifetime. He and his brother Frank were closer to Synge than any other members of the family. His knowledge and insight, his skill at sifting evidence derived from his years of legal experience, his understanding of Synge's genius and his devotion to his uncle's memory enabled him to assemble a record which would not have been possible for anyone else to do.

But telling the story of Synge's life has been my responsibility. The interpretations and conclusions in this book, and the actual writing, are my own. I am sure that my collaborator would have endorsed a good deal that I have written, but I am equally sure that he would not have agreed with some of my judgements. I can only say that in producing a book quite different from the one Edward Stephens projected I have used the same freedom any biographer would have considered essential.

Lilo Stephens' part in this undertaking and my indebtedness to her are something I cannot adequately spell out here. At her dinner table I met some of the surviving relatives of Synge and many other people who helped me. She and I talked constantly about Synge when we were not arguing about Irish politics or climbing over stone walls to explore ancient Irish churches or historic monuments of the Bronze Age. When the actual dimensions of my task became apparent she obtained permission for me to take all of the necessary documents back to the United States so that I could finish the writing at home.

It would be impossible to list all the people who have contributed to the making of this book, but I would like to express my gratitude to those whose help was essential. To those who gave information to Edward Stephens, whose identities I am not in all instances certain of, I extend thanks on his behalf as well as my own. I must mention also the people I talked to in 1939, who had known Synge and who were no longer alive when I started to write his biography— Molly Allgood and her sister Sara Allgood, W. G. Fay, and Synge's brother, the Reverend Samuel Synge. Miss Pegeen Mair gave me information about her mother Molly Allgood and allowed me to copy a large number of letters in her possession which Synge had written to her mother. Mr. Gerard Fay let me read the unfinished manuscript of a book about his father Frank Fay and his uncle W. G. Fay of the Abbey Theatre and numerous letters and documents in his possession. Mrs. W. B. Yeats loaned me letters among her husband's papers and talked to me about his relations with Synge. Mr. James Healy allowed me to copy letters of Synge in his possession. Professor Richard Ellmann loaned me his transcripts of Yeats' letters to Lady Gregory, doubly valuable because he had learned to read Yeats' handwriting.

To my student James Riley, who was killed in an automobile accident in Dublin before he could finish his doctoral dissertation on Synge, I am grateful both for his help and for the memory of the hours we spent together in New York and in Dublin. To the people of Aran, whom I stayed with first in the dead of winter and returned to in the summer when the seas were more beneficent, I am grateful and mention two in particular—Mrs. Bridget Johnstone-Hernon of Inishmore and Mrs. Michael Faherty of Inishmaan, the daughter of Synge's friend John McDonough. Synge's friends R. I. Best and Jack Yeats have both given me an impression of the man as he actually was. Miss Honor Betson, agent of the Synge estate, has been a constant source of help. My colleague Professor William M. Gibson read my manuscript and gave me valuable comments. My wife, Catherine Greene, has read every line as it has been written and rewritten and made concrete suggestions for its improvement. My editor, Cecil Scott, has been patient with me and skillful. Others, whose help has been peripheral but no less real and appreciated, are Miss Joan Allgood, Professor Douglas Bush, Mr. Ernest Blythe, Professor Oscar Cargill, Mr. and Mrs. Jack Carney, Mr. Edward F. D'Arms, Mr. Joseph Hone, Mr. Francis MacManus, Mr. John Marshall, Professor Vivian Mercier, Miss Ria Mooney, Mr. and Mrs. Sean O'Casey, Mrs. Mary Vaughan, and Mr. James Hardon Wright.

In telling the story of Synge's life and of his development as a writer many years after nearly all the people he knew are no longer living, I have had to depend more upon written records than upon living memories. In interpreting those records, however, I have tried to present the facts in such a way that the reader can form his own judgements. Synge once wrote, "the deeds of a man's lifetime are impersonal and concrete, might have been done by anyone, while art is the expression of the abstract beauty of the person." I would assume that the chief thing a biography can do is to record the deeds of a man's lifetime. The interpretations of those "impersonal and concrete" facts will be as many and as varied as the people who study them. It hardly needs saying that to Synge's art itself readers will still go for "the abstract beauty of the person himself."

Upper Montclair, New Jersey   David H. Greene
August 23, 1958

Contents

xi

Illustrations

One

THE SYNGE FAMILY. CHILDHOOD. RELIGIOUS
DOUBTS. IRELAND IN THE PARNELLITE ERA

*You should have had great people in your family, I'm thinking, with
the little, small feet you have, and you with a kind of quality name, the
like of what you'd find on the great powers and potentates of France and
Spain.*

The Synges are supposed to have derived their unique and happy
name from the fact that a member of the family had evoked royal
admiration for his singing in the court of Henry VIII—*cognominatus
quia canonicus fuit,* as the family tradition records it. The history of
the family does not tend to support the legend because the Synges
in later generations ran more to churchmen than to musicians. The
Irish branch of the family produced five bishops, beginning with the
first Synge who came to Ireland in the seventeenth century. The best
known of the bishops was Edward, Archbishop of Tuam, a contemporary of Swift and Berkeley and one of the great churchmen of his
day. He is remembered as a humane and liberal man who preached
a sermon before the Irish House of Commons in 1725 in which he
said that no magistrate had any right to use force against Catholics.[1]
He was also the author of *A Gentleman's Religion*—"a short and easy
draught of Christianity, and the grounds for it, as every man of a
moderate capacity may read without tediousness and understand
without difficulty."

The wealth in the form of vast landholdings which the Synges

1

came to own was not amassed by one of them but by John Hatch, whose father had been agent for Swift's patron, Sir William Temple, and who came to own large estates in Wicklow, Meath and Dublin. John Hatch's house on Harcourt Street, Dublin, is today the well-known private school for boys which W. B. Yeats attended. In 1765 John Hatch married a Synge. Subsequently the union of the two families was consolidated when his two daughters married their first cousins, both Synges and also brothers. Thenceforward the Hatch name was submerged, and the transfusion of wealth made possible the continued importance of the Synges in Irish life. John Hatch's son-in-law Francis Synge built the family seat, Glanmore Castle, on an estate which stretched for ten miles across County Wicklow. But Francis' lifetime marked the high point in the fortunes of the family. His son John, who was to succeed him as master of Glanmore, was a man of many interests, few of them having any application to the development of the estates he inherited. In 1814 John Synge met the famous Swiss educational theorist Johann Heinrich Pestalozzi and became interested in his theories of educating the young upon what would be called progressive lines today. John Synge set up his own printing press, and the books which came from it included *The Relations and Descriptions of Forms According to the Principles of Pestalozzi* and *An Easy Introduction to the Hebrew Language on the Principles of Pestalozzi*. More than that, he put Pestalozzi's principles to work in the school on his own estate.

Most landlords in Ireland organized and financed schools on their estates for the children of their servants and tenants. Opposed to these schools were the "hedge schools," which had flourished in Ireland for generations and which have been the subject of song and story and a vital part of the native tradition. The hedge school-masters had little formal education, but their heads were full of "bog Latin" and revolutionary idealism. They taught in any kind of barn or unused building which happened to be available. Each child brought his sod of turf daily to heat the school, and up to a few years ago in Ireland many an old man explained his inability to write his own name with the words, "I never carried the sod."

The teaching of the estate schools was unwelcome doctrine because in Wicklow, at least, where a revivalist movement within the Protestant Church was strong among the landlords and included

John Synge, the schools were used as an instrument of religious proselytizing. John Synge's own printing press turned out the lesson sheets used in his school. They were half the size of a sheet of newspaper, well printed, and included different arrangements of the alphabet, tables of weights and measures, Scripture, reading and geography, all done according to the principles of Pestalozzi. But John Synge's enlightenment appeared to be confined solely to educational theory, or at least to the welfare of the students, for his unfortunate teacher had a hard time of it. An entry in one of his old account books under the name "John O'Brien" reads, "commenced with me as schoolmaster on the 1st of May, 1833, at £1 annum, to have a house and an acre of ground at Tiglin and grass for a cow in the same place."

Glanmore was one of those elaborate houses built vaguely to resemble a castle which the gentry of the nineteenth century were fond of erecting. It fell on evil days after the death of "Pestalozzi John" in 1845. In 1850 it was put up for auction under the terms of the Encumbered Estates Act of 1848 and bought by Francis Synge, the son of Pestalozzi John, who would normally have inherited it if his father had been solvent. Glanmore Castle stood until well into the twentieth century when it was finally torn down for salvage. In its later years it became a symbol, of which Ireland had many, of the decline and decay of a once proud class.

J. M. Synge's mother, who was to survive his father by thirty-six years, was the daughter of Robert Traill, the Protestant rector of Schull in County Cork. Robert Traill was born in County Antrim, one of the six counties which form modern Ulster, and his religious convictions had been moulded in the dour Protestant atmosphere of the north, and later developed under the influence of the evangelical movement of the Protestant church. The north of Ireland, which has seen the clash of Protestant and Catholic for centuries, has always produced extremists like Robert Traill. His zeal was so intense that it apparently stood in the way of his ecclesiastical advancement, for his bishop saw to it that he remained in a relatively remote parish. "The bishop, who is well known as the enemy of all evangelical piety, objects to me on account of my religious sentiments," Dr. Traill complained. Thus he was fated to spend his whole career "in the bush," as it were, fighting the savage natives of Roman Catholic Cork.

"I have waged war against popery in its thousand forms of wickedness, until my life had nearly paid the forfeit," he once wrote. "None but those who have had the trying experience can possibly know the state of inquietude and feverish anxiety in which the Roman Catholics, especially in the country parts of the kingdom, keep the man who boldly denounces their abominations. It occurred to me on one occasion to be under the necessity of having two bodies of police armed for my protection."

Dr. Traill had one consolation—his classical scholarship. But he did not live to see the publication of his translation of Josephus' *The Jewish Wars*, which was going through the press when he died in 1847. It was the second year of the potato famine—the great calamity which destroyed or expelled half the population of Ireland and seared the national memory so cruelly that it is still spoken of in the country districts as though it had happened yesterday. When Dr. Traill died of the famine fever his widow and seven children moved to the suburbs of Dublin, where Kathleen, his fourth daughter, met and married J. M. Synge's father in 1856. She was eighteen and he was thirty-two years old.

John Hatch Synge, the third son of "Pestalozzi John," was a barrister whose practice was mostly confined to conveyancing. He had inherited some land in Galway which produced income for many years, and was a man of his class. History, however, was beginning to overtake the Ascendancy class. The famine was the prelude to the collapse of a feudal system, and the gentry looked on helplessly while their economic and political power gradually passed into the hands of the people. The decline of the Synge fortunes was symptomatic of the fate that befell many other such families. One of the ironies of modern Irish history is that the submerged masses were drawing their leadership from the very class they were seeking to destroy. Neighbours to the Synges of Glanmore Castle were the Parnells of Avondale, who were to provide Ireland with its greatest patriot leader of the age. Aunt Jane Synge, who had often dandled the infant Charles Stewart Parnell on her lap at Glanmore, used to say years afterwards that she wished she had choked him in infancy.

John Hatch Synge took his bride to live in a house at 1, afterwards 4, Hatch Street, in a part of Dublin developed out of the property which had belonged to his great-grandfather John Hatch. After the first three children were born, the Synges moved to Newtown Villas, Rathfarnham, a group of houses in what was then the country but is now a suburb of Dublin. There Edmund John Millington Synge, as he was christened, was born on April 16, 1871, four years after his brother Samuel. A year later John Hatch Synge died of smallpox, leaving his widow to bring up five children, the oldest of whom was fifteen. She had £400-a-year income from the Galway property, and this plus the legacies each of her children had received from an uncle enabled her to bring them up in a style conservative but befitting their class. The first thing she did was to move to 4 Orwell Park, Rathgar, about two miles nearer the city and next door to her mother, Mrs. Traill. Here she lived until her youngest son was a student in college.

Synge described his childhood in an autobiographical narrative buried in a dilapidated notebook which he used in Paris in the middle nineties. It was probably written for his own satisfaction only. Later he must have decided that it might be reworked and published because he rewrote it as an impressionistic narrative entitled "My Youth" and called his fictitious narrator Dora Comyn. The first version is a crude exercise, scarcely legible, while the second is only a fragment. But the memories and impressions "My Youth" records are based upon verified facts.

He describes himself as an impressionable child, intimidated by the fierce doctrine of sin and its punishments which his mother preached constantly. "The well-meant but extraordinary cruelty of introducing the idea of Hell into the imagination of a nervous child has probably caused more misery than many customs that the same people send missionaries to eradicate." This atmosphere of religious intensity engendered by his mother was something he could not overcome until he was eighteen years old and a student in college, and then he rejected it completely.

He was also a sickly boy, although none of his illnesses seems to have been very severe. "This ill health led to a curious resolution which has explained in some measure all my subsequent evolution. Without knowing, or as far as I can remember hearing anything, about doctrines of heredity I surmised that unhealthy parents should have unhealthy children—my rabbit breeding may have put the idea into my head. Therefore, I said, I am unhealthy and if I marry I will have unhealthy children. But I will never create beings to suffer as I am suffering, so I will never marry. I do not know how old I was when I came to this decision, but I was between thirteen and fifteen and it caused me horrible misery." The incident itself was one that any sensitive boy could have survived easily. The significant thing is that he not only remembered it in his middle twenties but attributed to it an influence upon "all my subsequent evolution." Synge's morbidity, which seems to have been a family characteristic, is most evident in his poetry. But the truth is that until he fell victim to the malignant disease which killed him at the age of thirty-eight he was capable of cycling sixty miles a day.

His childhood companion was a cousin named Florence Ross. They had rabbits, pigeons, guinea pigs, canaries and dogs to look after together. On rainy days they would draw animals in their copybooks, and compare their drawings. On good days he would wander with her through the woods of the large demesne of Rathfarnham Castle. Their passion was ornithology. They collected birds' eggs, and worked together on a notebook which has survived. "I remember telling—or intending to tell—her that each egg I found gave three distinct moments of rapture: the finding of the nest, the insertion of [the] egg successfully blown in my collection, and lastly, the greatest, exhibiting it to her." His passion for her found expression in his kissing the chair she had sat on and in tenderly preserving the little notes she wrote him. Later he began to realize that "though we were excellent companions we knew each other too well and were both eager for more exciting flirtations."

Summers were spent vacationing at Greystones, a small fishing village in Wicklow which later became a seaside resort. Mrs. Synge hired a house every summer; and except for a short visit to Glanmore Castle when he was one, a summer in Dalkey when he was two, and a trip to the Isle of Man when he was eleven, Synge spent every summer until he was twenty at Greystones. He was not allowed to swim because of his ill health. At Greystones, as at Orwell Park, the children he and his brothers were likely to see were all Protestant and their parents members of the evangelical movement.

At ten he was sent to Mr. Harrick's Classical and English School, 4 Upper Leeson Street, where his older brother Samuel was enrolled. Ill health continued to plague him, and his attendance was irregular. Three years later he transferred to a school in Bray but withdrew after one year of intermittent absences. Except for these four years of irregular schooling, all of his education until he enrolled at Trinity College, Dublin, was at the hands of a private tutor whom he saw three times a week in his own home. But there was nothing irregular or haphazard about his religious training, for his mother and grandmother ruled a household where the discipline was almost as strict as that of a religious order. Mrs. Synge and her mother had gone to school themselves to a harsh master. Their authority was the Bible, and they cited it constantly to all the children.

Not being able to swim or take part in sports with his brothers, Synge's only recreation was walking, and it was to remain the one great activity of his life. At first he was confined to the woods near Rathfarnham Castle, a sixteenth century building whose owner gave the Synges permission to walk in his demesne but inspected their baskets to see that they had not uprooted the wild flowers that grew everywhere. Later he walked with his brother Samuel to the valley of Glenasmole. The place has subsequently been changed by the building of reservoirs, but at that time it was as wild as the glens of Wicklow. Irish had been spoken in the valley of Glenasmole only forty years before, and stories were still told of ancient Gaelic heroes by the people of the valley, and the place names were redolent of Irish folklore—Bohernabreena, the Road of the Hostel; Glenasmole, the Glen of the Thrushes.

Synge's oldest brother, Robert, who had been graduated from Trinity College in 1879, was apprenticed to an engineer building a tunnel in England. In 1883 he went out to the Argentine with his mother's brother, Robert Traill, who had a large ranch and who was on his way to making a fortune. A "charge" of £2,000 was made on the Galway estate to finance the venture. For many years thereafter he made his home in the New World, though he came back home frequently for vacations. Synge's sister Annie married Harry Stephens, a young solicitor, and for most of Synge's life the Stephenses were next-door neighbours. Synge's brother Edward became land agent of the family estates in Wicklow in 1884, acquired the management of other estates in Cavan and Mayo, and in 1885 became the agent for the estate of Lord Gormanstown, whose standing in Ireland was unique because he was not only Ireland's premier viscount but also a Roman Catholic. Synge's other brother, Samuel, was to graduate

from Trinity College, take medical and divinity degrees and spend
most of his adult life as a missionary in China. With one son in the
"colonies," one managing landed estates, and one soon to be working
for the church in the land of the heathen, the fortunes of the Synges
were developing according to the pattern of their class.

A logical development of Synge's interest in nature studies was his
joining the Dublin Naturalists' Field Club, an organization founded
in 1886 by some of the foremost botanists, anthropologists and orni-
thologists in Ireland. Synge was an active member until 1888. He was
a boy of only sixteen when he resigned and he had contributed nothing to the association beyond his attendance at the meetings where
he listened to papers read by experts on such subjects as the collection and preservation of beetles, the migration of birds and the
preservation of butterflies and moths. But he owned a fine collection
of butterflies, moths and beetles, and worked systematically at his
hobby. In May of 1886 he went on a field trip with the club to
Howth, the long fist-shaped peninsula that forms the northern side
of Dublin Bay. Howth is full of traditions about ancient Celtic
heroes. On the crest of the hill of Howth is a cairn, or stone-covered
tomb, reputed to be the burial place of Criffan, an ancient high king
of Ireland. In the demesne of Howth Castle, a sixteenth century
baronial mansion, is a massive dolmen, or gallery grave, traditionally
known as the grave of Aideen, a heroine of the third century who was
said to have died of grief when her husband, Oscar, fell in battle near
Tara. Synge was familiar with Samuel Ferguson's poem "Aideen's
Grave" which begins:

> They heaved the stone; they heaped the cairn.
> Said Ossian, "In a queenly grave
> We leave her 'mong her fields of fern
> Between the cliff and wave."

His study of natural history widened and took on a more formal
aspect. He read and took notes on Charles Waterton's *Wanderings
in South America*, and then turned to Darwin. Unlike the orthodox
Roman Catholic Waterton, Darwin threw Synge's inquiring mind
into a turmoil. He wrote in "My Youth":

Before I abandoned science it rendered me an important service. When I was about fourteen I obtained a book of Darwin's. It opened in my hands at a passage where he asks how can we explain the similarity between a man's hand and a bird's or bat's wings except by evolution. I flung the book aside and rushed out into the open air—it was summer and we were in the country—the sky seemed to have lost its blue and the grass its green. I lay down and writhed in an agony of doubt. Till then I had never doubted and never conceived that a sane and wise man or boy could doubt. I had of course heard of atheists but as vague monsters that I was unable to realize. My memory does not record how I returned home nor how long my misery lasted. I know only that I got the book out of the house as soon as possible and kept it out of my sight till its departure, saying to myself logically enough that I was not yet sufficiently advanced in science to weigh his arguments, so I would do better to reserve his work for future study. In a few weeks or days I had regained my composure, but this was the beginning. Soon afterwards I turned my attention to works of Christian evidence, reading them at first with pleasure, soon with doubt, and at last in some cases with derision.

My study of insects had given me a scientific attitude—probably a crude one—which did not and could not interpret life and nature as I heard it interpreted from the pulpit. By the time I was sixteen or seventeen I had renounced Christianity after a good deal of wobbling, although I do not think I avowed my decision quite so soon. I felt a sort of shame in being thought an infidel, a term which I have always—and still—used as a reproach. For a while I denied everything, then I took to reading Carlyle, Stephen and Matthew Arnold, and made myself a sort of incredulous belief that illuminated nature and lent an object to life without hampering the intellect. This story is easily told, but it was a terrible experience. By it I laid a chasm between my present and my past and between myself and my kindred and friends. Till I was twenty-three I never met or at least knew a man or woman who shared my opinions.

The works on Christian evidence which he referred to were Locke's *Essay Concerning Human Understanding,* Paley's *Evidences of Christianity* and Butler's *Analogy.* As he said himself his reactions were at first pleasurable but soon characterized by scepticism. "To be indifferent which of two opinions is true," he wrote in his notebook, "is the right temper of the mind that preserves it from being imposed upon and disposes it to examine with that indifferency until it has done its best to find the truth and this is the only direct and safe way to the conduct of understanding." The doubts planted in his mind by

Darwin were never to be resolved. From this time on his indifference to religion, his refusal to attend Bible classes and his unwillingness to discuss religious questions with his mother opened the rift between him and the rest of his family which was only to widen with the years.

The Protestant minority, which saw itself succumbing to historical forces too great to cope with, no longer felt the assurance which its position of privilege had given it in Ireland for centuries. Fearful of the rising power of the Catholic masses and the loss of their lands, they were losing also the power of reasoned criticism which had animated the best of Anglo-Irish culture in the past. Like a threatened aristocracy they rallied behind their barricades of class supremacy and forced their members into rigid adherence to their own traditions and beliefs. By his disbelief Synge was dissociating himself from his own people.

Religion was not the only thing which created difficulties with his family. In 1879 the Land League had been founded by Michael Davitt, and for the next few years under Parnell's brilliant leadership Irish tenants fought their landlords in what came to be known as the Land War. In 1880 Parnell made his famous speech in Ennis which resulted in the practice of boycotting. In 1881 he was indicted and tried for "seditious conspiracy," but the trial was a fiasco and when the Gladstone government could not get a conviction they introduced a Coercion bill to bring the tenants into line. The act empowered authorities to arrest any person "reasonably suspected" and to hold him for a period of many months. Immediately hundreds of the "reasonably suspected," most of them league officials, were imprisoned. But the agitation continued, and rural Ireland was in the grip of terror. In 1881 a land act, intended to grant certain benefits to tenants, became law after it had survived a bitter battle in Parliament. But the new law was accepted grudgingly, and when the government decided that the league was sabotaging it new arrests and violence followed. Finally, in 1882, the boiling pot simmered down when Parnell, after confidential negotiations with the government, decided upon a tactful retreat and accepted certain concessions from the government as the price of truce. The truce, however, came to an abrupt end in a period of months when Ireland was shaken by the Phoenix Park murders.

Lord Frederick Cavendish, the Chief Secretary for Ireland, and his permanent Under Secretary were murdered as they were walking together along one of the avenues of the Phoenix Park in Dublin by an extremist group known as the Invincibles. The horror created by the assassination of the newly appointed Chief Secretary, who was believed to be liberal in his attitudes to Ireland, was deplored by Irish leaders attempting to fight Ireland's battle for freedom within the framework of the law. Parnell denounced the crime and offered Gladstone his resignation from Parliament. But the murder and the terrible justice which followed it, made possible by the defection of two of the plotters who turned state's evidence, touched the national consciousness in a way which was never to be forgotten.

In 1885 Synge's brother Edward was busily evicting tenants in Cavan, Mayo and Wicklow. When Synge argued with his mother over the rights of the tenants and the injustice of evicting them, her answer was, "What would become of us if our tenants in Galway stopped paying their rents?" To this he could find no answer and was forced to hold his tongue. In the summer of 1887 Edward's activities came much nearer home when he evicted a tenant from his aunt's estate at Glanmore. The cruelty and efficiency with which he went about his duties made it an event Synge never forgot.

The tenant, named Hugh Carey, lived with his two elderly sisters in a small farm on the poor townland of Ahowl near Carrick Mountain in County Wicklow. He had not paid any rent for some months. Edward Synge's technique was almost perfect, for he had learned it in the west of Ireland where the opposition was formidable. He first hired two "emergency men," whose job was to hold houses from which tenants had been evicted against any attempt to restore the occupants. Being an emergency man must have been a hazardous life, reserved for itinerants not likely to return to the neighbourhoods in which they worked. One can get an idea of the violence which sometimes overtook them from Synge's poem "The 'Mergency Man," written in 1905 when he was in Kerry.

Edward's next step was to approach the farm by an unexpected route early in the morning, rout out the occupants and install his emergency men before the news had spread through the neighbourhood. What happened next usually depended on whether the farm was worth saving or whether another tenant was brave or foolish enough to move into a boycotted house. If prospects were not favorable the house was frequently burned to the ground. The authorities then retired, leaving only a pile of burning embers behind them.

The account of Hugh Carey's eviction which appeared in *The Freeman's Journal* described a situation fairly typical of what was happening all over the country. The tenant was described as the sole support of his two sisters, one of whom was an imbecile. The crowds which watched the eviction included everyone of importance in the area, including three priests. Order was maintained by a detachment of eight policemen. Afterwards speeches were made by the angry spectators, and the name of Synge took on a meaning in the neighbourhood which it had not had in more peaceful years when landlords could afford to be generous to tenants without any fear of weakening their hold on them. A few days after the eviction Edward burned Hugh Carey's miserable cottage to the ground.

According to his mother, Edward Synge was not only acting in the best interests of his employer and his class but also according to what was morally right. Her theology, shaped by the evangelical movement, held that man was essentially wicked and, by justice at least, entitled to nothing but damnation. If he did not pay his rent he deserved eviction. To eliminate evictions was to traffic in the generosity of the landlords, and this was no time for the landlords to relax their already precarious hold on the rights and privileges that gave them their power. She was also inclined to see the problem of landlord versus tenant solely in religious terms, as a conflict between Protestant and Catholic. Truth lay with her class, and any weakening of one was a weakening of the other. Imagine her puzzlement and the dismay which swept over the Roman Catholic masses of Ireland when the Pope himself in 1888 pronounced boycotting, the only effective weapon the tenants had, to be unlawful. The Roman Catholic members of Parliament immediately condemned the papal rescript, and it had little actual effect upon Catholic Ireland despite the fact that the Pope confirmed his stand and was supported by one Irish bishop in Limerick.

Getting the Pope to condemn boycotting was a brilliant achievement of British secret diplomacy. But the effect upon the Catholics of Ireland was probably no more startling than it was upon the Protestants. Mrs. Synge was astonished at the sudden arrival of papal support for the Protestants. She was sure that some dark and

mysterious motive lay behind the papal rescript and was unable to
see that the Vatican could be used in the game of politics. Most Irish
bishops saw it as just this, for they explained in the pages of their
newspapers and from the pulpits of their dioceses that the Pope had
been misled and that the decree was inapplicable. They were supported by one important English bishop when Cardinal Manning
wrote to Archbishop Walsh of Dublin that he believed that the
landlords were morally wrong and that the Pope's declaration had
been made without consulting the Irish hierarchy for their side of
the question.

Synge was horrified by the brutal efficiency of his brother's methods
and resentful of his mother's attempts to translate the land war
solely into religious terms, but he was not alone in his sentiments.
Many other young people of his class were beginning to express
similar attitudes, and they were led by a young girl of great beauty
whose influence was dramatic if not always effective. In 1887 Maud
Gonne was twenty-one years old. She had had some training as an
actress, but her health had prevented her from going on the stage,
though she is famous for the role she played in 1902 as Yeats'
Cathleen Ni Houlihan. Yeats wrote of her, "She made Cathleen
seem like a divine being fallen into our mortal infirmity."

Her background was hardly the usual one for a social revolutionary.
Her father had been adjutant general of the British forces in Dublin,
and her mother came from a wealthy London family. As the events
of her life prove, her enthusiasm for the cause was neither a passing
fancy nor a mere outlet for her emotions. Her objective was a social
revolution which would give the poor people of Ireland a decent
living from the land they tilled. She knew very little Irish history,
cared nothing about papal rescripts or Protestant claims, and threw
herself into the peasants' battle with a torrent of energy, teaching
to ignorant men, as Yeats phrased it in a poem, most violent ways
and standing shoulder to shoulder with them in crying defiance of law
and landlord.

She was an effective street orator, in great demand as an election
speaker both in England and in Ireland. Her efforts naturally pros-
pered in an atmosphere intensified not only by the actual events of
the day but also by the new current of interest in the Irish past
which antiquarian researches and the study of the ancient literature

were generating. She became a symbol of ancient Ireland herself not only to the poor peasants but to the young intellectuals of Dublin. She later described herself in the title of her autobiography as *A Servant of the Queen*, but she was a most unruly one.

Synge was only a boy of seventeen in 1888. He had never seen Maud Gonne, and did not meet her until eight years later in Paris when Yeats introduced him to her. But the arguments he had had with his mother over the eviction of Hugh Carey must have watered the soil which those two ardent revolutionaries found so fertile.

Natural science had been the great interest of Synge's boyhood because it filled a void in his life and was a substitute for the activities which school and schoolmates would have supplied under normal circumstances. But as he grew older, collecting birds' eggs and mounting butterfly specimens were thin fare, especially when he had only his own reading and the occasional lectures of the Naturalists' Field Club to stimulate him. When he was sixteen he began taking violin lessons from a Dublin violinist named Patrick Griffith. Through Griffith he met other young people interested in music. Two years later he enrolled as a student at the Royal Irish Academy of Music. Music was now the important influence in his life. It took him to Germany a year after he had been graduated from college, and liberated him from a life at home which had become increasingly oppressive.

His mother was pleased at his new interest, because she did not take it very seriously. Later when he told her that he wanted to become a professional musician she was quite upset, but for the present at least she hoped for no other future for him than his entrance into Trinity College where his three brothers had been educated. If there was any crisis on this score, it was resolved temporarily, at least, in March of 1888 when he stopped taking his violin lessons in order to devote all his time to preparing for the college entrance examinations in June. He had a tutor to help him, but the prospects of passing were so grim that he spent an intense period of several months of study.

Synge passed his entrance examinations "with a squeak," as his mother wrote to Robert Synge. He realized that if he was to survive the competition that his college classes would present he had better continue his studying throughout the summer months while he was at Greystones with his mother. His literary education had been informal but no less orthodox than his religious training. The books in the family library had all passed the strictest entrance requirements themselves, and there were no magazines, current novels or other frivolous reading matter—one wonders where he got hold of the Darwin. He was in no position yet to apply to literature the same critical scepticism he had learned to judge his mother's religious teaching by. As he later noted in "My Youth": "English literature I read with much care, although I was painfully conscious of my uncertain judgement and formed my opinions reluctantly for fear a blunder might lower me in my own estimation. I believe I never allowed myself to like a book that was not famous, though there were many famous books, such as Tennyson's poems, that I did not care for."

His backwardness in spoken English was undoubtedly due to the influence of his mother, who abhorred vulgarity and sought divine aid in confining the already restricted speech of the period and the class she represented, in which expression of feeling was almost paralyzed. Synge's reaction found expression ultimately in his interest in the earthy language of the Irish peasant and in a fondness for profanity. Once, on recovering from an anaesthetic, he shouted, "Damn the bloody Anglo-Saxon language that a man can't swear in without being vulgar!"

Two

COLLEGE. MUSICAL STUDIES. COUNTY WICKLOW

Did you ever hear tell of the summer and the fine spring in places where the holy men of Ireland have built up churches to the Lord . . .

Trinity College, or Dublin University as it was known until modern times, was founded in the early part of the seventeenth century as a sister college of Oxford and Cambridge for the education of young men of the Ascendancy class. Its doors were closed to Roman Catholics, officially at least, until 1794. In 1873 any officer of the college except in the Divinity School could be a Roman Catholic.[2] But the removal of legal restrictions, important as they were in lowering the barrier between the governing class and the dispossessed majority, made little real difference in the position that Trinity held as the fountainhead of Anglo-Irish culture. If its doors were opened, few Catholics were willing to rush in. Some who did, in defiance of their parish priests no doubt, discreetly described themselves on the college rolls as Protestant. Thomas Moore, the author of *Irish Melodies* and one of Trinity's most famous graduates, always described himself as a Catholic. But he was entered upon the college books as a Protestant, though it is difficult to see how anyone could have been under any illusions about his religion.

The chief function of the college for generations was the training of clergymen who were expected to "soothe the native breast, to soften rocks, or bend a knotted oak," to quote one of its most famous sons, William Congreve. But the native breast had not been easily soothed and now the knotted oak was beginning to bend in the wrong direction, and Trinity had scarcely noticed the change. With her great traditions and her great men—Edward Dowden and J. P. Mahaffy who sneered at the very possibility of a Celtic revival—she had very little to offer the young people of the Ascendancy who were emerging into a different Ireland from that of Swift and Congreve, Burke and Goldsmith. Shaw once pointed out that the great cultural movements of Europe had passed Ireland by, but now the greatest cultural movement in Irish history was about to pass by the gates of Trinity College, and her only action was to disapprove of it to the extent that she was aware of it.

Trinity is still a Protestant foundation, although today one-quarter of its student body and some of its faculty are Catholic. It is now an Irish university in a way it never was in the past, and seems destined to become even more Irish, dependent as it is upon a native government which gives it a part of its funds. By American standards it is a small university, with a total of some two thousand full-time students, and a faculty of about four hundred. In 1953 it granted 567 degrees. In Synge's day it must have been somewhat smaller, but not appreciably so.

Every student who enters Trinity College is assigned a tutor from among the junior fellows who acts as his faculty adviser. Synge was lucky to have a relative as his tutor. His mother's cousin, Anthony Traill, became a fellow of Trinity very shortly after the office had ceased to be reserved for clergymen of the Church of Ireland, and he remained a layman at a time when most of his colleagues were in holy orders. He was a short, determined, thick-set man who had acquired little refinement from his wide learning and looked as if he would be more at home on his farm than guiding young college students through their courses of study. But neither his appearance nor his personality prevented him from rising to the topmost executive office of provost of the college.

Synge had other friends among the officials of the college. Charles Miller, an old friend of his family, managed the College Office, and Marshall, the chief porter, who "carried the mace," had grown up on the Glanmore estate. But Trinity was not to play as important a role in Synge's life as these facts might indicate. For one thing he did not occupy rooms in college, but continued to live at home. For another he gave his heart as well as most of his time and energy not to his college work but to his musical studies.

The college rules, which have been changed somewhat since Synge's day, required the student to attend lectures in only one of the three terms which made up the academic year. For one of the other two terms he was required merely to pass final examinations for which he could prepare by reading by himself. Synge decided to read by himself during the first, or Michaelmas, term and take the final examinations in January.

The notebooks which he filled during his first year in college reveal that he had acquired another interest—Irish antiquities. Ireland is a happy hunting ground for the student of the past, with its artifacts from the Stone Age, megalithic monuments from the Bronze Age, and its early Christian building and burial sites. The study of antiquity was much in vogue at the time, and though it was not to achieve scientific proportions until a generation later, some of the best minds in Ireland were attempting a colorful, if not too accurate, reconstruction of the Irish past. Sir William Wilde, the father of Oscar Wilde and one of Ireland's eccentric geniuses, had explored and written a book about the antiquities of the Boyne River and one on the equally interesting area of Lough Corrib in County Galway. The Royal Irish Academy, a center of scholarly activity on the subject, was publishing in its *Proceedings* papers by antiquarian researchers on prehistoric burial grounds, megalithic tombs and monuments, ancient Irish gold and silver ornaments and early ecclesiastical remains—churches, round towers and high crosses. The suburbs of Dublin itself were full of the remains Synge was reading about, and he made a point of seeing them. His notebooks contain drawings of doorways in ruined churches, a sketch of a round tower, and some ancient Gaelic inscriptions.

While he was focussing his attention upon the physical remains of Ireland's great and violent past he began reading Irish patriotic literature. "The Irish ballad poetry of *The Spirit of The Nation** school engrossed me for a while and made me commit my most serious literary error: I thought it excellent for a considerable time and then

---

* *The Spirit of The Nation* (1843) was a collection of patriotic poems which had appeared in *The Nation* newspaper, founded in 1842 by Charles Gavan Duffy, Thomas Davis and John Blake Dillon.

repented bitterly," he wrote in "My Youth." The apology sounds very much like the one Yeats made for a similar addiction to the same school of poets: "I knew in my heart that most of them wrote badly, and yet such romance clung about them, such a desire for Irish poetry was in all our minds, that I kept saying, not only to others but to myself, that most of them wrote well, or all but well."[3]

Synge's mother suspected that any interest in Irish tradition was linked up inextricably with popish superstition. His reading was probably furtive, therefore, and identified in his own mind at least with his escape from her religion, for he wrote in "My Youth": "Soon after I had relinquished the Kingdom of God I began to take a real interest in the Kingdom of Ireland. My patriotism went round from a vigorous and unreasoning loyalty to a temperate nationalism, and everything Irish became sacred."

While Synge was studying Irish antiquities his mother was writing to her son Robert on Christmas day, 1888, "Ned* came here last Wednesday on his way home from Mayo. . . . He likes these Mayo tenants. He has the unpleasant task of evicting a whole townland of them who are regular paupers. Some of them have not paid any rent for four years. It is well they are so quiet and don't fight him. A new priest has come, as the old one is superannuated. He was a good quiet old fellow. Ned is very much afraid lest the new one should sow discord. He† has begun by stopping a man taking an evicted farm."

Synge began attending his first college lectures in February. His mother reported to Robert: "He does not enjoy the lectures at all and is longing for them to be over, that he may begin his lessons on the fiddle again. . . . Oh! that I could say his soul is in health. I hope you pray for him, the only one of all my dear children a stranger to God." He made no acquaintances among his classmates, and when the term ended in March he resumed his violin lessons and read whatever books he liked. He was now nearly eighteen, and his ideas were becoming directed. He was shrinking increasingly from even an outward conformity with his mother's religion, and her alarm is evidenced in her letters. He had also reached a position where he felt that all further discussion of his convictions was useless. He was

* Edward Synge.
† The new priest.

through defending his attitudes—he would go his own way quietly. There would be only one more crisis, when he refused to be present at his brother Sam's first sermon.

His mother wrote in April: "Johnnie is taking more lessons from Griffith and spends a great deal of his time fiddling. He is learning harmony from books as well as he can and is always composing little airs and making out accompaniments for them on the piano, which I have to play. They are so badly written, I make mistakes pretty often. Poor fellow, I long and long for the day when he will no longer live to himself—that is what he is doing now—but to Him who died for him." A fortnight later she wrote: "He leads a queer solitary life poor boy. He plays his fiddle a great deal and reads and takes a walk. I wonder what he will turn into by and by. He is a great burden on my heart, but the Lord says, 'Cast thy burden on me.'"

The usual summer vacation at Greystones was interrupted by a week's visit to Glanmore Castle, now owned by the widow of his uncle Francis Synge. Synge had not stayed in the castle overnight since he was an infant, though he had visited it many times and knew the demesne and the woods of Glanmore and every corner of the Devil's Glen. Glanmore had fallen upon evil days, but it was still impressive enough. In 1889 the library was still intact, though the castle itself had settled gradually into decay. Ten years later the silver and the library, or most of it, were sold and the proceeds used to coax some fertility back into the soil which also had fallen upon evil days. As a boy of eighteen who still had not moved outside the restricted circle of his own family and class, he could not look with indifference upon Glanmore. One of his Wicklow essays, entitled "A Landlord's Garden in County Wicklow," inspired by a house called Castle Kevin where he stayed in later summers with his mother, shows how much he could be moved by the tragedy of the landlord class and the crumbling fortunes of his own family. "These owners of the land are not so much pitied at the present day, or much deserving of pity; and yet one cannot quite forget that they are the descendants of what was at one time, in the eighteenth century, a high-spirited and highly-cultivated aristocracy. The broken greenhouses and mouse-eaten libraries, that were designed and collected by men who voted with Grattan, are perhaps as mournful in the end as the four mudwalls that are so often left in Wicklow as the only remnants of a farm-house."[4]

When the summer was over the Synges moved back to Rathgar. The fall term opened at Trinity, but Synge had decided to forego lectures until the next term as he had done in his first year. His mother's apprehensions about his loss of religious faith were so great that she finally asked her minister to talk to him. The discussion which took place was not only futile but seems to have confirmed Synge's growing conviction that an open declaration of his unbelief was necessary so that the family would no longer indulge in the polite excuses they were beginning to fabricate to explain his absence from church. He announced that he would no longer attend church, that not only was it a form of polite hypocrisy but led people to con-clusions about him that he could not allow. His mother must have seen this development coming, for the restraint with which she wrote about it in her diary expresses the quiet tragedy in her heart. For Christmas day she wrote, "Johnnie would not come, very sad . . . my only trouble Johnnie." Other members of the family spoke of it with discretion, but from this time on he was looked upon as an outsider. Only his indifference and his unwillingness to argue pre-served the uneasy peace. The air of tension which his action had created tended to drive him in upon himself.

In November he began attending lectures in musical theory at the Royal Irish Academy of Music given by Sir Robert Stewart. For the next three years his formal musical training was at the academy. His subjects were violin, musical theory and composition. His mother wrote to Robert:

Johnnie is so bewitched with music that I fear he will not give it up. I never knew till lately that he was thinking of making his living by it seriously; he spares no pains or trouble and practises from morning till night, if he can. Harry* had a talk with him the other day, advising him very strongly not to think of making it a profession. Harry told him all the men who do take to drink! And they are not a nice set of men either, but I don't think his advice has had the least effect on Johnnie. . . . The sound of the fiddle makes me quite sad now. I used to think it was only a harmless amusement and it kept him out of mischief, but it seems now likely to lead to mischief.

* Harry Stephens, Synge's brother-in-law.

But at the academy Synge was associating only with young people of his own class and was in little danger of the corruption she feared.

The year 1890 was an eventful one for Ireland. The country appeared to be coerced into a state of inactivity, but actually the land war continued to smoulder and blaze out with violence in isolated districts. A year earlier on the Olphert estate in Donegal a police inspector arrested a priest—still in his vestments after Sunday mass—for his part in obstructing an eviction and was immediately murdered by the congregation. In February of 1890 Mr. Olphert announced that he would continue to evict and pull down the vacated cottages on his estate and use the lands for grazing if his tenants did not abandon the Plan of Campaign—a stratagem devised in 1886 whereby tenants pooled their rents in amounts they considered reasonable and offered the lump sum to their landlord. If he refused it, the amount was deposited with a trustee who would use it to support evicted tenants. Mr. Olphert's most formidable opponent was Maud Gonne, who appeared at every eviction on his estate, publicizing the plight of the tenants and encouraging them to resist. But the evictions went on nevertheless, and Miss Gonne finally had to evade arrest by fleeing to Paris, where she continued the fight.

In January of 1890 the step was taken which led swiftly to the downfall of Parnell and with him the hopes of the Irish masses. The power he had managed to achieve by uniting such diverse elements as the Catholic hierarchy and the Fenians had led Ireland to the brink of Home Rule when he was named as co-respondent in a divorce action brought against his mistress, who had borne him three children. The scandal immediately turned the church against him and broke the ranks of his party. He was deposed as leader, and his party was no longer a threat to an English government that had almost reached the end of its resistance to Home Rule. When the event was further dramatized a year later by Parnell's death, the whole country was thrown into a state of demoralization which appeared to be final and complete.

The effect of Parnell's downfall upon the popular imagination and the way in which it separated the turbulent factions who had submerged their differences to fight a common enemy has made the figure of Parnell a somewhat shadowy symbol of heroic resistance for poet, historian and man in the street. The admiration for Parnell took

on the proportions of a cult in which the chief doctrine was liberation
—not only from England but from the puritanical restrictions of
Catholic life in Ireland. The picture of Stephen Dedalus' father
sobbing for his "dead king" over an untasted Christmas dinner has
lost little of its meaning to Irish readers even today.

If Catholic Ireland was demoralized to a state of shock over the
downfall of Parnell, Protestant Ireland was delighted with it. Parnell
was a Wicklow landlord, sprung from one of the families most
prominent in the evangelical revival of the Protestant church, who
epitomized in his personality all the autocratic detachment one would
expect of his class. But he had devoted his genius to the emancipation
of his country from English rule and from the grip of the landlords.
Like Maud Gonne he had warred against his own class. How much
more vivid a figure of revolt he must have seemed to Synge, a member
of his class, than he had to the youthful James Joyce!

Synge passed his examinations for Hilary term in April and was
free of all college obligations until the following October. The
Stephenses had decided to move to a suburb known then as Kingstown and now by its ancient Gaelic name Dún Laoghaire. Mrs.
Synge decided that she would move with them. A door was built in
the wall connecting their attached houses, and for the next sixteen
years the two families lived as one.

Dún Laoghaire is seven miles south of Dublin and connected
with it by a railroad built in 1836. It has a deep-water harbour, from
which the Holyhead boat sails daily, and is fringed by a wide prome-
nade and seaside houses looking out over Dublin Bay. An article in
The Irish Times of 1890 described it as a "fashionable metropolitan
suburb" whose residents were "of the better class." Crosthwaite Park,
however, is not on the waterfront. The house Synge lived in, Number
31, was smoothly plastered and painted grey. The dining room and
drawing room, as in the other houses flanking it, had bow windows.
All the doors were shining with brown varnish, finished with artificial
graining, and the windows, porticoes and doorways were decorated
with stucco ornamentation. The park in front was surrounded by a
line of trees, and outside them was a spiked iron railing. Today
Crosthwaite Park looks much the same, except that one no longer
would describe it in the elegant terms used by The Irish Times in
1890.

The move may have meant a fresh outlook for both the Stephenses and the Synges, but Mrs. Synge's one great problem was still her errant son John. She wrote to Robert just before they moved: "Oh, my poor Johnnie, may God soon awaken him and reveal Himself to his poor soul. I very seldom speak to him on the subject, it distresses me so much, and it seems no use. He reads the Bible sometimes just because I ask him—but I wait, and pray and expect. Surely our God will hear and answer our prayers, for He is the Mighty God and He is able to break the heart of stone and bring my poor wandering child to His feet repenting and forsaking his sin and unbelief."

At the beginning of his third year of college Synge took the Little Go, or Final Freshman, examinations at Trinity, used to classify students into three groups according to their ability. Mrs. Synge wrote to Robert: "You will be glad to hear that poor Johnnie got a third class at the Little Go. He might have got a first if he had read for a longer time, but considering a fortnight's reading it was very good. He is now working away again at the music. He does the composition at night and exerts his brains so much that he often lies awake after it, and then sleeps very late in the morning." Music was now his whole life, and he was content with only a pass degree from college. At the annual examination in the academy in December he passed an oral examination held by two doctors of music who granted him a certificate for his knowledge of the rudiments and certified him for advanced study in counterpoint during the coming year. But the news of his success brought little comfort to his mother.

In January of 1891 he joined the student orchestra at the academy, which was directed by his violin instructor Herr Werner, and for the first time in his life was actually working and studying with other young people. He played in his first concert in March, held in the Antient Concert Rooms on Brunswick Street. The Antient Concert Rooms was to play its part in the history of the Irish Literary Revival because it was there in May of 1899 that Yeats' *The Countess Cathleen* and Edward Martyn's *The Heather Field* were performed as the first offering of the Irish Literary Theatre. Brunswick Street is now renamed Pearse Street, after the hero of a new Ireland, and the Antient Concert Rooms has been converted into a cinema. About six years after Synge played in his first concert, the Feis Cóeil, or Irish musical festival, was established, but in 1891 organized music in

Dublin had not been touched by the current of nationalism. The concert had been arranged under the patronage of the lord lieutenant of Ireland and drew its support and its attendance from a fashionable audience. The conductors were three well known local composers, including Sir Robert Stewart.

The concert was a great success and was well reported in all the newspapers, but Mrs. Synge derived little pleasure from it. She wrote to Robert: "I wonder when his eyes will be opened to see his folly in wasting all his time at that music. . . . He has not one friend who thinks he is wise in going on in his present course, but he is very determined and takes no advice from anyone. Poor boy, how I long to see his footsteps turned into the way of peace, and I pray continually for him." Had she known it, she might have drawn some consolation from the fact that he was exceedingly nervous about playing in public. Only in an orchestra, where his efforts were blended with those of other players, could he face an audience. Ultimately his shyness turned him away from music altogether. One of the most revealing things he wrote during his early years in Paris when he was desperately trying to achieve some kind of self-expression is a disturbing narrative about a violinist who collapses in the middle of his first important recital because he is nervous and unsure of himself. Though he later described it as "a morbid thing about a mad fiddler in Paris which I hate," he could not bring himself to destroy it. It was a chapter in the story of his private life and he could not have denied it.

After the concert he began preparing for the Junior Sophister examinations in April, and his notebooks show how assiduously he could study when he had to. He passed by a narrow margin and went back to his music again, knowing that the college would not ask anything of him again until the autumn. Playing in the orchestra now took all his interest and time. Years later he wrote in one of his notes:

Soon after my entrance to an orchestra we played the Jupiter Symphony of Mozart. It was in an academy and a Jewess was playing at the desk before me. No other emotion that I have received was quite so puissant or complete. A slight and altogether subconscious avidity of sex wound and wreathed itself in the extraordinary beauty of the movement, not unlike the sexual element that exists in all really fervent ecstasies of faith.

I had not long left puberty and, though vulgar sensuality did not attract me, I was haunted by dreams of a verdant liberty that reigned or seemed to reign, in pagan forests of the south. Often I threw my music aside and hid in the hollows of the hills, in the futile quest of an adventure. In the orchestra I found the mysterious mansion I had dreamed. I played with morbid assiduity, and remember particularly the long days of a June that I spent looking out over the four strings of my violin into the filling leaves and white erect florescence of a chestnut and a wilderness of plants beneath it, that crushed and strangled each other in a green and silent frenzy of expansion.

The house at Crosthwaite Park had one attractive feature—a view from the top floor of the Dublin mountains in the distance. It was also at the end of the street, and an aloofness from the other residents was easier to maintain. Mrs. Synge decided to spend the summer at home instead of going to Greystones. She wrote to Robert: "Johnnie is very well and is taking a rest from his fiddle, which is a relief and better for himself as he looks so pale and tired after spending hours practising. . . . He is studying German now. He wants to be able to read it, not to speak it. He likes good stiff work, and I am sure German must be rather hard to learn alone without a teacher. There is no sign of any softening towards God, or any desire to seek Him."

Samuel was a comfort to her. He completed his divinity course that spring but postponed his ordination until he should have the medical degree which would equip him for a career as a medical missionary. He and his mother carried on a constant campaign of prayer and propaganda directed at John. She reported to Robert: "Sam has lent him a book to read, written by a clergyman to those who have doubts and unbelief, and we are asking the Lord to speak through the book. We take ahold afresh of His promises." But the propagandizing was not all one-sided, for Synge talked her into changing her daily newspaper from *The Daily Express* to *The Irish Times*, which was unionist in politics but more liberal in its attitude to the Irish question. "I took it to please Johnnie," she wrote to Robert, "but I find it a rebel paper and praises O'Connell, so I gave it up."

As the summer drew to a close he began preparing for the scholarship examination in counterpoint to be given at the academy in December. At college he began to study Hebrew and Irish for the

prize examinations to be given in the next term. The teaching of
Irish at Trinity was prompted by a motive considerably different
from that which was shortly to inspire the study of Irish elsewhere in
Ireland. Being an activity of the Divinity School, it was the medium
through which the Irish Church Missions hoped to convert the
Roman Catholics of the west of Ireland to the Protestant faith. The
professor of Irish was a country rector who spent half the academic
year at the university and the other half in his parish in Skibbereen,
County Cork. The only text Synge read in class was the Gospel of
Saint John, and he actually acquired his copy of it from the Irish
Society, which distributed free copies of the Scriptures in Irish in
order "to instruct the native Irish, who still use their vernacular
language, with a view to spread among them Scriptural instruction."
Motivated by such an objective the course cannot have attracted
many students. There must have been some competition, however,
for Synge took first place on the prize examination and received £4, a
more lucrative prize than he got for taking first also in Hebrew, a
much less useful tool for converting the Catholic peasant.

Remembering his college course ten years later, he wrote, "In those
days if an odd undergraduate of Trinity . . . wished to learn a little
of the Irish language and went to the professor appointed to teach
it in Trinity College, he found an amiable old clergyman who made
him read a crabbed version of the New Testament, and seemed to
know nothing, or least care nothing, about the old literature of
Ireland, or the fine folk-tales and folk-poetry of Munster and Connacht."[5]

Synge's judgement of the Reverend James Goodman, who held
the post of Professor of Irish at Trinity from 1884 until his death in
1896, would appear to be a little too harsh. Professor Goodman's
interest in the native speaker may well have been directed more to
saving his soul than to studying his literature, but he can hardly
have cared nothing about the native tradition. For one thing he had
been surrounded by it on the Dingle peninsula in Kerry, the heart of
the *Gaeltacht*, where he was born and brought up as the son of the
Protestant rector. He was also a member of the governing body of
the Ossianic Society, a collector of Irish manuscripts, and is remembered today by students of Irish folk music for having collected and
recorded almost two thousand traditional Irish melodies, some of

which he played on a set of pipes in his rooms at Trinity for the enjoyment of his colleagues.[6]

It is possible that Synge owed more to his college course in Irish than he was later willing to admit. Professor Goodman must have succeeded by default, at least, in awakening in his student a curiosity about the literature, for outside the required work in the course Synge read the Irish texts of *The Children of Lir* and *Diarmuid and Grania* and listed them in his diary for 1892 among the books in Irish which he had read during the year. He could not have foreseen that his Irish studies were to have a more direct bearing on his career than the scholarship in counterpoint which he won in December at the academy.

In January of 1892 Synge played in his second concert, this time at the Molesworth Hall, a small auditorium on Molesworth Street where his first two plays were to be produced some years later. The scholarship in counterpoint was awarded to him on March 16th, and on that day he made his first entry in the pocket diary which he kept from 1892 to 1899 and from 1902 to 1903. His entries were written in English, French, German, Italian and occasionally Irish and mentioned the places he had been to, the people he had met and the books he was reading. He used pseudonyms for the women in his private life.

During his last year in college his interest in the Irish past revived. From *The Children of Lir* and *Diarmuid and Grania*, which he read very slowly in Irish, he went to Wakeman's *Handbook of Irish Antiquities*, Musgrave's *Rebellions in Ireland*, Froude's *The English in Ireland*, G. T. Stokes' *Ireland and the Celtic Church*, William Stokes' life of George Petrie, and Petrie's *The Ecclesiastical Architecture of Ireland*. Petrie was the greatest Irish antiquarian of his age. He had been a painter in his youth, published a pioneer book in 1855 on ancient Irish music and, in addition to his great work on Irish round towers and a study of the Hill of Tara, had worked on the Ordnance Survey with those two other giants of Gaelic studies, John O'Donovan and Eugene O'Curry. Petrie's theory that the round towers—those wonders of the Irish landscape—were places of refuge for Irish monks retreating from the fury of the Viking raiders who plundered the monasteries of Ireland throughout the ninth and tenth centuries is still accepted. Synge liked Petrie because Petrie liked

Wordsworth, his favorite poet. In his notes Synge commented, "Petrie laughs at O'Donovan's 'shillelagh style.' "

Petrie had been to the Aran Islands, and the notes he compiled there, quoted in Stokes' biography, may have been one of the things which interested Synge in Aran. Petrie wrote of the islanders, "They are a brave, hardy race, industrious and enterprising, as is sufficiently evinced not only by the daily increasing number of their fishing vessels [but by] the barren rock which they are covering with soil and making productive."[7] Synge also found in Stokes' *Life* the story told by Petrie of an old woman whom he met in Aran. Like Maurya in *Riders to the Sea*, her life had been overshadowed by the drowning of her son. She said to Petrie: "It was not the will of God to leave him with me long. It was too much happiness for this world. My boy, sir, while fishing, was drowned in a storm off the cliffs of Moher, and I had not even the consolation of embracing his corpse."[8]

In the spring of 1892 the foundations of the Irish Literary Revival were being laid. The year before, Yeats, whom Sean O'Casey has dubbed "The Great Founder," founded the Irish Literary Society in London. In 1892 he came to Dublin and after some conversations with other enthusiasts decided to establish a society like the London one. In a letter to the press he called for a public meeting and announced the objectives of the proposed society—to publish books and give lectures and discussions "upon notable figures in Irish history and notable epochs in the national life, and on problems and difficulties of today." When the meeting was held on June 9th Synge was busy with his Hebrew and Irish. Yeats' call to arms had not reached him, if he was even aware of it. It did not move many other Irishmen either, for most Dubliners of 1892 were so concerned with purely political problems that they showed no awareness of the little group of gifted translators and poets who were intent upon giving artistic expression to nationalist aspirations. Two days after the meeting, when he might have read the newspaper accounts of it, Synge noted in his diary that he had studied Hebrew for fifteen hours.

The measure of his isolation may be taken from the fact that when the inaugural meeting of the Irish National Literary Society was held in Dublin two months later and speeches were made by Yeats, Maud Gonne, John O'Leary and others, the young man who had just won a prize for excellence in the Irish language had gone to

Wicklow for the summer where his mother under police protection
had hired a boycotted house. The Kingdom of Ireland would not
make its next appeal to him until he fell under the influence of Yeats
and Cathleen Ni Houlihan herself in Paris more than four years
later.

Yeats was six years older than Synge, but there was a world of difference between his life and Synge's. He had received his political in-
doctrination, for one thing, in "the school of John O'Leary," and the
letters he wrote to Katharine Tynan during the period between 1887
and 1892 indicate where the rest of his orientation came from—the
reading of Irish patriotic literature. "We used to discuss everything
that was known to us about Ireland," he wrote later, "and especially
Irish literature and Irish history. We had no Gaelic, but paid great
honour to the Irish poets who wrote in English, and quoted them in
our speeches. I could have told you at that time the dates of the
birth and death, and quoted the chief poems, of men whose names
you have not heard, and perhaps of some whose names I have
forgotten."9

The boycotted house in which Synge spent the summer vacation
of 1892, and many summers thereafter, was a huge, grey stone house
surrounded by trees and standing on the crest of a hill in the townland of Castle Kevin, a few miles from Glanmore Castle in County
Wicklow where he had visited in 1889. The original Castle Kevin, of
which only a high green mound with a bit of the ancient stonework
still remains, stands at the foot of the hill, a short walk from its
modern counterpart. It was the manorial castle of the archbishops of
Dublin, built when the ancient sees of Glendalough and Dublin were
united in 1214. From it the Anglo-Norman archbishops had only
temporary success, however, in subduing the native chieftains. After
its first half-century of existence as a symbol of Anglo-Norman law
and order it changed hands frequently, being alternately destroyed
and restored, was then firmly held by native chieftains for two centuries and finally destroyed by Cromwell's artillery in the seventeenth
century. For Synge, who was immersed at the time in Irish history, it
was not the only visible sign of the historical and legendary associations which the district had. The countryside was dotted with the
remains of primitive burial sites and megalithic fortifications, and
five miles to the southwest was the remarkable collection of ruins at

Glendalough. In addition to the local myths about giants' graves and saints' beds, Synge knew the story of Red Hugh O'Donnell, the great Gaelic chieftain of the sixteenth century, who had stopped at Castle Kevin on his historic flight from Dublin Castle across the Wicklow mountains. He was shown the hill on which Cromwell's cannon had been mounted for the last assault upon the castle.

Confiscations, rebellions and devastations had left their mark on Wicklow. Almost all the domestic architecture had been destroyed, and the only impressive buildings left standing were those homes of the gentry which had managed to survive the rising of 1798 and were now falling into decay. A more subtle sign of the completeness of the conquest was the total disappearance of the native language and the large number of natives with English names whose origins were lost in the confusion of the centuries. The Wicklow countryman spoke a dialect which blended Gaelic syntax with an archaic English vocabulary and was the natural heritage of a conquest which had suddenly and violently imposed one language upon another. In other parts of Ireland more remote from the conquest this process came later and left more visible marks upon the speech of the people. As Synge tramped over the roads and mountains that first summer, listening not only to the talk of the servant girls but also to the stories told him by the tinkers and tramps he met by the wayside, he was impressed by the colour and vitality of the local dialect without realizing that it would one day provide him with a medium of expression. He did not begin to formulate his theory of language for the stage until he had learned to speak Irish and had lived with bilingual peasants in the west of Ireland.

The modern Castle Kevin is an attractive and rather massive stone house of three floors, the lowest at ground level being accessible only from the rear and containing service rooms and servants' quarters. A courtyard in the rear is surrounded by stables and outhouses, and there is a large high-walled garden covering an acre or so a few yards from the entrance to the stable yard. The garden and terraced grounds are well kept, and the view from the front steps looks over the Wicklow hills stretching for miles into the distance. In Synge's day neither the house nor the grounds had been maintained for years. The hill upon which the house stood was almost entirely surrounded by bogs and streams, passing traffic having been diverted by a new road made early

in the nineteenth century. Most of the people who lived on the estate
had left, and the big house had been lying empty and boycotted for
ten years. Round the town land was a road, but the part across the
southern slopes of the hill had degenerated into a grassy track; and
the rest, unfrequented, had become edged with grass margins where
tinkers used to camp.

The particularly forbidding stone wall which enclosed the overgrown garden was a mute symbol of defiance to a new generation of
rebellious natives. In a rare moment of sympathy for his own class
Synge later wrote, "The desolation of this life is often of a peculiarly
local kind, and if a playwright chose to go through the Irish country
houses he would find material, it is likely, for many gloomy plays that
would turn on the dying away of these old families. . . ."[10] It was to
provide him with the subject matter of the first play he wrote.

The Synges had more than the ruinous state of the house to remind
them that a new generation of natives resented the people in the big
house. The police constable stopped every day; the local blacksmith
refused at first to shoe horses from a boycotted house; and scribbled
in pencil on one of the doorposts, Synge discovered, were a few lines
of verse. He copied them and afterwards published them in a different
context.

> In the days of rack renting
> And land-grabbing so vile,
> A proud, heartless landlord
> Lived here a great while.
>
> When the League it was started,
> And the land-grabbing cry,
> To the cold North of Ireland
> He had for to fly.[11]

The Synges returned to Crosthwaite Park in September, and he
wrote in his diary for the first three days after his return, "Wrote airs
in E♭ and G," "Polished air in G," and "Worked at Sonata in D."
In October he took his first composition, which he called "Andante
in F," to Sir Robert Stewart and two weeks later a "violin fugue in
G." He filled his notebooks with analyses of concertos and symphonies by Mozart and copied out whole passages from treatises on

musical composition. "Two dangers beset the beginner—vulgarity and morbid effort for originality." "A melody which can only be harmonized awkwardly can never produce perfect music." None of his musical compositions has survived.

He also began to write verse, and sent a poem to Father Russell, the editor of *The Irish Monthly*, entitled "A Mountain Creed":

> A mountain flower once I spied,
> A lonely height its dwelling,
> Where winds around it wailed and sighed
> Sad stories sadly telling.

When the flower is asked how it survives its lonely existence, the answer is Wordsworthian:

> I live not here to pine and mourn
> O'er what is not my making,
> But to fulfill my fate inborn
> And hold myself unquaking. . . .

Father Russell returned it with the words, "Your pleasing poem has some defects, I think, which allow me to carry out my general policy, which now tends towards a diminution of our supply of verse." His criticism was directed towards the title, two rhymes and the inappropriate use of two adjectives. Synge immediately eliminated the objectionable passages and changed the title to "A Mountain Flower." But Father Russell, whose helpful letters could hardly have been the most effective way of encouraging the "diminution of our supply of verse," as he tactfully put it, returned it again with a short note of congratulation on the improvements.

In the second week of December he took his final examinations and "passed in the second class." When he received his degree on December 15, 1892, he would have had to admit that he had given the college as little as it had given him. Except for his work in Hebrew and Irish, he attended the minimum number of required lectures, ignored all student activities, made no friends and visited his tutor only when required to. He was given what was known as a gentleman's or pass degree, and the college authorities must have thought that a gentleman was all he was capable of becoming.

His mother discreetly said nothing to him about his plans for the future. He joined an instrumental club, attended concerts, continued playing in the orchestra and studied music by himself. The family were pleased when he brought his violin to small family gatherings and even took pride in his playing. He might well have settled down to a relatively harmless career as a member of a little circle of musicians in Dublin except for one event which altered the whole course of his life.

Three

FIRST LOVE. GERMANY. PARIS. ITALY

You've made a choice wise men will be glad of in the five ends of Ireland.

In March of 1893 a distant cousin of Mrs. Synge's came from England for a visit to Dublin. Mary Synge was a concert pianist and music teacher whose orthodox religious views enabled her Irish relatives to overlook the fact that she was a professional entertainer. She had thick white hair which seemed to stand on end, and was considered an unconventional but interesting person. She was immediately attracted to Synge, especially when she heard him play and realized that he wanted to make a career of music. Before she had quite realized it she was planning his future for him. When she announced her intentions of giving a piano recital in the Antient Concert Rooms he hired the hall, took charge of the publicity and engaged three Dublin musicians to appear with her. The recital was held on April 17th, and he was delighted when *The Irish Times* published a detailed and complimentary report of her performance.

Whether the idea of flanking herself with local musicians in order to assure a solid attendance and favourable critical reception was his idea or not is not clear, but she was grateful for his help and pointed out that they were now musical colleagues. She decided that he should go to Germany to study, and set about convincing his mother. She would go herself with him to Germany in July to see that he did not fall in with thieves and arrange for him to stay with friends of hers on the river island of Oberwerth, near Coblenz, in a boardinghouse

35

kept by four sisters, the von Eikens. When she left for London at the end of April, their plans to meet in London in July and continue on together to Oberwerth were made.

In the interval Synge continued his violin lessons, brought an increasing number of musical compositions to Stewart and on May 20th wrote in his diary, "Started words and music of an opera on Eileen Aruine." He also resumed the study of German, which he had started in the summer of 1891, by taking lessons from a private teacher. He amused the Stephens boys by playing on a dandelion stalk, an art which had taken him some time to master and which he described in his diary: "Practised on a dandelion stalk till I mastered the reed sound and brought three corncrakes across a field by it." He also fell in love.

He had met Cherry Matheson, a girl of his own age, at Greystones, but he had not got to know her very well until her family moved to Crosthwaite Park, three houses away from his. Cherry's father was a leader of the Plymouth Brethren and directed the religious activities of his family with a vigour even Mrs. Synge could barely rival. His daughter was short, plump, quick of gesture and remarkable for a brightness of manner which Synge found attractive. She was not unduly oppressed by her father's strict discipline and ascetic creed, but she accepted them nevertheless with unquestioning faith. It soon became apparent that she would never form any real intimacy with a man who could not assure her and her father that he believed in salvation. Synge seems to have sensed the hopelessness of the situation from the very beginning, though he did not admit it for a long time.

At the end of July Synge left Dún Laoghaire by boat, met Mary Synge in London and continued on with her to Coblenz. Except for a brief visit to the Isle of Man with his mother when he was eleven, he had never been out of Ireland. The von Eiken house, where he was to stay, was near the left bank of the Rhine, above the town of Oberwerth and just below the gorge where the river, overlooked by many castles, twisted for about forty miles among vine-covered hills. The von Eiken girls—Hedwig, Emma, Claire and Valeska—were daughters of a German army officer who had died leaving them without any money. Together they ran a boardinghouse in a large building which had once been part of an old convent. It was the first and the last house Synge stayed in on the Continent, for he returned to it years afterwards for a brief visit a few months before his death.

He arrived at Oberwerth on July 29th. The next day he made only one brief entry in his diary and it was written in Irish: "The day of Valeska!" Valeska was the youngest of the sisters. She nicknamed him "Holy Moses," from an oath he used, and he called her "Gorse." When he told her about his love for Cherry Matheson and about how his unorthodoxy was separating them, she dubbed Cherry "The Holy One." She agreed to teach him German.

Before he had been in Oberwerth a month he wrote to his mother to propose a longer stay than the two months he had planned. She approved and sent him more money. When Mary Synge left for home in October he saw her off and thanked her for bringing him into a world he never knew existed. He was now living among people who regarded music as an important profession and who accepted his ambition quite naturally. With Valeska, who would have shocked his mother, he talked openly about himself in a way he had not done since childhood with Florence Ross. He wrote his mother such an enthusiastic letter about his life that she was offended and wrote in her diary, "'I had a long letter from poor Johnnie. He has a bad cold. Curious letter attributing his unsociableness to his narrow bringing up and warning me! I wrote to him, [but] did not say much on that subject."

He did not forget, however, that he was in Germany to study music, for when his violin lessons ended on December 18th he began to wonder if the pleasant life at Oberwerth afforded him the best opportunity. He made inquiries about Cologne, but decided that he would go to Würzburg instead. He wrote in his diary on January 22nd, "Left Coblenz by train at 11:30 and arrived in Wurzburg at 5:30. *Ochone! Ochone! Ochone!*" His mother wrote to Robert:

The Von Eikens, whom he has just left have been very kind and pleasant, and he feels as if they were his oldest friends instead of his newest! What a pity that, when thrown among strangers, we only show ourselves as amiable and agreeable and taking everything in good part—while at home we show ourselves sometimes in a very unpleasant aspect, and temper often spoils our comfort, and certainly the comfort of those we live with. Poor Johnnie forgets this, and I won't remind him. I am glad he is happier than when he was at home, but I am very sorry it was out of my power to make him happy, though I did all I could for him. He tells me that he has got complete control over his temper.

He wrote to the von Eikens as soon as he arrived in Würzburg and was rewarded with letters from Emma, Claire and Valeska. Valeska's letter began, "Dear Mister, Master, Mr. Edmund John Millington Synge, Holy Moses, Unholy Michael, Esq., B. A." and concluded with "kind regards from the cloistered maidens." Her banter made him sorry that he had left Oberwerth.

His new lodgings were in a house at Hanger Ring 16, and he arranged to take his meals at the Railway Hotel. He also hired a piano and made arrangements to take lessons beginning on February 10th with a teacher recommended to him by his friends at Oberwerth. The only person he knew in Würzburg was a girl he had met at Oberwerth, but before calling upon her he wrote to the von Eikens to ask about the propriety of it. Both Emma and Claire replied to him in separate letters that his caution was well taken. Claire wrote, "In Germany it is just the same as in England—no gentleman visits a lady." It was apparent to him that life with the von Eiken girls in Oberwerth was going to be difficult to duplicate in another city.

He was beginning to examine his own attitudes, and apparently reflecting on some slight tactlessness he wrote in his diary: "Let A and B be two women. If A is your particular friend or near relative, never say anything to her in B's favor, or at least never more than once in your life time, and then with care and judgement." Life in Würzburg began to open for him, however. In February there was a carnival, and the streets were full of good-humored crowds. On the third day of the carnival he found himself mixing with the students. But he missed the von Eikens and wrote Valeska a long letter telling her so. She replied, addressing him as "Dear Herr, Mr., Master, Mr. Edmund John Millington Synge, B. A., Holy Moses, *etc. etc.*"

Probably a little disturbance in your lonely life of art and science at which you are now so busy will do you good. Therefore I shall disturb your peace today and write you this ordinary letter which is neither a scientific nor an artistic essay.

First of all many thanks for your letter which pleased me very much on account of your German. I did not think you capable of sending such a long letter so soon. Your talkative people at table must be very interesting. Why did you not break the ice and start a conversation with them? They probably think you do not know any German, otherwise I cannot understand such stiffness in Germany. . . .

None of Synge's letters to Valeska von Eiken have survived, apparently; but sometimes, when his German was so shaky that he had to write out his letter first in the rough and then correct the mistakes before he made a final copy, his notebook provides a fragment. He wrote, "Many thanks for the pleasant disturbance which arrived on Friday morning, and to which I can reply comfortably as the weather today is unpleasant for a walk. I think that the other letter I wrote you was throughout foolish, ridiculous and tasteless, but then I was terribly sentimental for a few weeks. As I always have to write such sensible and well-behaved letters to Ireland it is very pleasant to let myself go when I can, as just now, and talk about foolish and silly things for a change."

In another letter to Valeska he wrote that he had taken her advice about striking up conversation with his dinner companions:

Once, when I was alone at table with a young gentleman, I started to talk to him and now we chatter together in quite a friendly way. He is a young doctor, from North Germany, who has studied in Berlin and Leipzig. He is a terribly anxious fellow. At first my power of imagination was quite exhausted after dinner, but now fortunately I am in practice. For instance, at table yesterday he started again, as usual, and asked me what the population of Belfast was—100,000 or 300,000? I replied with anything that came into my head and asked him how many madmen there were in Wurzburg. He thought about it industriously and gave me a long reply. Then I asked him, how many madwomen are there? mad children? and so on as long as the smallest trace of curiosity remained in his poor face.

But the only friend he made in Würzburg was an American named Robert Peers, who wanted to reform spelling in the English language upon phonetic principles. When Synge returned to Ireland they corresponded briefly on the subject.

Talking with German students convinced Synge that his own university education had been inadequate, and he began to think of enrolling for graduate study in a German university. He wrote in his diary, "Heard from a German student that in the last exams in the Gymnasium here the youths must translate *unseen* Greek, Latin and French and also translate into three languages." When he was out for long walks in the mountains, he talked to country people as he did at home, but the picture which Yeats later drew of him "playing his fiddle to Italian sailors, and listening to stories in Bavarian woods" is quite fanciful.

In March he went back to Oberwerth to spend a week's vacation at Easter with the von Eikens, and on the way to Würzburg made a side excursion to Frankfurt am Main to visit the house where Goethe had lived as a child. In Würzburg he found a letter from his mother telling him of the death of Sir Robert Stewart, his teacher at the Royal Irish Academy of Music. He wrote to Valeska:

Since my return I have not had a pleasant time as I got a bad cough, I do not know how or where. Moreover I have had sad news from Ireland that my beloved harmony teacher died on Easter Saturday in the evening from a stroke, and with him the cleverest Irish musician and one of the kindest of men of the century has gone from us. In recent years, it is true, he was not a strict teacher, but yet he had definitely more genius than Hubner and Van Zeyl have together. . . .

On Friday morning, when I woke up, I found the postman opposite my bed. As you can imagine I was a little surprised, but he quietly fetched a pen and I wrote my name in his book. But then I had to get up to find him a tip, and the fellow seemed greatly amused when he saw that I slept in stockings; however he did not say anything except to ask me how much my watch cost. . . .

Many thanks for your letter and the united good wishes. Since my last letter to Oberwerth nothing extraordinary has happened in Wurzburg, except that owing to the warm and dusty weather people seem to drink much more beer and are therefore frequently drunk. I don't deny I am delighted to see that Germans sin just as the Irish do, a fact which I always believed.

He began writing verse again and filled a notebook with poems and snatches of poems. In 1908, when he was preparing a volume of his verse for publication, he wrote on the flyleaf of the notebook, "These boyish verses are not to be printed under any circumstances." But he resurrected and revised two of them. One of these, entitled "Pre-lude," owes more to Wordsworth for its title, its description of the speaker "in converse with the mountains, moors, and fens," than to Wicklow, which is mentioned in the second line. No Wicklowman would have described anything in his native habitat as a *moor*. The other poem—one of two with the same title, "Epitaph"—is also derivative. The speaker is "a silent sinner," lamenting his loneliness and the fact that he is little loved. But the fixation on death, too sentimental to have the astringent morbidity of a later poem like "To the Oaks of Glencree," is more characteristic. The most interesting, and certainly the most original, is a debate in ballad style between an old man of the roads on his way to the poorhouse and the speaker, a young man from one of the big houses in Wicklow, presumably Synge himself:

> "Good evenin', Misther, niver more
> My face you'll see again.
> I'm so filled full of emptiness
> So drownded with the rain
>
> That I'm jist goin' to the House,
> Jist goin' to be a pauper,
> To axe her gracious Majesty
> For a life of meals and torpor."
>
> "Why, ragged bones, 'twere better choose
> A schoolin' in Glencree,
> Where you'd be taught a dacent thrade,
> With duds and eatin' free."
>
> "There's none goes there but them as steals.
> I'm honester nor you.
> I niver stole, a starvin' thief,
> As yours are proud to do!"
>
> "'Tis but the course of equity,
> We work for laws and right."
> "Och, Misther Honey, spake the thruth,
> You're jobbers all for might."

He outlined a play and may even have written a substantial part of it, for his diary entries indicate that he worked on it during his last few months in Würzburg. It was to be about a young Irish landlord who returns from Paris and marries a girl of the lower classes from a cottage on his own estate. The hero and his widowed mother were not the only autobiographical elements: the girl's two brothers, one a wastrel and the other a poet, possibly represented the two aspects of his own character—as his family saw him and as he saw himself. In a reminiscence which Cherry Matheson later wrote of him, she quoted him as having said to her once: "I am a poor man, but I feel that if I live I shall be rich. I feel there is that in me which will be of value to the world."[12] The words do not impress one as being something he ever actually said, but the concern about his poverty and whether he would live long enough are certainly characteristic. His conception of himself as a vagrant owed more to his own idea of himself than to any the family had.

His first attempt at a drama was probably as derivative as his poems, but unlike them it seems to have given expression, however inadequately, to a theme which he was to return to in his mature work. His first completed play, which he showed to Yeats and to Lady Gregory about seven years later, is about the same young Irish landlord who returns to Ireland from Paris and falls in love with a nun. He also projected another play while he was still in Würzburg, this too based on his own life. In the fragment which remains a stern father prohibits his daughter from marrying a penniless hero. "I tell you, you can't be engaged to a beggar. Long before he had money enough to marry, you would be tired of him, [and] then his second state would be worse than his first."

There is no evidence, either in his letters of the time or in his notebooks, that he had made the decision to abandon music for writing, but during his last two months in Würzburg he was undoubtedly on his way to making it. When he left Würzburg on June 1st for Oberwerth, where he spent twelve days before returning to Ireland, his mind must have been made up. From what he wrote later it is plain that his chief reason was that he was convinced that he could never perform as an instrumentalist before an audience. As for musical composition, he had probably been told that his talent was too limited.

His vacation at Oberwerth he spent playing in quartets with the von Eikens and discussing with Valeska his decision to give up music. On June 12th he left for Dublin, where he looked forward to seeing

Cherry and spending the summer months in Wicklow with his mother and the Stephenses. Ireland, with its political agitation and the restricting influences of the narrow society he was returning to, must have seemed like a world he was most fortunate to have been rescued from. At Crosthwaite Park he learned that Cherry Matheson was away and would not return to Dublin until next month. He was probably grateful for the necessity of postponing a painful reunion. Since his correspondence with her has disappeared, one can only gather from indirect evidence and cryptic entries in his diary just what state his mind was in.

In her letter to Robert two weeks after Synge's homecoming, his mother described him as "low and depressed" and lamented the fact that he had not changed his basic attitudes to religion. "Sam talks with him now and then, and he told me last night that there is a great change for the better in Johnnie's mind, looking back a few years; he allows so much more now than he did then. But alas he won't receive Christ and thinks He is not a Saviour for him. But he allowed last night, to Sam, that Christianity is good for depraved humanity such as cannibals and the heathen in general, whose lives are so cruel and miserable till the Holy Spirit transforms them through the preaching of the gospel." She was also worried about a mysterious lump which had developed on each of his wrists. She wrote Robert, "I don't think I told you he had got a lump on each wrist, underneath where all the sinews are, from playing the piano so much." She persuaded him to show them to a Dublin doctor, who remarked that he didn't think they would go away by themselves. They eventually disappeared, but one is tempted to think that they might have had some connection with the lump which eventually formed on his neck and brought his death with it.

His family were surprised to hear him playing the piano. His mother wrote, "Sam heard him playing the piano at Greystones—they made him play for them—and was quite surprised at his style, altogether so different from his former style. He told Sam afterwards that he had composed the little piece he played. It was the only thing he could play by heart. He has never played for me, though I asked him. He seems shy of doing so."

Cherry Matheson came to Castle Kevin to spend two weeks with the Synges in the summer of 1894. In her recollection, written nearly thirty years later, she described Synge as "a strongly built man with a rather thick neck and large head, a wonderful face with great luminous sad eyes, and though he was tanned from being constantly out of doors, there was a sort of pallor on his face that gave it a look of delicacy belying his figure, which was that of a hardy mountaineer . . . he had acquired a guttural way of speaking which made him seem almost foreign. When he was interested he spoke with the greatest rapidity."[13] They talked about their favorite poet, Wordsworth, and about art, especially Corot. One day when he was playing the violin for her, "a lovely wild melody of his own," his small nephew Edward Stephens disturbed him and he suddenly stopped playing and retreated from the room. "He told me that he had thought of taking up music as a profession, but his master in Dublin told him he could never make a success of it on account of his extreme nervousness."

Synge's version of the incident, and of the crisis he had gone through with Cherry, is embodied in a collection of verses he wrote during this visit of Cherry's. Some years later, when he was able to look back on the incident as closed, he collected these poems under the title *Vita Vecchia* and connected them by short links of prose narrative in which he told the story of his affair by disguising personalities and real events:

A young girl of the Roman Catholic Church spent nine weeks in the house where I lodged when I was studying music in Germany. Two days before she moved on to Venice I promised to play for her on the violin. The following night I dreamed that I did so, and that when I began a crowd of people rushed into the room with such noise and disturbance that I stopped playing and threw down my fiddle on the floor with the horror of nightmare. The next morning I played for her as she wished, and as I was in the middle of an old love song I had chosen, a number of children ran into the room and began to make fun of my performance. I was playing from memory. I began to lose notes, and in the end I broke down utterly.

At the end of the summer he announced his plans to give up music permanently and concentrate on learning foreign languages. He told his mother—who was only partially relieved by his announcement—that he would return to Oberwerth but only for a visit before moving on to Paris where he would take courses at the Sorbonne and support himself by giving English lessons. When he left Dublin at the end of October he was as pleased with the prospects of his new career as he had been with the old one.

He stayed only two months at Oberwerth and spent most of his time studying German, with Valeska, and French, a new language for him. On New Year's day, 1895, he left for Paris with the address of a Breton student named Albert Cugnier, whom he had met at Oberwerth. Cugnier got him a room at 94 rue Lafayette with a family named Arbeau. He wrote to his mother that he hoped to earn enough teaching English, and possibly German, to earn his own tuition at the Sorbonne. Valeska wrote to him on January 4th, telling how much he was missed by the "cloistered maidens" and of the legend on one of the "crackers" she had pulled during a game, which expressed her feelings for Holy Moses. "It means 'Nothing can destroy our friendship; time and the future will only enhance it.' " Knowing also that he was still upset about his relations with Cherry, she added: "If you want to unburden your heart about the Holy One I shall keep your secret. Let your *ordinary* letter follow soon and look into the future with confidence and trust in God." He was careful, apparently, to distinguish between the letters he wrote for her alone and those she was expected to show her sisters.

On January 11th she wrote again, apparently after he had responded to her invitation to unburden himself, with more intimacy than she was willing to accept.

Dear Holy Moses, who begins his letter with "a slip of the pen" and just writes "Dear Valeska" without adding "Miss" to it. What do I think of it? You see, Monsieur Moses, for this your friend has not given you permission, so in the next letter please don't make the "slip" again.

Don't think that I am angry with you because of that, but to be really good *friends* one ought to behave in the manner due to true friends as otherwise no friendship can exist. Perhaps you think because we call each other by the first name with Titi Fenwick, so we two could do it just the same. But you see that is different; we knew each other from childhood and always called each other by the first name. These are customs and it won't disturb our friendship when you continue to call me Miss V.

Why do you think that you might be disappointed in your friendship with us? Even if you have had bad experiences in your friendships, it is no reason to think that the same might happen with your friends from Oberwerth. Maybe your other choice of friends was not the correct one; probably they were too young—maybe even of your own age? I think that that is never good, because they are never real friendships. Too often there appears between such people a different feeling called "Love." But if your friends are so much older, as is the case with us, so that no jealousies *etc.* can appear, then a real friendly feeling can exist between a Holy Moses and a Gorse, and if the Holy Man should marry one day the Holy Woman, so will the Gorse be very much pleased about the good luck of her friend. But now we had better finish with this subject. So— for true friendship!

It must have been a douche of cold water to discover that his "friend" was worried only about the proper formality due her. He met her objections to his "slip of the pen" with a long letter on January 16th:

Dear Gorse, Do you know the country where the yellow gorse blossoms? Unfortunately you have never seen those lovely flowers. They are lovely to look at. The color is so charming and warm, and they smell so beautifully that even the saints in heaven would feel still more divine if they could only smell them. Sometime, in my past youth, I was tempted to pluck these flowers and take them home. But, Good Heavens, I found they were full of thorns; so I was forced to sit down on the cold rock and, like the pious Linnaeus, to thank God for having created so much that is beautiful in this world. It reminds me of a little story that my mother often read to me when I was a small and well-behaved boy sitting in my chair at her feet. This is the story of the Holy Moses when he stood in excitement in front of the Burning Bush and remarked how it burned and burned without ever burning out. He is stated to have taken off his shoes in reverence, but this I could not do as my stocking had not been darned.

Another good thing about gorse is that you can always find beautiful flowers on it; throughout the whole year you can take delight in it, whereas everything else in the world looks cold and desolate. The thought has occurred to me that this property is dead this winter, and I shall soon write to the "Flea" to find out whether this is really true.

After all this symbolic dreaming I must thank you very much for your long letter which arrived last evening at 9 o'clock. I immediately sat down in my arm-chair to be able to read it comfortably and when I pulled out my watch it was past 12 o'clock. For three full hours I had been dreaming without ever noticing the time. Then I went to bed and dreamt on and on. This was my dream. I stood in front of a great iceberg. On the top of it grew the loveliest gorse bush. I wanted to climb up to look at the beautiful flowers more closely and to enjoy their smell, but it was all so smooth and cold and slippery that it seemed impossible. Then I noticed some small blue flowers. They were forget-me-nots! Where they grew it was not so slippery and I could climb and climb until I got near the beautiful gorse; when I got there the forget-me-nots had disappeared, and when I wanted to jump over the last bush I fell and fell until I woke up very frightened. . . .

You ask if you may tell your sister about my letters. You ought to have known for a long time that if you really desire something, I cannot have anything against it, but before doing such a thing think of what might happen by doing so. A letter is written to the person who reads it; it does not matter whose name is on it. Human beings on the whole are so similar that when you write two letters to different people at the same time, these letters will be found very similar, so that if you do a thing like that again, I shall never be able to write to *you* again. Letters to a family are quite a different matter, which I do not like. It does not matter whether one likes the family. When I write a letter to my mother, it is for her and not for the others. That's how I feel about it. Do you know the beautiful quotation from Bacon, "One doubleth a joy when one imparts it to a friend and a sorrow loses half its pain?"

Unfortunately I shall only see you very little from now on and even then only for a very short time. And in the meantime you want me to write nothing but stupid compositions about the weather. Such a thing would have surprised me when I was younger. Oh yes, do as you please. Don't mind me.

His allegory was apparently effective, for she wrote back, "When I wrote to you a short time ago, it was with many interruptions and in great haste as Claire wanted to go to town and was begging me to hurry up." Then after urging him to call on the people she had given introductions to, she added that they were expecting an Irishwoman at Oberwerth. "I wished it were your Holy One. In that case I would tell her a few things (of course only bad things) about you. From your last letter I gather that you are not too pleased at my sisters' reading your letters. I am sorry about that, for I would like to continue our harmless exchange of letters. As soon as there are secrets in them they cease to be harmless and I would not care for that. I would be sorry not to have a conversation in writing with Holy Moses from time to time." She had apparently forgotten that she had invited him to unburden himself and that she would keep his secret.

In another letter she asked him to clear up the mystery of Monsieur Arbeau. "You wrote us lately that he was an agent for tooth-powder and now you say he is a professor." Actually Monsieur Arbeau was a professional cook who supplemented his income by selling tooth-powder of his own manufacture. His wife made women's hats, and Synge appears to have assisted occasionally in both operations. But the women who made the hats, he complained, looked upon him as unsophisticated, uninteresting, and helped him very little in his attempts to learn French.

The house provided a strange contrast to the one he had left in Oberwerth. When he wasn't in the living room, surrounded by women's hats or batches of toothpowder, he sat in his attic room alone before a small fire and listened to the sound of the street noises in the strange city. He wrote a poem about homesickness,

> But to my soul it seemed my eager feet
> Tread once again the heather, rock and peat
> Of Wicklow glens, where now the free winds blow,
> Chasing in wild delight the vagrant snow
> From hill to hill, seeking a safe retreat. . . .

Cherry wrote that she received long letters from him during this first stay in Paris, "telling about his life, his hardships and experiences. Though he had hardships I don't think he minded them much; they were all more or less of an adventure. He said the weather was bitterly cold, so he used to stay in bed to keep warm. It was the only way. Also he said his landlady's servant warned him not to eat the meat, and told him it was cat's meat. That amused him very much. These letters were closely written in a small, pointed hand and often misspelt. Sometimes he began a word in the middle, as if he were thinking much faster than he could write."[14]

His French improved rapidly, and he joined a students' club where he could meet other people. He also began to write steadily. According to his diary he wrote a "critique" and on January 28th sent it to *The Irish Times*, but it seems not to have been published. On March 24th he "wrote St. Kevin 1-110," apparently a poem on the Irish saint associated with Glendalough. The poems he wrote during these months are not only quite undistinguished but with few exceptions appear to be unfinished, as though they were attempted in one sitting and never returned to again. They are full of the consciousness of death, as all his work is. Perhaps the self-pity and self-dramatization are not unusual in the work of a young man a long way from home.

At the students' club he met a man named Edward Denny, probably a fellow Irishman, who sent him a philosophy student from Heidelberg who agreed to exchange language lessons. On April 1, 1895, he had had enough of toothpowder and women's hats and moved to a single room in another private home at 2 rue Léopold Robert. In April he began to take courses at the Sorbonne in modern French literature with T. M. Faguet, medieval literature with Petit de Julleville, and general and comparative phonetics with Paul Passy, a rather impressive start in his new field of interest. He attended lectures regularly until the end of the term in June and received certificates signed by each of the three lecturers.

He was reading French authors. His notebook contains a long passage of thirty-six pages, mostly quotations, from Taine's *La Philosophie de l'Art*, and dated May 25, 1895. He was reading Pierre Loti also. Loti was to become one of his favourite authors, but the influence of Loti on his work has been exaggerated. In the article on Loti and Huysmans which he wrote for *The Speaker* in 1903, he actually praised Anatole France at Loti's expense. Of Loti's *Pêcheur d'Islande*, which he read for the first time in 1898 just before he went to Aran and which is supposed to have inspired his remark about doing for the Irish peasantry what Loti had done for the Breton fishermen, he observed in his Aran notebook that Loti had erred in his portrayal of peasants.

Early in June his friend Denny sent him another student of English, a French girl named Thérèse Beydon. She was an art teacher in a girls' school, a devout Protestant, interested in politics and in the feminist movement, and a defender of Dreyfus. The only attachments he had had so far had been with women—Florence Ross, Cherry Matheson and Valeska von Eiken. He was shy and inclined to silence with men, but all too willing to lay bare his troubles and his dreams to a sympathetic and sensitive woman. It was to be the pattern of his entire life, for the letters he received from the many women he knew provide a startling contrast to those he received from men. The testimony of friends like Yeats, R. I. Best and others about his brooding silence and impersonality make one realize that they saw only one side of him. The hero of his first completed play reads a letter from a friend who writes, "Have you noticed all the wit one lavishes on women? It would be possible to write an article on the 'Lost Gems of the Jester,' to show the misery of a man who is only articulate with girls, and spreads out humor and fancies before them which he knows are never understood. . . . I have never said anything to a man that was worth saying to a woman, and rarely said anything to a woman that was not fit for a man." It was an observation he had previously made about himself and written in his notebook.

He attended two public lectures by the anarchist Sebastian Fauré in June, but he was not too impressed by what he heard. Of the first he wrote in his diary, "*très interessant mais fou*," and of the second, "*Il a montré que si l'anarchism etait fondé, il faudreut à tout le monde travailler pour 4 heure par jour.*" After his first exposure to revolutionary doctrine he later returned to it again, and for a time at least described himself as a socialist. When he left Paris for Ireland on June 28th, with his courses at the Sorbonne successfully completed and a good deal of writing done, he had reason to feel that he had made a start, at least, in a new direction. In one of his poems he wrote a farewell to music:

> For thee I would have led my life,
> Have braved a breadless, barren strife.
> I was not destined for the glee
> True musicians find in thee.
>
> Now I am poor but poor alone,
> No music answers to my moan,
> My heart is hard as hardest stone.

The technique is scarcely impressive, but the sentiment is clear.

His mother had hired a farmhouse near Lough Dan for the month of July, and for August a house on the side of Castle Kevin hill. Since the farmhouse was secluded he announced that there would be no necessity for his going to church with his mother on Sundays as he had

Synge at the Abbey Theatre. Pencil sketch
by J. B. Yeats. January 25, 1907.

done in previous summers to keep up appearances. He fell back into his summer routine of walking, fishing and reading. He voted at a general election in July but did not record how he voted. From a letter he wrote later, however, it appears that he was still opposed to Home Rule on the ground that it might produce a religious conflict. He was not willing to face the possibility of a violent upheaval in the class structure. He began rereading Petrie on Irish antiquities and picked up his Irish text of *The Children of Lir* which he had studied three years before. Perhaps the thought occurred to him that a student of languages should not be entirely uninterested in the language of his own country. He also continued to write verse, using the same notebook he had used in Würzburg and Paris. The dominant note was still his love for Cherry, and one of the poems written this summer later appeared in *Vita Vecchia* in revised form.

> Then a footfall faint arose,
> Timid touched the way,
> Of one that many loved,
> In days passed away.
>
> Soon I faltered, found my feet,
> Bound me to her side,
> Wandered for years and years,
> Till she dropped and died.

When he returned to Dublin at the beginning of September he seems to have been in some doubt about his next step. He went into the city every day and read Herbert Spencer in the library of Trinity College, took Italian lessons from a private teacher, and finally made his mind up to make one more attempt to win Cherry before leaving for the Continent. He took her to the Sketching Club and the National Gallery. She lent him religious books in the hope of converting him, and he replied in a composition entitled "Sir John and Scherma," probably a short skit dramatizing their differences. He later destroyed it, but the name he had invented for her stuck. From this time on she was always Scherma in his diary. She later remembered his saying to her, "It is very amusing to me coming back to Ireland to find myself looked upon as a Pariah, because I don't go to church and am not orthodox, while in Paris amongst the students I am looked upon as a saint, simply because I don't do the things they do. . . ."[15]

Before he left for Paris he had his photograph taken for Cherry by the Dublin photographer Chancellor. It was later used as the frontispiece for Volume III of his collected works, published the year after his death. It shows him with a head of thick, wavy hair, a full moustache and goatee, and a face with rather pronounced features and lines under the eyes, and lends strength to the description of him by Masefield, who did not meet him until eight years later, that he had a face which looked like a blacking brush. The Synges were not as a rule dark, and his swarthy complexion, which a good many people commented on, was just one more feature that set him off from the rest of his people.

Since he planned to stay only a month in Paris before leaving for Italy, he took a room at the Hotel Corneille opposite the Odéon Theatre rather than to go into lodgings. The Hotel Corneille had had a history. Du Maurier described it in *Trilby*, and Thackeray in *The Paris Sketch-Book* wrote of it, "If you are a poor student come to study the humanities, or the pleasant art of amputation, cross the water forthwith, and proceed to the Hotel Corneille near the Odéon. . . ."[16] John O'Leary, the old Fenian, had lived there for many years during his political exile from Ireland, Yeats had stayed there, and it was there that James Joyce stayed when he left Ireland for the first time in 1902. A Dublin literary man named D. J. O'Donoghue described it as a "Bohemian resort," but Yeats' description of it as a "students' hotel" was probably more accurate, for a photograph of room Number 47, which is among Synge's papers and must have been of the room he lived in, shows a recessed bed, neatly covered, with matching drapes on a drawstring to shut it off from the rest of the room. There are also a chest of drawers, with student's lamp on top, and two chairs, one with an upholstered back standing before a small table or desk covered with papers. The woodwork is dark but appears to be in good condition. It was obviously a luxury accommodation after the house of the toothpowder mixer.

It was now that Synge met a fellow Dubliner, Dr. James Cree, whose family he had known in Dublin. Cree was from Synge's own class, but his people had been Parnellites and he was an Irish nationalist practising medicine in Paris. He and Synge became good

Four

NEW FRIENDS: W. B. YEATS, MAUD GONNE AND STEPHEN MAC KENNA. "THE KINGDOM OF IRELAND"

Let you come this day, for there's no place but Ireland where the Gael can have peace always.

In Paris, in October of 1896, Synge returned to the Hotel Corneille. There was now very little, he felt, to bind him to Ireland, except for his mother and for the fact that the money she sent him made him an Irish landlord. "My compliments to the little Irish pigs that eat filth all their lives that you may prosper," writes a friend to the hero of his first play. But even on these grounds he was beginning to question his orthodoxy. The year before he had described Fauré's lectures on socialism as madness, but now—in fact before he had left Ireland —he had begun reading the literature of socialism—*The Communist Manifesto*, the writings of William Morris, and other books whose titles he entered in his diary—*Problems of Poverty, Principes du Socialisme, L'Anarchie, Basic Socialism.* "He says he has gone back to Paris to study Socialism," his mother wrote to Samuel, "and he wants to do good, and for that possibility he is giving up everything. He says he is not selfish or egotistical but quite the reverse. In fact he writes the most utter folly. . . . I felt as if I ought not to support him there when he may only be getting himself into trouble and mischief." Socialism on top of atheism must have seemed like the last straw to her.

He had other interests however. He had discovered Thomas à

Kempis. He began reading *The Imitation of Christ* in November and read it almost daily until the middle of January. He returned to it again, as his diary records, many times in the years to come. Among his papers is a fragment of an imaginary conversation between the saint and Rabelais.

St. Thomas. Rabelais! How you must thank the Almighty that he has a place for even you among the saved!

Rabelais. Why? His peculiar glory is His mercy. If all were pious they would be unfulfilled.

St. Thomas. Could you lend me an old copy of *Gargantua?* I am suffering from a sore throat and have some time to read.

Rabelais. All are sold for a fancy price. The sum shortened my Purgatory by centuries. And the *Imitation?*

St. Thomas. No demand in Hell. Here it has no interest. It is too heavenly.

Rabelais. If I wasn't Rabelais I would be Thomas à Kempis. The cool but passionate ecstasy. . . .

St. Thomas. The sad ecstasy I write in would have little to attract you. You had a thousand readers for my one!

An example of the impact which the *Imitation* made on him is contained in the strange document entitled *Etude Morbide, or Imaginary Portrait.* In it a violinist writes in his diary the account of his love for two women, "two components of one ideal," one his mistress, whom he calls the Celliniani, the other his pupil whom he calls the Chouska. When he breaks down with nervousness in the middle of his first public concert and retires in confusion and humiliation from the stage, the Celliniani, who is in the audience, collapses and is taken to an insane asylum where she dies. The hero contemplates suicide but is saved by finding a copy of the *Imitation* on the street. "All thought of suicide seemed to leave me in an instant and I walked home up the Bd. St. Michel, wondering how the book had fallen there. Then I read it till daylight and grew as quiet as a child." As he reads and rereads the book he writes in his diary:

The unyielding quiet of this book has rescued yet appalled me. . . . I am trying to co-ordinate the inner life of this monk and my own inner life as a musician. It seems as I read him that his joy is the same as my own. Perhaps as all thirst is quenched by liquid, so the inner longing of the personality is assuaged by an ecstasy which is as multiform as the varieties of liquid and exists as essentially in prayer as in the sound of the violin. Even in the half-technical discipline of the cloister there is much that resembles the effort of the artist. "*Adjuva me, Domine Deus, in bono proposito, et sancto servitio tuo, et da mihi nunc hodie perspecte incipere, quia nihil est quod hactenus feci*" is, in a different form, the daily cry of the musician. In another way we have the same joy in progress, the same joy in infinitely fine manipulation—the saint with daily actions, the artist with his materials—and the same creation, for the saint creates, in a real sense, the strength and beauty of his personality.

A few days later he notes, "In the *Imitation*—'*Fili non poti perfectam possidere libertatem nisi totaliter abneges temet ipsum. Demitte omnia et invenias omnia.*' I have realized at length that the nearly miraculous power of the saint lies in his system of daily self-suggestion. I will try something similar." Four days later, "I have never been so happy. . . . I take some beautiful thing every morning and dwell on it till my admiration turns to a moment of passionate ecstasy, which is my equivalent for the adoration of the saints." But the optimism fades gradually into scepticism, and he writes some weeks later, "I question sometimes whether this religious ecstasy I live in is not a morbid growth—a glad infatuation I have wrought to heal the sad one." Then the Chouska recommends that he read Spinoza "as a change from the saints." Some months later he goes to Brittany where his daily readings of the saints and Stoics have lost their interest, and he gets more satisfaction from living with the people. "I have my fiddle here and I make the peasants dance in the evenings. My skin shivers while I play to see that in spite of the agony of the world there are still men and women joyous enough to leap and skip with exultation." Finally, back to normal and happy in his love of the Chouska he concludes, "I am sick of the ascetic twaddle of the saints. I will not deny my masculine existence nor rise, if I can rise, by facile abnegation. I despise the hermit and the monk and pity only the adulterer and the drunkard. There is one world of souls and no flesh and no devil."

One cannot be sure of the exact date when Synge wrote this strange spiritual autobiography. The period of his life with which it deals was the months following his break with Cherry when, according to his diary, he had discovered and immersed himself in *The Imitation of Christ*. If Cherry was Celliniani—he got the actual name from a girl he had met in a pension in Florence—one can only guess at the identity of the Chouska. The name was obviously a variation of Zdanowska, but the Polish girl was a devout Roman Catholic and would not have recommended his reading Spinoza as a change from the saints, nor would Thérèse Beydon, a Protestant whose Christian orthodoxy was just as sound as the Polish girl's. Hope Rea, the only other woman in his life at the time, to whom he went for help directly following Cherry's dismissal of him and whom his mother described as a "modern sceptic," was a more likely model. Like the Chouska she helped restore him by her own good sense and, as with the Chouska, there was no possible marital relationship. The Celliniani was like "some growth of the sea," but the Chouska was like "a mountain birch or fir tree."

In December he resumed formal study at the Sorbonne by enrolling for lectures on Petrarch by Professor Gebhardt, on La Fontaine by Professor Faguet, and on French literature by Professor Petit de Julleville. Later in the month he moved from the Hotel Corneille into lodgings on the rue Léopold Robert. Yeats and Maud Gonne were both in Paris. Before audiences that frequently numbered a thousand, Miss Gonne preached the cause of Irish nationalism. She had just returned from a lecture tour in the United States and was at the height of her fame. With the help of Arthur Lynch, an expatriate Irish journalist, she was publishing her newspaper *Irlande Libre*. Yeats believed that she had a messianic role to fulfill and was "the fiery hand of the intellectual movement."

Yeats' active career as a revolutionary had reached its peak. He was a member of the Irish Republican Brotherhood, the secret society which was the center of all conspiratorial activity in Ireland, and by the end of the year was busy in the preparations for the centennial celebration in Dublin for Wolfe Tone, the hero of the rising of 1798. Before coming to Paris he had been in the west of Ireland with his friend Arthur Symons, staying with Edward Martyn, whose money was to finance the first performances of the Irish Literary Theatre. Through Martyn he had met Lady Gregory, and both he and Symons had sailed over to the Aran Islands from Galway, where they both recorded hearing the story upon which Synge later based *The Playboy of the Western World*. At the end of the year Yeats was staying at the Hotel Corneille, as was Synge, and he and Maud Gonne were laying the foundations for a Paris branch of the Young Ireland Society.

Synge recorded the date of their first meeting in his diary on December 21, 1896—"*Fait la connaissance de* W. B. Yeates" (*sic*). In the account of the meeting which he wrote in his preface to *The Well of the Saints* Yeats put the event two years later—a mistake which he later corrected:

Six years ago I was staying in a students' hotel in the Latin quarter, and somebody whose name I cannot recollect introduced me to an Irishman, who, even poorer than myself, had taken a room at the top of the house. It was J. M. Synge, and I, who thought I knew the name of every Irishman who was working at literature, had never heard of him. He was a graduate of Trinity College, Dublin, too, and Trinity College does not as a rule produce artistic minds. He told me that he had been living in France and Germany, reading French and German literature, and that he wished to become a writer. He had, however, nothing to show but one or two poems and impressionistic essays, full of that kind of morbidity that has its root in too much brooding over methods of expression, and ways of looking upon life, which come, not out of life but out of literature, images reflected from mirror to mirror. He had wandered among people whose life is as picturesque as the middle ages, playing his fiddle to Italian sailors, and listening to stories in Bavarian woods, but life had cast no light into his writings. He had learned Irish years ago, but had begun to forget it, for the only language that interested him was that conventional language of modern poetry which has begun to make us all weary. . . . I said, "Give up Paris, you will never create anything by reading Racine, and Arthur Symons will always be a better critic of French literature. Go to the Arran Islands. Live there as if you were one of the people themselves; express a life that has never found expression." I had just come from Arran and my imagination was full of those gray islands, where men must reap with knives because of the stones.[18]

The Irish League, or L'Association Irlandaise as Maud Gonne's organization was called, was founded at the end of 1896 and held its inaugural meeting on New Year's Day of 1897. Its objective was Irish independence, and in providing an opportunity for Irish nationalists in France to coordinate their efforts to this end it hoped also to enlist sympathy for its aims among the French people by collecting a library and by propagandizing through the pages of *Irlande Libre*. Miss Gonne later admitted that "we never did much effective work, except sending votes of congratulation (or the reverse) to political groups in Ireland."[19] At least she had some historical justification for believing at the time that France would be a fertile soil for her efforts, since the Irish cause had always found sympathy in the country that had twice sent fleets to invade Ireland.

Maud Gonne was cautious about accepting new members in the League. Synge, who "seemed by nature unfitted to think a political thought," as Yeats once wrote of him,[20] could hardly have seemed a likely member. Though his lack of interest in politics has been greatly exaggerated, he was, after all, an Irish landlord, even if he had partly liberated himself from the convictions which that implied. The fact is that he did become a member, and an active one. He was present, as his diary indicates, at the inaugural meeting in Maud Gonne's apartment, and he attended subsequent weekly meetings throughout the succeeding months until his departure from Paris on May 13th. In addition to the regular meetings he went with the members on St. Patrick's day to Versailles to lay a wreath at the statue of Hoche, the commander of the French forces at Bantry Bay in 1796, and then visited Hoche's house and went to dinner with Miss Gonne afterwards. He spent a good deal of time with Miss Gonne and Yeats, when politics and the activities of the league must have been the chief topic of conversation.

But he was unwilling to go as far as they in their zeal. On April 6th he wrote a letter of resignation to Miss Gonne, though he continued to attend meetings:

Dear Miss Gonne, I am sorry to trouble you again so soon, but I have something to say which it seems better to say by letter than in one of our meetings, as there French members might misconstrue our difference of opinion. You already know how widely my theory of regeneration for

Ireland differs from yours and most of the other members of *Jeune Irlande*.

I do not wish to enter the question which of us may be in the right, but I think you will not be surprised to hear that I cannot possibly continue to be a member of a society which works on lines such as those laid down for the *Irlande Libre*. I wish to work in my own way for the cause of Ireland, and I shall never be able to do so if I get mixed up with a revolutionary and semi-military movement.

I have considered the matter very carefully, and I see there is no course open to me but to ask you to take my name off your list of members. If you think well I shall be glad to attend your meetings in a purely non-official capacity, but that is for you and the committee to decide. As member I should have henceforth to contend every point raised in reference to the journal (wasting your time and creating disunion) but as spectator I can still help you where and whenever it is in my power and for the rest keep an uncompromising silence.

Miss Gonne accepted his resignation, in a letter written by her secretary, and expressed the hope that he would continue to come to the meetings. But an interesting comment on Synge's motive in resigning came from his mother, who wrote to her son Robert:

I asked him in one letter how he could be mixed up with nationalists, and he said I was not to think he is a rebel, but he thinks Ireland will come to her own in years to come when socialistic ideas spread in England, but he does not at all approve of fighting for freedom. He thinks things will change by degrees in the world and there will be equality and no more grinding down of the poor. . . . I have come to the conclusion I will support him at home, but I will not give him any money to go and live in Paris idle. . . . He has nearly £40 of his own now,* and he can do what he likes with that. It makes him fancy he is independent which is a very great mistake.

If his mother's account is an accurate reflection of the way in which his "theory of regeneration" for Ireland differed from that of Maud Gonne, one may reasonably question whether he was "unfitted to think a political thought."

The importance of his meeting with Yeats and Maud Gonne was that at the very time in his life when he was beginning to feel that

* *I.e.*, an income of £40 a year.

he had turned his back on Ireland he found himself among people whose only thoughts were about Ireland. He began reading Yeats' books. In his diary he lists *The Wanderings of Oisin, The Countess Kathleen and Various Legends and Lyrics, The Land of Heart's Desire, The Secret Rose* and, though he does not specifically list it with the others, *The Celtic Twilight.* He also turned to the work of other young Irish writers like AE (George Russell) and to books about Ireland like John Mitchel's *Jail Journal* and Escande's *Hoche en Irlande.* Yeats may also have been responsible for interesting him in psychic phenomena. In his diary for February 19th he writes, "Meeting Irish League. Saw manifestations," but he does not enlarge on the connection between the two. He began reading such works as Paulam's *Nouveau Mysticisme* and the *Proceedings of the Society of Psychical Research.*

During the first three months of 1897 Synge exchanged letters with Cherry. Miss Zdanowska wrote about the middle of April telling him to resolve his differences with Cherry and to join the Catholic Church. "It is painful to feel spirits in search of truth and to see them make useless efforts because they will not take the unique and only way which is the Catholic religion, the only one which is true and which can lead you to your ideal." She did not realize that Roman Catholicism would have been just as objectionable to Cherry as atheism and, with the political implications which such a conversion would have assumed in Ireland, probably worse.

In April he attended a lecture on Brittany by the Breton folklorist and writer Anatole Le Braz and was so excited about it that he spoke to Le Braz after the lecture. He began to read Le Braz's books— *Au Pays des Pardons, Vieilles Histoires du Pays Breton* and *La Légende de la Mort chez les Bretons Armoricains*—and then turned to other books about Brittany whose titles he entered in his diary— *Les Grandes Légendes de France et Bretagne* and *Populace de la Basse Bretagne.* In Brittany, he discovered, a handful of enthusiasts were attempting to preserve the only remaining Continental vestiges of Celtic civilization. Other Breton writers like Pierre Loti and Ernest Renan, whom Synge had read, were calling attention to the fact that the language and ancient customs of their native province were rapidly disappearing.

Nearly two years later, when Synge's essay on Le Braz appeared in a Dublin newspaper, he had learned something about the Celtic revival in his own country, had spent his first summer on Aran, and could contrast Le Braz' anguish over the waning of his native language and customs with his own optimism about the Gaelic survival in Ireland. "If an Irishman of modern culture dwells for a while in Inishmaan, or Inisheer,* or, perhaps, anywhere among the mountains of Connacht, he will not find there any trace of an external at-homeness but will rather yield himself up to the entrancing newness of the old."[21] His interest in Brittany led him eventually to study Breton and to visit Quimper for two weeks in the spring of 1899. But in 1897 he had had no contact with the Celtic revival of his own country, like most Dubliners had probably never heard a word of Irish spoken outside of Professor Goodman's class at Trinity College, and was yet to realize the influence it would have upon his development as a writer. When Yeats convinced him to give up an unsuccessful career as book reviewer and go among the Irish-speaking peasants of the west of Ireland for his material, he brought with him a linguistic equipment which his colleagues could only envy and an insight sharpened by his knowledge of Continental Celticism.

Among his new friends was Stephen MacKenna, journalist, linguist, and student of philosophy. His father, who died when he was eleven, was an officer in the British army who deserted to join Garibaldi. His father's sisters adopted him and sent him to a Roman Catholic boarding school in Leicestershire. When he failed the entrance examinations for London University because of inadequacy in English, he entered a religious order but stayed in it only a short while. He then worked for five or six years as a clerk in a Dublin bank, spent one year as a reporter for a London newspaper, and in 1896 went to Paris as correspondent for an English Catholic journal. In school MacKenna had been a brilliant student in the classics, published a translation of *The Imitation of Christ* while he was working in the bank, and had a passion for Greek which eventually resulted in the first translation into English of the complete text of the *Enneads* of Plotinus.

When the Graeco-Turkish War broke out in 1897 his sympathy for the Greeks led him to enlist in the Greek army. His military career was brief, and the stories about it which survive are, accord-

* Two of the three islands that comprise Aran.

ing to his biographer, "pleasing but mutually contradictory."[22] By the time he got to Greece and was "in the field" the Greek army had already been routed. He was soon back in Paris and faced with the more prosaic battle of earning a living as a journalist. In 1899 he came to New York, worked on the *Criterion* for a time, and went back to Paris where he married an American girl and headed the office of the New York *Herald* until personal difficulties with the owner eventually led to his resignation in 1907. He went to Dublin, got a job as an editorial writer for *The Freeman's Journal* and devoted most of the next twenty years to his translation of Plotinus.

Brought up as a Catholic, MacKenna eventually repudiated all religion. He was an ardent nationalist all his life, believed in the Gaelic language revival, and in 1924 refused to accept a gold medal from the Royal Irish Academy because its title suggested a connection between Ireland and the English throne. In the same year he moved to England because he believed the Free State a betrayal of the Republic and because "I couldn't bear to live where I must ask a minister of Church or State whether I may or may not read Anatole France."[23] MacKenna was living on the top floor of a house at 90 rue d'Assas with an impoverished Armenian scientist he had befriended, named Michel Elmassian, when he met Synge at the end of 1896 or beginning of 1897. Their long friendship must unfortunately be viewed mostly through MacKenna's letters because MacKenna mutilated Synge's beyond all salvage by scissoring out names and whole sentences he considered harmful to his friend's memory. Of his friendship with Synge, MacKenna wrote:

. . . we were the most intimate of comrades and talked days and nights through, and mainly on literature and the technique of it; but except for the *Aran Isles* [sic] and his critical work for some London journal— *The Speaker*, I think—I never knew what he had on the loom. He often read me an isolated sentence from the sheet on his Blick*—often an entire day's work—but I never knew where the sentence fitted. I did know, curiously, a good deal about his unpublished work; I imagine because he never intended it for publication. He gave me once an immense wad of his verse to read and return; we never spoke of it; I have wondered what he did with it.[24]

* Synge's typewriter. See p. 114.

The Ireland Synge came back to in the middle of May in 1897 was beginning to look different. The first Feis Cóeil was held in May. In June, Unionist Dublin was getting ready to stage a huge celebration of Queen Victoria's diamond jubilee. Synge lunched several times with Maud Gonne and Yeats and listened in amazement to their plans of staging a counterdemonstration and sabotaging the displays of Unionist merchants by cutting electric wires at the right moment. The nationalists led by James Connolly climaxed their demonstration with a mock funeral procession down O'Connell Street, carrying a coffin to represent John Bull, while they slowly yielded to the baton charges of the police. It was the first violence Synge had ever witnessed in his native city, but his only diary entry for the day was "To town—evening."

For July the Synges stayed at the small house on Castle Kevin hill they had hired the summer before, but in August they moved to a house on the estate of Charles Stuart Parnell at Avondale, one of the beauty spots of Ireland, between Glenmalure and the famous Vale of Avoca. The greatest Irishman of his day had died in defeat six years before. The "Chief's" house stood empty, and the trees on his decaying estate, now being felled by the Forestry Department, must have reminded the people of the finality of their defeat. The hills of Avoca contained veins of copper which had been worked at different times and mined on a large scale in the seventeenth century. Avoca is once more being actively mined today, but when Synge knew it first in 1897 the landscape was disfigured with yellow dumps and the huts of the departed miners were in ruins. Little changed by the coming and going of either miner or tourist, the people who remained worked the poor hill farms, and life was nearly as primitive as it was for the more secluded people of the glens. Synge noted, "Here and there in County Wicklow there are a number of little known places—places with curiously melodious names, such as Aughavanna, Glenmalure, Annamoe, or Lough Nahanagan— where the people have retained a peculiar simplicity, and speak a language in some ways more Elizabethan than the English of Connacht, where Irish was used till a much later date."[25]

Glenmalure is one of the longest glens in Ireland, being nearly ten miles long, with high boulder-covered hills on either side and the Avonbeg River running the entire length of it. There in 1580 the

native chieftain Feagh McHugh O'Byrne put to rout the cavalry of
Lord Grey, and the poet Edmund Spenser witnessed it. During the
rebellion of 1798 the rebel leader Michael Dwyer made his head-
quarters at the head of the glen in Harney's cottage, which is still
standing. In Synge's day the cottage had become less accessible than
it had been a hundred years before, for the road leading through
the pass to it had fallen out of use and was overgrown with heather.
In bad weather the river, normally a mountain stream, rose to such
a flood that not even a farm cart could reach the cottage from the
glen. The Harneys were two bachelor brothers and their unmarried
sister—not an uncommon sight even today in rural Ireland—and
they were almost completely secluded from the outside world. Their
turn of speech was noticeably different from that of the people
living farther down in the glen, and the loneliness of their lives
impressed Synge so much that when he looked round for a suitable
setting for his play *In the Shadow of the Glen* he thought of the
Harney's cottage and wrote for his stage directions, "The last cottage
at the head of a long glen in County Wicklow." The play was based
on a west-of-Ireland folk tale, but the "mists rolling down the bog"
and the "wind crying out in the bits of broken trees were left from
the great storm, and the streams roaring with the rain," which
Nora complains about so poignantly, provide the setting and the
mood which Synge remembered from this desolate and lonely place
in the Wicklow hills. Glenmalure also provided him with the narrative of an article, published a few years later, entitled "An Autumn
Night in the Hills."

Synge wrote to Mlle. Beydon that Cherry had refused even to
see him, and she replied, "I pity you with all my heart, but just the
same, and without wishing to hurt you, I must tell you as I did last
year, that I understand your friend very well, and that I would have
done exactly as she has done (considering her ideas). There has
been only one mistake, and that was not to have broken off with you
completely from the beginning." When he protested she wrote again:
"I am not at all of your opinion and see no connection between
one's own wife and one's woman friends! It has no more resemblance
than a cock and an ass. I do not at all confuse the idea of a husband
with the idea of a friend, since what is to prevent you having both?
It is then you will experience the difference." She added that they

had better not exchange French and English lessons again when he came back to Paris, since they were only a pretext. "We know each other too well and chatter too much to have any mutual benefit from the language. I think it is better to meet simply as friends." She was resisting his attempt to make her a substitute for Cherry.

When Synge returned to Dublin in September he found Mac-Kenna, whom he had left in Paris, back from the Graeco-Turkish War and full of stories about his adventures. But from the long undated letter MacKenna wrote him about this time the subject that interested them most at the moment was psychic phenomena. Neither Synge nor MacKenna ever became as interested in the subject as Yeats or AE, though Synge went to at least one meeting of the Theosophical Society in October with AE. After giving Synge a list of books to read on the subject—which Synge actually began to read and enter in his diary—MacKenna wrote:

There is no doubt Paris is the place for these studies—an immense *richesse* of the literature of the subject from the elementary matter of Magnetism, Hypnotism *etc.* to deepest Magic. I have some rough biblio-graphical notes made in Paris which I will look up for you. But we must meet and talk this business over much—not over-much, *ne quid nimis* Terence taught us. And, again apropos, I have several purely practical works on Magnetism and Hypnotism—Binet and Féré of the Salpetrière, Moll of Nancy, Gregory (1851) of England (with much on clairvoyance by crystal-gazing, *etc.*) and a really good little book—a general, non-self-committing study from the *Bibliothèque de Merveilles* (Paris). These I do not send, since they are *applied mysticism*—if mysticism at all—not *pure*, like the theosophical things. But ask and you shall have. . . .

Remind me when we meet to give you a note to a delightful Irishman in Paris, who lives the things of the Spirit and is one of the most charm-ing chaps that exists—a jewel of a man with great knowledge and reading and real uncantified culture. Perhaps you know him? Richard Best?

Synge did not know Richard Best, but when he returned to Paris in January of 1898 he went round to Best's room at 90 rue d'Assas where MacKenna had lived the year before, knocked on the door and announced himself to Best with the words, "*Je suis Synge—pas singe.*" Best was a Belfast Protestant come to Paris to study Celtic. Unlike MacKenna, he was not interested in political nationalism and was a little startled by the claims his enthusiastic compatriots were making in behalf of the Irish cause. He and Synge looked at each other in bewilderment when they once heard Maud Gonne tell a Parisian audience that Queen Victoria was personally responsible for the Irish potato famine. Best later became Librarian of the National Library in Dublin, a noted Celtic scholar and, like a good many unwilling Dubliners of the time, a character in James Joyce's *Ulysses*. Best's most vivid memory of that first evening is of Synge's homespun stockings and heavy boots, so out of place in an atmosphere where everyone else, including Irishmen, wore buttoned patent leather or suede shoes.

In the autumn of 1897 Synge's hair suddenly began to fall out, and a large lump formed on the side of his neck. His doctor prescribed ointments for his scalp and surgery for the "enlarged gland," as it was described. It was the first manifestation of Hodgkins Disease, or lymphatic sarcoma, which was to kill him. On December 11th he entered the Mount Street Nursing Home and was operated on. In a short piece entitled "Under Ether," written soon after the operation but not published until after his death, Synge described his experiences in the nursing home and his sensations under anaesthesia. The doctors must have known the nature of his disease and that its symptoms might recur, but they did not tell him. It was not until 1905 that the lump appeared again on his neck and 1907 before he submitted to another operation.

Although Synge suffered from asthma all his life and was a desperately ill man for the last year of it, he was a normally healthy man, capable of cycling sixty miles a day over the hills or tramping from dawn to dark over the bogs of West Kerry or Connemara. The intense preoccupation with death that is characteristic of his work cannot be attributed, as it has been, to the fact that he was ill. His morbidity had its source in something deeper. One of his ancestors in the seventeenth century was described by Ware, in his account of the Irish bishops, as "*vir gravis admodium et doctus*." There is ample evidence that the words describe a type which persisted in the family during three centuries. Synge's description of the fear of death planted in him as a child by his mother's religious teaching, which he recoiled from as soon as he was old enough, is a better explanation for his persistent morbidity.

It was past the middle of January, 1898, when his doctor told him that his recovery from the operation was complete and that he could leave for Paris. He left Dublin on the 19th, stopped off in London for a few days to see Yeats and Hope Rea and arrived in Paris on the 23rd. His mother wrote to Robert, "He looks very like a Frenchman now with a wig which is black like a Frenchman's hair, and he he has to wear turn-down collars now and a soft felt hat, which looks quite French, and he speaks French so well he might easily pass for a Frenchman if he got mixed up in a row." A sketch in his notebook describes an experience he had on the train from Calais to Paris. Whether it was based on an actual experience or not, it reveals the frame of mind he was in. A company of eight ballet girls who shared a compartment with him went to sleep leaning against one another.

. . . Some had laid aside their hats and thrown loose shawls over their heads. Others had retained their hats but allowed them to work down gradually with their unfolding hair upon their ears and gave the impression of feminine weakness and disorder, which produces a potent yet human influence on a man with a conscience. What were these weak and tired girls that they should be compelled nightly to exhibit the stripped nudity of their limbs to amuse the dregs of masculine cupidity. Opposite from myself one who lay back in the corner before me with one wisp of hair pushed out beneath the shawl she held tightly round her small half-childish face recalled with grotesque yet irresistible irony a picture of Little Red Riding Hood and the Wolf that I had delighted in, in one of my first picture books. Her face was still radiant, even in fatigue, with the imperial grace and purity of childhood, although her age had probably not attained seventeen or eighteen.

The strong coffee I had taken when leaving the boat kept me awake. I looked out every few moments into the wonderful purity of the blue dawn of September, then back again to the gallery of sleeping girls. Is life a stage and all the men and women merely players, or an arena where men and women and children are captives of destiny to be torn with beasts and gladiators—who appear only to destroy and be destroyed. . . .

After a while I grew so bitter in my strange and solitary watch that I sprang up and cried out to them that we were nearing Paris. They aroused themselves with stiff and dreary expectation. In a few [moments] their tradition of boisterous gaiety restored the chattering that had preceded their hour of slumber. They threw aside their shawls and hats and began to do their hair with combs and looking glasses, plying me with questions about Paris life and theatres, throwing in at times a remark of the rankest obscenity.

Morituri te saluto. The pity I felt changed gradually to admiration as I warmed myself with their high spirits and good humour.

For the next three months Synge stayed in a small hotel called the St. Malo at 2 rue d'Odessa, which cost him £5 a month, with fire, light and laundry extra. His mother wrote to Robert: "He is living on his own money now. He drew £60 of the principal and is living on that. I have wasted too much on him in the past. I don't know what he is doing, but I believe he wants to become a reviewer of French literature." In the middle of February he began to attend lectures at the Sorbonne by Professor H. d'Arbois de Jubainville, "*sur la civilization irlandaise comparée avec celle d'Homer,*" as he described them in his diary. De Jubainville, who was one of the foremost Celtic scholars in Europe, was a friend of Maud Gonne, and interested in the Irish cause. Maud Gonne later claimed that she recommended Synge to De Jubainville for a position as assistant, but it is unlikely that Synge ever held any such post.[26] He recorded his high regard for De Jubainville's achievements in his essay "*La Vieille Littérature Irlandaise,*" which appeared in *L'Européen* in 1902 and again in 1904 when he reviewed Best's English translation of De Jubainville's *The Irish Mythological Cycle and Celtic Mythology* for *The Speaker.*

Although Synge was studying the ancient culture of his own country, it had as yet no meaningful relationship with what he was writing. He sketched rough drafts of possible plays, but whether he finished any is doubtful. He began a novel and, according to his diary, finished the first draft on February 19th. The few pages of it which he kept, because they were in a notebook with other things, indicate that it was to be a tract on the hard working conditions of nurses. That he should have attempted something so completely beyond him is probably attributable more to his sympathy for the nurses he had known in the hospital than to any knowledge of his subject matter. He was naturally attracted to women and capable of achieving an intimacy with them quite easily. Among his papers are letters from five different nurses who had taken care of him in the hospital.

Before he left Paris for home at the end of April he had met another girl. Margaret Hardon was from Boston, where her father was a school principal, and had come to Paris four years before to study art after graduation from Wellesley College and the Massachusetts Institute of Technology. Her father had been brought up on a farm in Mansfield, Massachusetts, and had little sympathy with his daughter's ambitions or desire to study in Paris, although the article she wrote for the Boston *Evening Transcript* entitled "In the *Quartier Latin*, The Truth About the American Girl's Life," must have assured him and the fathers of other Boston girls that her life was respectable. Synge spent five evenings with her in the three weeks before he left Paris. They corresponded during the summer, and when he returned in the fall he nicknamed her *"La Robe Verte"* and fell in love with her.

When he came back to Dublin he found that his mother had sent her servants away and gone to a Greystones lodging house for a change of air. He stayed in the empty house and took his meals with the Stephenses next door. Cherry was only a few doors away and they could not prevent meeting. On May 4th they met by appointment at the museum, but there is no record of what they said to each other.

Five

THE ARAN ISLANDS

Did you ever hear tell of a place across a bit of the sea, where there is an island, and the grave of the four beautiful saints?

Synge's visit to the Aran Islands in 1898 must be one of the most remarkable examples on record of how a sudden immersion in a new environment converted a man of ostensibly mediocre talent, a complete failure, in fact, into a writer of genius. The decision to go was made at Yeats' suggestion, and Yeats was not reticent about claiming credit for it. He wrote to Lady Gregory in 1911: "Tell Bourgeois* that I met Synge in Paris long before he had ever been in Arran. I met him in 1896, and our conversation about his going to Arran was published in the introduction to the first edition of [*The*] *Well of the Saints* during Synge's lifetime."[27] Yeats had been on Aran during the summer of 1896 when he sailed over from Galway to get material for his novel *The Speckled Bird*. The opening scene of the novel was to be laid on the islands, and Yeats wrote to John O'Leary: "I have already been to the Aran Islands to study them and am going again. The book is to be among other things my first study of the Irish Fairy Kingdom and the mystical faith of that time, before I return to more earthly things."[28] He neither finished the novel nor returned to Aran, but his imagination was "full of those gray islands."

Yeats' advice came when Synge was at his wits' end. Except for a

* Maurice Bourgeois, author of *John Millington Synge and the Irish Theatre*, London, 1913.

74

poem in his college magazine, he had not managed to write a publishable line in five years of desperate trying. His verse, Yeats thought, was quite unpromising. If Aran could not provide him with material for journalistic pieces, it could at least offer him the opportunity to live with Irish speakers and carry on his study of Gaelic.

Synge was not actually the first member of his family to walk the limestone wastes of Aran. In 1851 his uncle, the Reverend Alexander Synge, had been the first Protestant missionary to the islands, and the accounts of his life there which survive in letters to his brother Edward Synge are a striking contrast to what his nephew was to write about the islands:

Here I am Lord of all I survey—surrounded with dirt and ignorance. We have not got our schoolmaster yet, but we expect him shortly. It is a very wretched island, the soil very scanty, almost all a barren rock. We have a little church, two to twenty-five make our congregation, mostly of the families of the coastguards. I have two services each Sunday. I am at present living in a very small inn but intend next week D. V.* to move into a "private" lodging, a house with a kitchen and two small rooms overhead. I shall have one dirty little chap for my man Friday, who I expect will always be where I don't want him to be and never to be had when he is wanted. However, we must not be nice. It is very hard to make off a living here some times. Fresh meat we never think of—I have it once in five weeks—and the chickens are very scarce. . . .

I want a vessel for my self woefully. I am a regular prisoner. I get on with the people so far very well, but how will it be when we begin to attack their bad ways, religion *etc.*, I don't know. The proprietors of the island are fitting up a house for me which will be a very great comfort when it is done. The noise and dirt of my present situation is very bad indeed. We have not a wheel machine, cart or wheelbarrow on the island. The women carry everything on their backs. . . .

A month later he wrote, "I have succeeded in putting a stop to a ball match that used to go on here every Sunday. I attacked them very sharply the other Sunday, and the next Monday the priest was the first to begin to pulling down their wall—though the rascal had seen them playing there a hundred times before. But when I went to them and spoke about it he took it up at once. However it is well

* *Deo volente*, God willing.

to put it down." The Reverend Alexander unfortunately did not con-
fine himself to such relatively innocent assaults on the native customs.
He bought a motorboat, fitted it out with fishing gear and started
netting fish for the Galway market in direct competition with the
fishermen who would certainly have assaulted him if he had not
armed his captain and crew.

The Protestant church is still standing on Inishmore, deserted by
the families of the coast guards and the British officials who departed
in 1922 when Ireland achieved its independence, and the young men
of Inishmore still play handball on a Sunday afternoon, unhampered
by either of the two priests who serve the island. There are no Protestants left among the permanent residents.

Despite its barrenness and isolation, the three islands which com-
pose the group, like some others off the west coast of Ireland, are rich
in monuments of the past: massive stone forts, the most remarkable in
western Europe, from the Bronze Age; oratories and beehive-like
stone houses, called *clocháns* in Irish, which mark the site of medieval
ecclesiastical settlements; holy wells, inscribed stones, saints' beds
and ruined churches of a later period; and the remains of two castles
one of which enjoys the distinction of being probably the only
castle in Ireland which Cromwell did not tear down but actually
fortified. Soldiers walked its battlements when French pirates and
the fabulous female chieftain Grace O'Malley sailed the waters of
Galway Bay. The only ships it looks upon now are the little steamer
that brings freight and passengers to the three islands twice a week
and the Spanish trawlers which fish the waters in defiance of an
Irish naval corvette. The only other remains of Aran's violent past
are names like Hernon and Dirrane, which belong to islanders whose
ancestors were the soldiers of Cromwell.

Synge's first visit in 1898 lasted from May 10th to June 25th, with
two weeks spent on the main island and four on the middle island. He
returned in the four succeeding summers and spent altogether a little
more than four and a half months in the islands. His book *The Aran
Islands* is based on his first four visits.

The building Synge stayed in on Inishmore was the Atlantic Hotel,
still in use but no longer a hotel. Arthur Symons, who had stayed
there two summers before, described it as "a very primitive hotel;
it had last been slept in by some priests from the mainland, who had

come on their holiday with bicycles; and before that by a German philologist* who was learning Irish. The kitchen, which is also the old landlady's bedroom, presents a medley of pots and pans and petticoats as you pass its open door and climb the little staircase, diverging oddly on either side after the first five or six steps, and leading on the right to a large dining room, where the table lounges on an adequate number of legs and chairs bow over when you lean back on them."[29]

Today, because the islands are known throughout the English-speaking world and because several thousand tourists visit them during the summer, guest-house accommodations on Inishmore are far from primitive; and if one can put up without electricity, running water, telephone and any mechanical means of transportation, life for the tourist is quite as comfortable as it is on the mainland. But in 1898 the only regular visitors to the islands were government officials and students interested in the antiquities and the language. In the summertime, when the weather is good and fish are plentiful, the islands are a delightful place; but in the mist and fog of a wintry day when one sees them for the first time looming up out of the sea, like the island apparitions described in Irish medieval voyage literature, one can have some sympathy with Yeats' effort to invoke fairies in so unusual a place. Synge was more interested in flesh-and-blood Irishmen, but he too noted how the landscape of Aran could produce manifestations, particularly after a week of sweeping fogs.

More Irish is spoken today on Inishmore, the main island, than in Synge's day, because the Irish government has tried to preserve the native language. In 1898, when Ireland was part of the United Kingdom, instruction in the schools on Aran was in English; today it is in Irish. On the two smaller islands, where contact with visitors from the mainland is considerably less than it is on Inishmore, the children speak virtually no English, and the only adults who speak it with any fluency are those who received their schooling under an English government. Synge noted this fact and soon decided that Inishmaan would be better for his purposes than Inishmore.

Martin Coneely, who was his tutor on Inishmore, had taught Irish to the European philologists Finck and Pedersen, given stories to Jeremiah Curtin, and known the antiquarians Petrie, Stokes, and

* Most probably F. N. Finck, author of *Die araner Mundart*, Marburg, 1899.

Sir William Wilde. On Inishmaan Synge's tutors were Martin McDonough, the "Michael" of his narrative, and Martin Flaherty, who emigrated to America in 1906 and is still living in New York City. Synge listed in his notebooks the words and idiomatic expressions which he was hearing for the first time and made translations of them into English. He had difficulty understanding the rapid Irish of the native storytellers, but he soon discovered that they were bilingual. "I have given up my attempts to collect the tales till I am more perfect in Irish," he wrote during his first visit, "as the English versions they give me are very poor and incomplete." As his Irish improved from day to day he was finally able to follow them, and wrote, "I feel more every day that it is criminal to deprive these people of their language and with it the unwritten literature which is still as full and distinguished as in any European people."

He was interested in the people and in every aspect of their lives, from the colourful homespun dresses of the women to the intonations of their voices and the more subtle manifestations of how they looked at the limited and desolate world around them. Though he had long been a student of antiquities he seems to have considered the rich array of megalithic monuments as being little more than the incidental scenery for the life that interested him so much more. And for this he developed quickly a scrupulous regard, an unerring ear and eye, for the actualities of the life he was observing. "In the pages that follow," he stated in the introduction to *The Aran Islands*, "I have given a direct account of my life on the islands, and of what I met with among them, inventing nothing, and changing nothing that is essential."

He saw on Aran a life that had all but disappeared from the rest of Ireland. The women all dressed in red flannel skirts and plaid shawls, so lurid against the grey background of limestone shelf and sandy shore, the men in blue turtleneck sweaters, homespun trousers and vests, grey as the rocks, and wearing the kind of cowhide moccasin called a *pampootie*, ideal for walking cat-footed over the rocks or for rowing a *curragh*, the traditional canoe of the west of Ireland made of tarred canvas and laths. The kelp industry and the old women keening by the open grave, which he described, have disappeared, but other aspects of island life have changed little from what he saw over half a century ago.

The islands are limestone shelf, sloping gradually from sea level on the eastern side upwards to precipitous cliffs on the western side, which in some places tower three hundred feet above the seas. On the brink of the highest of these cliffs on Inishmore is Dún Aengus, an ancient stone fort of gigantic proportions shaped like a horseshoe and surrounded by three rings of outer fortifications which impede the steps of the visitor who toils up the hill as they did the approach of an attacking army in the centuries before Christ. Dún Aengus is only one of four such megalithic constructions on Inishmore. There are two more on Inishmaan, including Dún Conor, across the road from the McDonough cottage where Synge stayed and where the original father-slayer from Connemara, the prototype of the Playboy, hid in a passage and listened to the heels of the police grating on the stones over his head.

All three islands have very little ground which has not been cleared by sledgehammer and fertilized with seaweed brought up from the sea in panniers slung over the sides of donkeys. Keeping the soil, so laboriously created, from sliding down into the sea is achieved by building stone walls, so that all three islands present a maze of small fields enclosed by interlocking walls, broken only by the road which bisects each of the islands. Since there are no bogs, all the turf burned on the islands is brought from Connemara. In the springtime the cattle, which have been foraging among the rocks all winter, are shipped to the mainland for fattening on Connemara grass, and one of the great sights on Aran is the islanders swimming their cows out from shore behind their *curraghs* to be hoisted aboard the steamer. One man kneels in the stern, watching for the thrashing legs to tire before he seizes the frightened animal by the horns, maneuvers her onto her side and brings her head to rest on the stern.

Synge's book about Aran is the best account one could ask for of the daily life of the people—of the way they burned kelp, fished from a *curragh* or huddled in their darkened cottages and spoke in hushed whispers when the islands were lashed by storms. But it is also an interesting document in the case history of a writer's evolution. In 1907 he wrote to a journalist acquaintance: "I look on *The Aran Islands* as my first serious piece of work—it was written before any of the plays. In writing out the talks of the people and their stories in this book—and in a certain number of articles on Wicklow peasants which I have not yet collected—I learned to write the peasant dialect and dialogue which I use in my plays."[30]

The people of Aran had provided him with the material and the idiom with which he could construct an art completely different from any he had even dreamed of. On this first visit he heard the two stories which gave him the raw material for *In the Shadow of the Glen* and *The Playboy of the Western World*, even though he transplanted the first—which is a folk tale—to Wicklow, and the second —which was not a folk tale but an actual incident—to Mayo. And if island life gave him the stuff of his plays, the language of the bilingual man of Aran gave him the language which became his hallmark. In the east of Ireland Irish had gradually disappeared, leaving the field to English. But in the west the English which survived the Cromwellian conquest had been forced to maintain itself alongside the native language. Under such conditions any language, especially one imposed by conquest, would find it difficult to develop with the times. The English spoken by western peasants in Synge's day was still largely a seventeenth century English, full of archaisms, based on a rich substratum of Gaelic syntax, and characterized by the kind of construction which results when the idiom of one language is blended with that of another. In Synge's plays it has sounded to some people, including Joyce's Buck Mulligan, like a parody of English, a new kind of stage Irish. But Synge insisted that it had come from the actual speech of the people, and the Celtic philologist Van Hamel, who studied it carefully, described Synge's language as "a very realistic and vigorous Western Anglo Irish."[31]

During his first two weeks in Aran, when Martin Coneely was showing him the sights on Inishmore and telling stories about places and people, he went to see a holy well near a ruined church called the Church of the Four Comely Persons, just off the road from Kilronan to Kilmurvy and near the village of Cowrugh. When he got back to the inn he recorded the story in his notebook, and one can see from the last line, which he omitted from his book, that it was the dramatic potentialities of the story that interested him.

A woman of Sligo had one son who was blind. She dreamed of a well that held water potent to cure. So she took boat with her son, following the course of her dream and reached Arran. She came to the house of my informant's father and told what had brought [her], but when those around offered to lead her to the well nearby she declined all aid, saying she saw still her way clear before [her]. She led her son from the [house] and going a little up the hill stopped at the well. Then kneeling with the blind child beside her she prayed God and then bathed his eyes. In [a] moment his face gleamed with joy as he said, "Oh mother, look at the beautiful flowers." Twice since, the same story has been told to me with unimportant variation, yet ending always with the glad dramatic cry of the young child.

When he was not out walking with Martin he met other people. He called on the Reverend William Kilbride, the Protestant clergyman, and got to know Father Farragher, the priest who served the islands for more than twenty years. At the inn he talked with a fellow visitor from whom he bought a camera. It was made of polished mahogany and was carried in a black leather case in which eye holes were cut for the lens and the view finders. He loaded it by night, changing the plates in their holders, and placing them one by one in the magazine. He took a good many photographs of the islanders, and one can see from their letters to him how much they enjoyed the prints he sent them.

On Inishmore he saw only one other visitor, but he did not meet her. Lady Gregory afterwards wrote: "I first saw Synge in the north island of Aran. I was staying there, gathering folklore, talking to the people, and felt quite angry when I passed another outsider walking here and there, talking also to the people. I was jealous of not being alone on the island among the fishers and sea-weed gatherers."[32] He sat by himself on the cliffs, watching the sea and listening to the birds. He wrote in his notebook, "When the sun is covered, six distinct and beautiful shades still blend in one another—the limestone, the sea leaden at my feet and with a steel tinge far away, the mountains on the coast of Clare and then the clouds transparent and opaque."

He had brought books with him—*The Life of Guy de Maupassant*, AE's *Earth Breath, Madame Bovary, Aucassin and Nicolette*, Dante Gabriel Rossetti's poems, works by Swedenborg and Pierre Loti. As he saw opened before him the strange life of the people, so much a part of sea and rock, his books kept him from losing himself. He was interested in the stories and conversations, the new words and phrases in Irish he was learning, and the curiously rhythmic English which came from the mouths of a people who would be described in a sophisticated society as illiterates. But his mission was to interpret their lives, not to participate in them.

The women interested him more than the men. His notebooks are full of his observations about their wild beauty, their colorful dress and the grace of their movements. "I have noticed many beautiful girls whose long luxuriant lashes lend a shade to wistful eyes." Another time he writes, "I am so much a stranger I cannot dare under the attention I create to gaze at a beautiful oval face that looks from a brown shawl near me. The girls are singularly unconscious, unaccustomed to receive attention. I notice no walking out* of young men and girls. Courtship is I believe not considered a necessity." And still later on the same day, when he couldn't get out of his mind's eye the picture of the "oval face" that looked at him from the brown shawl, he wrote, "The face came with me all day among the rocks. She is madonna-like, yet has a rapt majesty as far from easy exaltation as from the material comeliness of Raphael's later style. . . . The expression of her eyes is so overwhelmingly beautiful that I remember no single qualities of her." As his visit was drawing to a close he noted:

One woman also has interested me in a way that binds me more than ever to the islands. These women are before convention and share many things with the women of Paris or London who have freed themselves by a desperate personal effort from moral bondage of lady-like persons. Many women here are too sturdy and contented to have more than the decorative interest of wild deer, but I have found a couple that have been turned in on themselves by some circumstances of their lives and seem to sum up in the expressions of their blue grey eyes the whole external symphony of the sky and seas. They have wildness and humor and passion kept in continual subjection by the reverence for life and the sea that is inevitable in this place.

He was very careful when he published his observations not to reveal the profound and even disturbing effect which the girls had made upon him.

* Courtship.

The McDonough Cottage, Inishmaan, Aran Islands.
Photograph by the author, July, 1956.

After two weeks on Inishmore he moved to Inishmaan, where "Gaelic is more generally used, and the life is perhaps the most primitive that is left in Europe." The middle island is slightly more than a mile from the main island, but from Kilronan to the Callamore pier on the north side of Inishmaan the distance is at least four miles. His first ride in a *curragh*, the "rude canvas canoe of a model that has served primitive races since men first went on the sea" gave him "a moment of exquisite satisfaction." It was rowed by four men who ran up a small sail as soon as they were well out of Kilronan harbor. From the small pier where they landed on Inishmaan it was a short walk "between small fields and bare sheets of rock" to the McDonough cottage where he was to stay.

Patrick McDonough's cottage was probably the largest habitation on the island, containing three rooms in addition to the large, windowless kitchen with an earthen floor, an open fireplace at one end and two doors, one on the west and one on the east. It was also the post office, where the mail slung into a *curragh* from the steamer was sorted and passed out. The house has not changed much to this day, though the kitchen now has a concrete floor. From the back door one looks down a hill dotted by tiny fields and broad expanses of sloping rock. From the front, one sees a small yard paved naturally with limestone. Beyond the small road which goes by the house and is the island's only road, one can see perched upon a hill of limestone outcropping, twenty feet high, the ring fort called Dún Conor, its walls of unmortared limestone blocks, eighteen feet thick and twenty feet high. After Synge's time the McDonough cottage continued to receive visitors to the island, including Padraic Pearse and Thomas McDonagh, the heroes of the Easter Rising.

Inishmaan is considerably smaller than Inishmore, being only three miles long and a mile wide. The island slopes down on all sides from a narrow ridge in the middle where the cottages are clustered in three or four groups of tiny villages. There is one school and one church, where mass is said on Sundays and holy days by the priest who is rowed over in a *curragh* from Inishere. There is no doctor, no policeman, and today, though not in Synge's day, communication with the outside world is by radio-telephone. There were no wheeled vehicles and the children, it was said, had never seen a donkey cart.

The tendency of island people to live in a closely knit, self-sufficient society still prevails even today on Inishmaan to a degree that is hard to believe. Synge noted the almost incredible amount of intermarriage and observed that there were only ten family names distributed among the four hundred inhabitants.

Pat Dirane, the old storyteller Synge listened to in the kitchen of the McDonough cottage, and John Joice, another storyteller on Inishere, were lineal descendants of the ancient bards, and they kept the tradition alive with a skill and a dedication that Synge found incredible. If one could capture in English, he thought, some of the vitality of the stories they recited in Irish one could reproduce the very face and mind of Ireland itself. "There exists yet in lonely places," he noted, "the unlettered literature which was the real source of all the art of words. In the Gaelic-speaking districts of Ireland, for instance, recitation is of extraordinary merit."

He thought a good deal about what a written literature could learn from an oral one. In an essay which never got beyond his notebooks, he argued that poetry had a dual existence, or should have— in the voice of the poet and in the voice of the reader, who is, or should be, a kind of performer. Modern poetry, he complained, had lost much of its vitality and was like pressed flowers, without odor, faded and one-dimensional. The intonation of the poet's voice was gone from the poem, and the reader was depended upon to restore the important element which the printed page could not convey. But where the poetic tradition was oral, as it was in the west of Ireland, the intonation of the original poet's voice still echoed in the storyteller's voice, for he had acquired the poem orally and for him it had no other existence. Synge wrote: "In primitive times every poet recited his own poem with the music he conceived with the words in his moment of excitement. And his hearers who admired the work repeated it with the exact music of the poet. This is still done among the Aran islanders. An old man who could not read has drawn tears to my eyes by reciting verse in Gaelic I did not fully understand."

Pat Dirane did not survive beyond Synge's first visit to Aran, but several of his stories appear in *The Aran Islands*. He told Synge the story which later became the basis of *In the Shadow of the Glen*, about the man who pretends to be dead to see if his wife will remain faithful to his memory. Arthur Griffith, the ebullient editor of *The United Irishman* who was to lead the attack on Synge, accused him of palming off on the Irish peasants of the west an excretion from the pages of the Roman writer Petronius. But it was one of the great folk tales of western Europe, and Synge had heard it from Pat Dirane.

In another story which Pat Dirane told about a faithful wife, two motifs are combined—the bargain of flesh, made famous in *The Merchant of Venice*, and the ordeals a virtuous wife passes through, which folklorists know as the story of patient Griselda. As Pat Dirane told it, the tale had been completely adapted to an Irish environment, with peasants reaping in a landlord's field and a settle bed—standard item in an Irish country cottage—provided for the villain to hide in. Synge sketched out the rough scenario of a play, following the main outlines of the story but transferring its locale to the mainland. The passages of verse dialogue he wrote show how he was working towards a control of dialect:

Lady Conor. I'm thinking it's well for you all your life,
　　　　　　Walking the world, while I, when wet clouds lift,
　　　　　　Look only all the day on the seas and clift.

Captain.　　You have silky pillows for your bed,
　　　　　　And golden combs, I'm thinking, comb your head.
　　　　　　It's roasted hares you'll eat and dearest wine,
　　　　　　And lay your feet on mats of Persian twine.
　　　　　　While we live shut in ships that roll and pitch,
　　　　　　Eating salt till our shin marrows itch,
　　　　　　And drinking filthy water from a barrel,
　　　　　　Our crew half naked through their ripped apparel.

During his first visit he heard about the man who murdered his father in Connemara and fled to Inishmaan where the people hid him from the police. The oldest man on Inishmaan "often tells me about a Connaught man who killed his father with the blow of a spade when he was in a passion, and then fled to this island and threw himself on the mercy of some of the natives with whom he was said to be related."[33] Synge saw in the story a revealing glimpse of an attitude that was traditional in Irish rural life. "This impulse to protect the criminal is universal in the west. It seems partly due to the association between justice and the hated English jurisdiction, but more directly to the primitive feeling of these people, who are never criminals yet always capable of crime, that a man will not do wrong unless he is under the influence of a passion which is as irresponsible as a storm on the sea. If a man has killed his father, and is already sick and broken with remorse, they can see no reason why he should be dragged away and killed by the law."[34]

In a country where the law was equated with oppression, lawlessness tended to be patriotic. The great Irish storyteller William Carleton, who came from peasant stock and lived through the terrible years of the famine and tithe wars in Ireland, wrote a tract on the deep contempt which characterized the Irish peasant's attitude to the law.[35] The late Professor Tomas O'Maille of University College, Galway, assembled the facts about the real-life Playboy,[36] but nobody on Inishmaan today seems to have heard of the incident, including the old man who lives—as he did in Synge's day—next door to the McDonough cottage and owns the land Dún Conor stands on. But the event was remembered and recounted on the island long before Synge. It had been told to Yeats and Arthur Symons two years before;[37] and the antiquarian Thomas Johnson Westropp, who visited Aran twenty years earlier, left an account of it.[38]

The keening, or lamentation for the dead, which Synge saw on Aran and used with good effect in *Riders to the Sea*, has disappeared in Ireland. Like the art of the storyteller it was a surviving remnant of the traditional life and represented what must once have been a highly developed mode of expression. Edmund Spenser witnessed keening in the sixteenth century and described it as "dispairful outcries and immoderate wailings."[39] The fact that it still managed to survive on the islands until Synge's day is an indication of how deeply the life was rooted in the Gaelic past.

Synge may have exaggerated the primitive elements in Irish peasant life, but they attracted his attention more than anything else. Because religion, for example, was to him only an idle superstition, he was particularly insensitive to the part it played in moulding the facts, if not the fancies, of Irish rural life. Some of his critics, who would have objected to his realism in any event, challenged the plausibility of his description of a funeral at which there was no priest and the only officiator was an old man praying against a background of "voices that were still hoarse with the cries of pagan desperation."[40] But the keening was a fact of island life, and the absence of the priest is explained by a passage in his notebook which he characteristically omitted from the published account. "The priest had held service the day before over the dead and had now been recalled to Aranmor, so when at last the grave was completed an old gray-haired man knelt simply on a stone and repeated a prayer whose words I was not able to understand." This fact will not strike anyone who knows the islands today as abnormal.

As his first visit drew to a close, Synge wrote in his notebook:

A wet day with a close circumference of wet stones and fog showing only at my window and inside white wash, red petticoats, turf smoke, my long pipe and Maeterlinck. I take stock slowly of my knowledge gained in Inishmaan. I cannot yet judge these strange primitive natures closely enough to divine them. I feel only what they are. I read *Grania* before I came here and enjoyed it, but the real Aran spirit is not there. The peasants are pure and spiritual, yet have all the healthy animal blood of a peasant and delight in broad jests and deeds. The young men are simple and friendly, never speaking however to strangers till they are addressed. The old men are chatty, cheerful and inquisitive. The girls are inclined to deride me when there are a handful together. Singly they are at first shy, or pretend to it, but show exquisitely bright frankness when the ice is crushed. Older women are full of good fellowship but have mostly little English and my Gaelic does not carry me beyond a few comments on the weather and the island.

To write a real novel of the island life one would require to pass several years among the people, but Miss Lawless* does not appear to have lived here. Indeed it would be hardly possible perhaps for a lady for more than a few days. . . . Take the passage in *Grania* where the heroine makes up the fire of kelp before she goes home to her rest as an example [of] how superficially travelers speak. The kelp fire lasts at most twenty-four hours and is tended all the time by some half dozen who pile on the weed continually. At least such is now the custom, and I am told none other could exist. Miss Lawless if she has erred has not done so deeply as Pierre Loti in his *Pêcheur d'Islande.* . . .†

The thought that this island will gradually yield to the ruthlessness of "progress" is as the certainty that decaying age is moving always nearer to the cheeks it is your ecstasy to kiss. How much of Ireland was formerly

* Emily Lawless (1845–1913), the daughter of Lord Cloncurry, wrote four novels about the west of Ireland. The action in *Grania* (1892), her first novel, takes place in Aran.

† A page is torn out at this point.

like this, and how much of Ireland is today Anglicized and civilized and brutalized?

On his last Sunday on the islands he wrote, "Am I not leaving in Inishmaan spiritual treasure unexplored whose presence is a great magnet to my soul? In this ocean alone is [there] not every symbol of the cosmos?"

Two days before he left the islands he received a letter from Yeats inviting him to come to Coole Park, Lady Gregory's estate in Galway, before continuing on to Dublin. "We can then talk about Aran and your work there. I spoke to my publisher, Bullen of Lawrence and Bullen, about your proposed book, as I thought you might care to try them if you have no other publishers in your mind. I think you should have no difficulty in placing some articles. I wonder if you have got any mythology. Try if the people remember the names of Aengus and Mannanan and the like, and if they know anything of the Dundonians, as I have heard the De Dananns called."*

On Saturday, June 25th, Synge climbed into one of the *curraghs* which came out to the steamer and bobbed on the waves as it waited its turn to come alongside. From the deck of the steamer he waved goodbye and watched the *curraghs* heading back into shore as the steamer moved across the bay to Galway city. Though he had not yet explored the "spiritual treasure" which was a "great magnet" to his soul, he had at least found it.

* Aengus is the Adonis of Celtic mythology and Mannanan the Poseidon. The Tuatha De Danann—People of the Goddess Dana—were one of the pre-Celtic peoples who conquered Ireland.

Six

COOLE PARK. BEGINNINGS OF THE IRISH
LITERARY THEATRE. PARIS. BRITTANY.
SECOND VISIT TO ARAN

Everyone is used in Ireland to the tragedy that is bound up with the lives of the farmers and fishing people; but in this garden one seemed to feel the tragedy of the landlord class also. . . .

Coole Park is in County Galway, twenty-two miles from Galway city. Today almost nothing remains of Lady Gregory's "modest white-fronted house rather like a large Italian farmhouse," as Joseph Hone described it.[41] "All the rooms and passages are gone, and saplings root among the broken stone," wrote Sean O'Casey parodying Yeats' moving tribute.[42] But the long tree-shaded avenue that led up to it is still there and also the lake from which Yeats' nine-and-fifty swans have flown away. Lady Gregory was the widow of Sir William Gregory, Governor of Ceylon, and in her middle forties with a son at Harrow when, through her neighbor Edward Martyn, she met George Moore and W. B. Yeats. Earlier in the year she had listened in London to Yeats' plans of "building a little theatre somewhere in the suburbs to produce romantic drama." Since that time the project had materialized to the extent that she and Yeats had drafted a formal letter announcing their plans of producing in Dublin in the spring of every year "certain Celtic and Irish plays," which would appeal to "an uncorrupted and imaginative audience trained to listen by its passion for oratory" and would embody "the deeper thoughts and emotions of Ireland."[43] The letter went to a group of well-to-do people who might be persuaded to underwrite the hiring of a Dublin theatre and the cost of performing Yeats' *The Countess Cathleen* and Martyn's *The Heather Field*. When Synge arrived at Coole Park on June 27th, Lady Gregory and Yeats were drawing up the list of potential subscribers. Edward Martyn took the responsibility of paying the deficit which the sale of the tickets did not cover.

Edward Martyn is somewhat ingloriously referred to in the official Dublin guidebook as a "wealthy County Galway landowner" who endowed the Palestrina Choir of the Pro-Cathedral in Dublin,[44] but his memory deserves more than this. He also deserves something better than George Moore's brilliantly malicious portrait in *Hail and Farewell*. Martyn's contribution to the birth of the Irish Literary Theatre was considerable, even if his personal influence was slight. The story of his difficulties with his fellow founders Moore and Yeats has been told by Moore, and one is tempted to conclude that if his ascetic personality had not clashed with Yeats' personality his addiction to Ibsen and the naturalistic drama of the Continent would have been an equal obstacle in the creation of Yeats' theatre of beauty. Martyn lived at Tulira, a modern manor house attached to a large Norman castle which had belonged to his ancestors and in which he had built his study. According to Moore it contained "a table taken from a design by Albrecht Dürer, and six oaken stools with terrifying edges," and was reached by a flight of "cold, moist, winding stairs."[45] Martyn's most recent biographer says only that it was panelled in oak, fitted with a simple table and chairs, bookshelves, reading stand, at which he wrote Greek verses standing up, and a high desk.[46] Whatever facts or fancies people wrote about Martyn's asceticism, it was no myth.

Coole Park, which had originally been part of the Martyn estate, was only five miles from Tulira, and on his second day there Yeats took Synge over to visit Martyn in Lady Gregory's dog cart. Whatever part Synge took in the discussions about the theatre is not known, but perhaps it was no mere coincidence that Yeats invited him to attend them. From this point on his friendship with both Lady Gregory and Yeats was the most important in his life, and he must have divined that whatever his future as a writer would be, it was bound up with theirs.

Yeats and Martyn went to Dublin in July to hire a theatre, and learned that the ordinary theatres were too expensive and that it was illegal to produce plays anywhere else, except in the Rotunda Maternity Hospital which had been deliberately excluded from the law passed more than a century before by the Irish Parliament. Lady Gregory then wrote to Lecky the historian who was then a Unionist member for Trinity College in the House of Commons, and he agreed to help by attaching a rider to the Local Government (Ireland) Act which became law on August 12, 1898, allowing the Dublin Corporation to grant licenses for the production of plays. The Irish Literary Theatre and its successor the Irish National Theatre Society existed under the provisions of this law until the group acquired its own theatre in 1904, and a warrant for the grant of letters patent was issued covering the Abbey Theatre and held by Lady Gregory in trust for the donor, Miss Horniman.

Synge was in Wicklow in July and knew nothing about the legal difficulties Yeats had encountered. On August 15th he went in to Dublin to see the Wolfe Tone Centenary celebration and saw both Yeats and Maud Gonne. The festivities in honor of the patriot were really an excuse for a massive demonstration. The immediate occasion was the laying of the cornerstone of a memorial, and Yeats was among the speakers who addressed the huge crowd. It was the second nationalist demonstration Synge had seen.

At Castle Kevin, where he spent the summer, he wrote among other things his first article, "A Story from Inishmaan," which appeared in November in *The New Ireland Review*. He also drafted an article which described a well known Wicklow itinerant who claimed to be over a hundred years old. In Ireland, which has more than its share of vagrants in the form of gypsies and tinkers and where the migratory instinct has been a fact of history, the vagrant and the ordinary tramp are never looked upon as outcasts or degenerates. For Synge—indeed for many Irish writers and painters—the vagrant is the personification of a romantic element in Irish life and an antidote to the devouring concern for land that has dominated Irish life for centuries. The vagrant came either from a peasantry which had vitality enough to create an occasional temperament of distinction, Synge wrote, or from the middle classes where "the gifted son of the family is always the poorest—usually a writer or artist with no sense for speculation." His life as a tramp had many privileges. He was untroubled by the law, lived in a climate that was always mild, and he enjoyed good health and good humor. But in all tramp life plaintive and tragic elements were apparent, even if only on the surface. "In these hills the summer passes in a few weeks from a late spring, full of odour and colour, to an autumn that is premature and filled with the desolate splendour of decay; and it often happens that, in moments when one is most aware of this ceaseless fading of beauty, some incident of tramp life gives a local human intensity to the shadow of one's own mood."[47] Either through envy or self-pity Synge began to see the tramp as a shadow of his own mood. In his love letters to Molly Allgood later he usually signed himself "Your Old Tramp," and it is clear that the tramp who appears in his play *In the Shadow of the Glen* had a private meaning for him.

During this summer he filled his notebook with fragments of verse, but passages of criticism indicate that he was a much better critic than creator:

The friends of music halls and churches like company, but those who worship on the hill go alone. Continual attendance mars the spirit, and marriage is only useful when it creates a wish for solitude. It is wiser to be in company and wish to be alone than to be alone and wish to be in company. A man who is ill may desire health, but the desirer of illness is a lunatic. With a person of the opposite sex one seeks a quiet corner to converse, but people of the same sex go in herds and this is why quite cultivated men often tolerate females. Gregarious animals are imbecile and solitary animals noble. The flea is also a nobler being than the ant, with an individual character and a sense of comfort like an Englishman. All nations with a talent for political life are individually stupid, while the French are delightful.

The intellectual superiority of the classes comes first of all from their privacy. The poor are always in flocks. An absolutely solitary existence would be incapable of small crimes being brought by some social instinct perverted, and indeed in countries where there were many gods they were never better than men in like case.

This attempt at an essay on solitude, which seems to be a defense of his own personality, is followed by some notes on Goethe which reveal his own conviction about the advantages to a writer who works in an atmosphere of intense nationalism:

Goethe's weakness [is] due to his having no national and intellectual mood to interpret. The individual mood is often trivial, perverse, fleeting, [but] the national mood broad, serious, provisionally permanent. Three distinctions to be sought: [a] work of art must have been possible to only one man at one period and in one place. Although only two suffice to give us art of the first importance such as much of the Gothic architecture, folk songs and airs, Dutch painting *etc.*, the great artist, like Rembrandt or Shakespeare, adds his personal distinction to a great distinction of time and place.

The profound is always inimitable. This feeling that a work of art is unimportant when it could have been produced by anyone at any time is inherent in the nature of art and altogether healthy. Things have always a character and characters have always a mood. These moods are as perpetually new as the sunsets. Profound insight finds the inner and essential mood of the things it treats of and hence gives us art that is absolutely distinct and inimitable—a thing never done before and never to be done again. Tennyson's complaint that all could grow the grain now that all possessed the seed is the proof, if any were needed, of his limitations. Pope also was very easy to imitate.

On the whole his notebooks at this time, with their passages of crisp, coherent prose alternating with scribbled-over fragments of poorly conceived verse reveal the state of his mind, poised as it was between the objective he had been trying to achieve before he went to Aran and the possibility of producing an art based upon the lives of the people he had lived with on Inishmaan. He was increasing his study of Gaelic tradition, but he did not see where this might lead beyond the writing of some articles for magazines. When he left for Paris again on November 14th he had not altered his intention of equipping himself to do critical work.

In Paris he moved into an unfurnished room at 90 rue d'Assas, which his friend Best found for him. It cost two hundred francs a year and was his permanent address in Paris until 1903. If one can overlook the errors in fact that distinguish nearly everything that George Moore wrote about Synge, his description of how Best helped Synge furnish the room is picturesque:

Synge was very helpless in the actual affairs of life; he could not go out and buy furniture; Best had to go with him, and they brought home a mattress and some chairs and a bed on a barrow, and then returned to

fetch the rest. There was a fiddle hanging on the wall of the garret in
the Rue d'Arras [*sic*], but as Synge never played it, Best began to wonder
if Synge could play, and as if suspecting Best of disbelief in his music,
Synge took it down one evening and drew the bow across the strings in a
way that convinced Best, who played the fiddle himself; and, as if satisfied,
he returned the fiddle to its nail, saying that he only played it in the Arran
Islands in the evenings when the peasants wanted to dance. "They have
no ear for music," he said, "and do not recognize a melody." "What!"
exclaimed Best. "Well, only as they recognize the cry of a bird or animal,
not as a musician." "Only the beat of the jig enters their ears," Best
replied in a voice tinged with melancholy.[48]

Snyge brought his fiddle to Aran only once, for his fourth visit in
1902, but nothing that he wrote lends support to this statement that
the islanders had no ear for music. His only complaint was that he
could not play rapidly enough for their dancing.

Marie Zdanowska was in Paris, living in a convent—or perhaps it
was a hostel for single girls run by a religious order—and Synge saw
a good deal of her. They went to the Louvre together and she lectured him on art and religion. He also saw Margaret Hardon frequently. Whether she or the memory of Cherry inspired the poems
he was writing, they were full of unhappiness over unrequited love
and quite as undistinguished as his previous verse.

A short poem which seems to have been inspired by a community
of nuns whom he used to see walking in their garden from a window
in Best's room in the rue Boissonade is untitled:

> Pigeons are cooing cool thoughts on the eaves.
> Insects pursuing their lusts on the leaves.
> The dust of the paper is hot to my skin.
> Rise little sisters and let me in.
>
> White-hood-sisters sit at their prayer
> Their droning beats at my breast with the air.
> "You are fragrant and cool and white,
> Sisters of Mercy, Love is delight."

He met T. P. Gill, the editor of *The Daily Express* (Dublin), and
was invited by him to write some book reviews. His review of Maeterlinck's *La Sagesse et la Destinée* appeared on December 17th, but

the ungainliness of his opening sentence, which is ninety-five words
long, indicates how little he had learned about journalism:

In these days, when many are looking with still perhaps uncertain hope
toward the gaining spirituality of art and abstract thinking, it grows a
serious duty for the critic to mark the attitude of workers in this newer
class, pointing out those to whom transcendental belief is but a wider
sphere for vulgar melodrama and those who (as, I think, Villiers de l'Isle
Adam) unite the highest endeavor with lower morbid sympathy, and
lastly, announcing the few books of pure and perfect conception, such
as *Wisdom and Destiny*, the volume Maurice Maeterlinck has lately
issued.

His second review, which appeared on January 28th, was a happier
effort because it was on the work of Anatole Le Braz. Synge was
studying Breton, as Yeats noted in a letter to Lady Gregory,[49] had
decided to go to Brittany for a fortnight in April, encouraged no
doubt by Cugnier and by another Breton enthusiast named Piquenard,
a neighbor of Cugnier at Quimper. Piquenard was an amiable fanatic
on the subject of the language revival in his native province. He
celebrated Synge's visit to Quimper by dedicating a poem to him—
Un fils de l'Irelande"—which appeared in October in the newspaper
Le Bas-Breton and was in Breton and French. It had the practical but
unpoetic title of *"Aimez Votre Langue Bretonne!"* A letter which
Piquenard wrote in September of the next year, when Synge was
planning another visit to Quimper, carries some of the flavour which
must have characterized the movement in Brittany. An *eisteddfod**
was to be held, and Piquenard wrote: "At that time all the Irish,
Scots, and Gauls who truly love their common nationality will assemble here and we can offer you a very pleasant room. You will
see our great bards—Valée, Le Tusbec, Yaffrenous *etc.*, and you will
see what progress the idea of Breton nationalism has made. . . . The
most important government officials have come over to our side, and
from now on the teaching of literary Breton is to be an elective in
the secondary schools. . . . As you can see, the hour of awakening
has finally come for us, and Brittany has generously taken the hand
of her valiant brothers over seas. . . . We are peaceful conquerors;
we are, therefore, sure to live and live a long time." Synge never

* An annual congress of bards and literati.

returned to Brittany and consequently did not hear the great Valée, Le Tusbec or Yaffrenous. But his knowledge of Breton and his brief encounter with Breton Celticism made him realize the advantage he had as an Irishman over "writers in places where the springtime of the local life has been forgotten."

During the autumn, plans for the Irish Literary Theatre had been at a standstill. In January the legal obstacles were removed through Lecky's help, and Yeats asked the National Literary Society to sponsor the enterprise and on January 12th published a letter in *The Daily Express* informing the public about the project. Then Edward Martyn, who had agreed to free the society of any financial liability, was granted in May a license to produce plays in the Antient Concert Rooms. Now the way was clear. When Synge arrived in London on the evening of May 8th, on his way home from Paris, an audience in Dublin was settling in their chairs to witness the first offering of the Irish Literary Theatre. Synge arrived in Dublin the next morning with a cold which put him in bed, but three days later he was able to get up and on the evening of the 12th witnessed the performances.

Lady Gregory, Yeats and George Moore have all left their own accounts of what happened in the months before the tumult which greeted the first performances of *The Countess Cathleen*. Moore entered the picture on Martyn's invitation and immediately took charge of the arrangements Yeats had made with Florence Farr to assemble a company of English actors. Meanwhile controversy had arisen over the principles of the movement itself. The opposition came not from the Protestant minority, who might understandably be antagonized by the political orientation of the movement, but from the nationalist Catholic majority. Ireland had largely a rural society, the Catholic population consisting mostly of people who worked the land for their living and had as little knowledge of the theatre as might be expected. Much of the material for the new Irish drama was to be drawn from their lives. It was to be a peasant theatre but not a theatre for peasants. In the period that had elapsed since Catholic Emancipation in 1829, the Protestant minority had used its influence to prevent the Catholic masses from ever losing their self-consciousness. To this the masses responded, as history has shown, in a way which committed them even more deeply to Catholicism and only broadened the base of their hatred for the landlord class.

Irish nationalist politicians since the 1840's had appealed to the people in the name of their former greatness. They were the literal descendants of Oscar and Cuchulain, and they were the natural heirs of a great body of literature written in their own distinctive language. But except for the peasants in the west and south of Ireland, where the native language was still a reality and the native literary tradition, diluted by centuries of neglect, still existed, few Irish people knew anything about their literature and not much more about the heroes whose exploits it recounted, the bards who had created it, or the scholars who had preserved it. A downtrodden people had merely been made to feel proud of the fact that they were Irish and that they had once had a noble past, some of the flavor of which it was still possible to recapture. As a result, the atmosphere of class hatred in which the Gaelic past was being rediscovered and the political uses to which it was being put made it almost inevitable that any literary movement drawing its inspiration from the Gaelic past would be expected to subordinate itself to the broader aims of Ireland's political destiny. Yeats and his associates were dedicated to their mission, but they were quite unwilling to become mere propagandists for politicians. They felt quite naturally that their first objective was to create an art that would be local without at the same time being provincial and would bring honour to Ireland because it was notable, not because it was a defence of the national character.

One of the ironies of the Irish Literary Revival was that it was founded by people whose origins were not Celtic and whose knowledge of the tradition they were attempting to identify themselves with was slight indeed. They were able eventually to resist all efforts to make them prostitute their movement to the cause of political nationalism because their involvement was purely an emotional one. They had no stake in the class that stood to gain from political liberation. Ireland merely provided them with excellent material for their art. But they did not see that the theatre they created, which indeed brought honour to Ireland beyond their wildest aspirations, would actually be repudiated by many Irish nationalists. Although they believed they were glorifying the Irish peasant, most Irishmen believed that it was their intention to ridicule him. Moreover, even though their original manifesto announced that their theatre would produce "a Celtic and Irish dramatic literature," and would be a manifestation of Celtic revivalism, they wrote their plays in English. These facts may help to explain why the Irish dramatic movement for the first twenty-six years of its history, from the performance of *The Countess Cathleen* to that of Sean O'Casey's *The Plough and the Stars* in 1926, was turbulent on occasion.

Edward Martyn had conceived the idea that Yeats' play, which is about a woman who offers her soul for her people, was heretical. After having his suspicions confirmed by his confessor, he refused to be associated with it. Yeats responded by getting contrary opinions from the Irish Jesuit Father Finlay, editor of *The New Ireland Review*, and an English priest—which resolved Martyn's doubts. While Yeats was trying to pacify the pietist Martyn and keep the blasphemous Moore, who was fuming at Yeats for submitting his work to theologians, from antagonizing Martyn, an attack came from outside the camp in the form of an anonymous pamphlet written by Frank Hugh O'Donnell and entitled *Souls for Sale*. The cover of the pamphlet carried a quotation from one of the demons in the play— "There soon will be no man or woman's soul unbargained for in five score baronies"—over the words, "Mr. W. B. Yeats on Celtic Ireland." It was given wide distribution and pushed into the mailboxes of everyone who might be effectively aroused. The cause of O'Donnell's enmity to Yeats is somewhat obscure. He was an impoverished journalist and thwarted politician who had entered Parliament in 1877 on the Parnellite ticket but later broke with the leader of the Irish Party out of personal jealousy and resigned his seat in extreme bitterness.

Trouble also came from Cardinal Logue, who issued a public statement warning Catholics that if the play was as it had been described to him—he admitted he had not read it—they should boycott it. The effect of the cardinal's letter immediately created discussion in Catholic circles, and letters to the press only stirred up the controversy further. But Martyn held firm because, as he had to admit, the cardinal had not read the play and his judgement could not be as good as Father Finlay's. Then Arthur Griffith entered the picture. He had just returned to Ireland after almost a three-year absence to edit *The United Irishman*, a newspaper which made its first appearance on March 4, 1899, and he was active in the most extreme nationalist circles. Griffith offered Yeats "a lot of men from the Quays" who would "applaud anything the Church did not like" to act as a strong-arm squad on the night of the first performance. Yeats had the wisdom to refuse, but then committed almost as serious a blunder by asking for police protection. The police were a strange contribution to a nationalist enterprise, but, as Yeats found out, their efficiency was unquestioned and they guaranteed that the play would be performed in an orderly fashion.

Yeats later admitted that he had asked for a good deal of the trouble. "In using . . . traditional symbols I forgot that in Ireland they are not symbols but realities. . . . The play itself was ill-constructed, the dialogue turning aside at the lure of word or metaphor, very different, I hope, from what it is to-day after many alterations. . . ."[50] The trouble over *The Countess Cathleen* was only the first test for his foundling theatre—"this Proteus that turns and changes like his draughty seas." Actually the Dublin press notices were friendly, even if Yeats' play was hooted at on each of the five nights of performance. Martyn's play was enthusiastically applauded. The élite of Dublin literary circles turned out, and some of the foremost London drama critics, including Max Beerbohm,[51] wrote enthusiastically about the whole enterprise. But outcries from nationalist circles continued for some weeks afterwards in the pages of *An Claidheamh Soluis*,* the organ of the Gaelic League.

It is not easy to picture the kind of theatre Yeats hoped to create, from the pronouncements in his original prospectus, letters to the press, and program notes in the issue of *Beltaine* sold at the first performances. A certain vagueness of phrase may have seemed advisable, so that it would offend no one. But a letter he wrote to Fiona McLeod in January of 1897 shows that he was thinking of a theatre which would "make the Irish, Scotch and other Celts recognize their solidarity." He wrote: "My own theory of poetical or legendary drama is that it should have no realistic, or elaborate, but only a symbolic and decorative setting. A forest, for instance, should be represented by a forest pattern and not by a forest painting. One should design a scene which would be an accompaniment not a reflection of the text. . . . The acting should have an equivalent distance to that of the play from common realities. The plays might be almost, in some cases, modern mystery plays."[52] How so ethereal a drama was to

* Ir., The Sword of Light.

make the Irish, Scotch and other Celts recognize their solidarity he had obviously not thought very much about. As he admitted, what he considered to be symbols a good many Irish people were accustomed to looking upon as realities. When Synge's influence turned the dramatic movement into precisely the opposite direction, into realism, Yeats had the integrity to admit Synge's achievement and even to fight for it. In the end his own plays had little influence, and the Abbey Theatre came to stand for something quite different from what he had planned.

During the spring of 1899 Synge asked Margaret Hardon to marry him and was gently refused. He continued to see her, however, and when he wrote to her from Castle Kevin in June of 1899 she replied, "Please do not delude yourself by any signs in dreams that you consider favorable. You know I have always been interested in you and your work and this winter considered you as a friend. But beyond that there is nothing and never can be. If you let this come so definitely into your life you will make yourself and me very unhappy, and the end will be that I cannot see you any more. But I hope that time and a certain distance has already mended that. Perhaps you would be interested to know that my ex-fiancé has announced his engagement to a friend of mine. It doesn't hurt now."

Thérèse Beydon wrote to him in August about a different matter—they had been discussing religion. "You shocked me very much at Versailles when you told me I was not any more religious than you! If you asked my American friend, who is a 'Reverend' and therefore someone to whom I could often speak openly on these subjects, I assure you that he would not at all share your opinion, but with you how could I ever discuss these sacred objects; it would seem to me that I was profaning them. I hope I am not hurting you in telling you this, but it is impossible to be myself with you as regards these questions; therefore it will be a side of me that you will never know."

On September 5th the Synges returned to Dublin from Castle Kevin, and four days later Synge left on his second visit to Aran. He spent two days in Galway, where he saw Martin McDonough, who was working in a lime factory and homesick for Inishmaan, landed at Kilronan, on Inishmore, on the 12th, and went immediately by *curragh* to the middle island. The people welcomed him warmly, and he wrote in his notebook, "Last year when I came here everything was

new and the people were a little strange to me, but now I am familiar
with them and their way of life so that their qualities strike me more
forcibly than before." But though he had got closer to an understanding of them he still realized how formidable the task of writing
about them was. "In some ways these men and women seem strangely
far away from me. They have the same emotions that I have and the
animals have; yet I cannot talk to them when there is much to say
more than to the dog that whines beside me in a mountain fog." The
comparison may not be very flattering but it reveals the kind of affection he felt for them.

What the people thought of him is in their letters. His Aran correspondents included Martin McDonough, his brother John, his father
Patrick, and his cousin Martin Flaherty—all on Inishmaan—and two
girls on Inishere. His Inishere correspondents wrote in English, but
the letters from Inishmaan are wholly or partly in Gaelic. In his
earliest letters to Synge, Martin McDonough was dubious of Synge's
ability to read Gaelic and appended English translations of what he
had written. None of Synge's correspondents was very sure either of
their English or of their Irish. English was used in the school, but
most of the people had had little schooling and some none at all.
Synge noted that on the two smaller islands only the men appeared
to have any command of English. The people learned Irish, of course,
from the cradle, but if the schoolteacher happened not to be a native
speaker, which was frequently the case, they got no formal training
in their native language and consequently the degree of illiteracy in
Irish was high. The Gaelic League, which was founded in 1893, was
attempting not only to teach Irish to English speakers but also to
eradicate illiteracy among Irish speakers. But it did not become active
on Inishmaan until the late nineties; its effects were not felt until
considerably later. Both the Irish and the English of Synge's correspondents are western dialects, inaccurately written by people orally
fluent in one and unsure in the other.

The letters have a strange formality, characteristic of a people unaccustomed to writing and due partly no doubt to the influence of the
old-fashioned schoolmasters who taught them to use formal saluta-
tions and observe certain conventions in their letters. But the letters
are valuable because they reveal quite clearly the source from which
Synge was learning the dialect he was to use in his plays and which

owes as much to his own literal translation of Gaelic phrases as it does to the Gaelic constructions which the people themselves used when they spoke or wrote in English. Perhaps most typical of the letters in Gaelic is one by Martin Flaherty, written on November 4, 1900, after Synge's third trip to Aran:

Dear Friend, It's a good while ago now since I sent you the last letter. And I do hope that you are good in your health, and more power to you. And myself is good, and all the neighbors. It's not long ago since Michaeleen O'Hickey was here with me and Agnes O'Farrelly, and they were friendly with the people and they put up a big *feis** and there was a big gathering of people. A lot of people came to the *feis*, but the island is empty now. Martin McDonough is at home and Johneen is married. We have a new priest here now by the name of Father White. We have a new school-inspector here now. And we have Mr. Coonan† and they are both good. Small Michaeleen is talking now and he is a good little boy. We have nice, fine days now, and you would like to be on the sea in a *curragh* and to be going swimming, and the days are very warm now. I am your friend, Martin Flaherty.

John McDonough could not write Gaelic at all and had to dictate a letter in English to his brother Martin, who turned it into Irish:

It is a great cause of shame to me not to send you a letter before this, but I was waiting until Martin had time to write an Irish letter to you, because you know that I can't write Irish. We got the money safely and also of course there was the clock. And it was going when it came here, and it had the right time too—I think. I am very thankful to you for it, and it has a good stroke as it ever had. I was very glad to hear that you were safely home and that you and your family had their health. We are sending you all our seven thousand blessings and every friend you have here—Miss Hedderman‡ and Mr. Coonan. It is lonely we were for a long time when you left. But now we are getting out of it when we are used to being lonely. Martin will be expecting a letter from you. And I too, soon. We did not get any news of Miss Drury§ yet. If you see her send me news quickly. I have nothing much else to tell you except farewell and goodbye. I am your friend always.

* A festival.
† The schoolteacher.
‡ The island nurse.
§ Apparently another visitor from Dublin.

One of the two young girls Synge had met during his first visit to the south island in 1900 wrote to him in English:

I thank you very much for sending the photographs to me. Violet Wallace got hers. She told me she was going to write to you. The big girl, her heart was well broken when she seen how she looked, hoping that you will be able to sketch us better next year. This place is very cold now. We wouldn't be able to go to the crosha* only for we got a stove. We are getting on very well with it. Miss McHught is well. She got one of the photographs from you, hoping that you admire the lace better next year. When you will come out have lots of jigs and reels next year. We will have a better dance, I hope. Hoping you are quite well and enjoying your music, wishing you the best compliments of this season, from your little friend, Barbara Coneely.

Barbara Coneely's words, "wishing you the best compliments of this season," were later to turn up in the mouth of Pegeen Mike in *The Playboy*.

We learn more about the lacework on Inishere from another letter of Barbara Coneely's, of slightly more than a year later:

You must forgive me for not answering your letter before this. I thought every day to write to you so. The times is so busy with that lace work we can't spare a minute. All the girls is first rate with it now. There is an evening class going to start soon so Miss McHugh will have a lot of work to do then. Miss McHugh is quite well. She will be going for her holidays at Easter. She didn't leave at Xmas at all. Violet Wallace is quite well. And so is every one. The winter is near out now. This place is not much in the winter time. It's all fish. I don't work at the crosha house now at all but I go there sometimes to see Miss McHugh and the girls. But I will be going there soon again. I am a coffee stall keeper for the Board.‡ Down in near the sea shore I work. So we will soon have summer now, hoping that we will soon see you back with us. The summer is near out always when you come, so come early this year and bring some of your music boxes with you. I am your friend, Barbara.

Some of Martin McDonough's letters are in Gaelic, some in English, and some in both. Synge used five of them in his book,[53] but

* Crochetting.
† The crochet instructress.
‡ The Congested Districts Board. See p. 185.

he not only reversed the order in which they were written but also made changes and deletions to conceal the identity of the writer. In one he deleted Martin's "I will write this letter in Irish but I do not know are you able to understand it," and in another his query about how well Synge was progressing with his Irish. He also reworked Martin's English idiom in the interest of clarity by changing "I now see that your time is coming on for the future to come to Inishmain" to "I see now that your time is coming round to come to this place." If some of Synge's critics who described his language as bogus could have read Martin McDonough's English they would have realized that except for the linguistic refinement that goes into any work of art, Synge's characters speak a language which must have been very close to that used by the islanders.

Martin wrote, after Synge's first visit,

O Loyal Friend, I got your letter a few days ago and indeed I was happy and delighted about it being written in Irish. And it was a nice, friendly, exultant letter and there is great exultation on me, you to be in your good health. I am delighted myself that you got the book which I sent to you. I never saw anyone as lonely as I. I have not got any gentleman or lady to be teaching Irish to. I was hard worked since you left me teaching Irish as you saw. I had Stephen Barrett, Padraic Pearse* and Miss Agnes O'Farrelly learning Irish from me, and I hope that you will write a letter to Mr. Stephen Barrett. . . . I have another story to tell you that the post is coming to the island twice a month to see if they can have a post in it, but they have no post office there yet. Myself and my family are in good health and I went to Kilronan and I got news that Mr. Kilbride† is well in his health. Every other friend is well also. [Continuing in English] I want you to write a letter every week. We are wanting to get the post office here and it is coming twice a month here. A canoe‡ from Kilronan is paid by coming here with it. Please I want you when you go to France to send me a small pocket knife. I am your friend forever.

Ten days later he wrote again to thank Synge for the clock, which must have been a fairly useless but novel possession on the island. A year later he wrote to tell about his job in Galway for which he was

* The hero of the Easter Rising.
† The Protestant minister on Inishmore.
‡ Martin translates the word *curragh* into its nearest English equivalent.

to get £11 a year. In February of 1902 he wrote to tell of the tragedy which struck the family when his brother John's wife died, apparently in childbirth:

Johneen, Friend of My Heart. A million blessings to you. It's a while ago since I thought of a small letter to write, and every day was going until it went too far and the time I was about to write to you. It happened that my brother's wife, Shawneen, died. And she was visiting the last Sunday in December, and now isn't it a sad story to tell? But at the same time we have to be satisfied because a person cannot live always. But Shawneen is good, but he is very lonely. But if he is, he has to be satisfied. I am afraid you will be cross with me, but I say to you it was through no fault of my own. I got the letter you sent me and the postcard. And I am happy to know your health is good. I said to my father and to my mother that I was ashamed that I did not send you a letter and that maybe you might be cross with me. Michael O'Hickey is good and myself, and small Michaeleen, and he makes tricks with his fingers as you did. . . .

Martin's simple eloquence on the subject of his brother's tragedy—"But at the same time we have to be satisfied because a person cannot live always"—was to be echoed in the final speech of the old mother in *Riders to the Sea*: "No man at all can be living for ever, and we must be satisfied."

In October of 1902 Martin wrote that Martin Flaherty had gone to a seminary at Tuam in Galway to study for the priesthood. In August of 1903 he wrote that he was now married himself and had a child and asked Synge to send "a long wire as long as the snood" and added in brackets that a *snood* was fishing tackle and was five yards long. In February of 1904 he answered a letter of Synge's asking for a pair of pampooties and some of the native flannel so that Willie Fay could see how to costume the actors in *Riders to the Sea*:

O Friend John. I should not have forgotten you for so long without sending a letter to you, but I must beg your pardon. I had a lot to do and I was putting it off from time to time until it went too far. But I had to make a small space now. I must say to you that I did not expect a letter from you for ever. I was thinking that you were not alive. Be sure I was greatly delighted when I got your letter at last and not only myself but my father and my mother and all my family. They were very satisfied too.

Now about the pampooties. The price is half-crown a pair. But if you want a pair yourself I'll send them to you and welcome. But I wouldn't like to give them to anybody else without a half crown if they want them. You send me word and you'll have them quickly. [Continuing in English] Sending you a little bit of flannel, but I have to say to you that it is very dear and very scarce, although I might be able to get some, if you want me to do so. The price of it is from 3/ to 3/6 per yard.

We are very badly without fire (turf) here this year, although we have plenty coal and some timber. We did not get much turf at all this year, on account of the rain and rough weather. I was told that the Connemara people was burning coal, that they cannot take the turf from the bog. It is not a very good year for fishing either, the weather being too rough, no snow, nor frost here. There was a man from Belfast here for the last fortnight, and he told me that there was a great lot of snow at home when he left it and he told me also that this place (island) is like summer, that it is warmer than Belfast.

As Synge's second visit drew to a close he crossed over to Inishmore in a rough sea with the warnings of the priest and the schoolmaster, who advised him not to attempt it, ringing in his ears. The *curragh* with its four rowers stood on end at times, but he enjoyed the trip. "Down in this shallow trough of canvas that bent and trembled with the motion of the men, I had a far more intimate feeling of the glory and power of the waves than I have ever known in a steamer." On Inishmore Martin Coneely, "Old Mourteen," was waiting for him and they walked northwards from Kilronan along the ridge of the island to the village of Cowrugh, where a number of *clocháns* nestled on the side of the hill below the shattered remains of a prehistoric stone fort. He and Mourteen lay down in the corner of the field, and Synge allowed the "antique formulas" of the story the old man told him to "blend with the suggestions from the prehistoric masonry I lay on." When the story was finished, Mourteen asked him, "Do you never be thinking on the young girls?" and passed judgement on the condition of bachelorhood in words that were later to come with slight modification from the mouth of Michael James in *The Playboy*—"a man who is not married is no better than an old jackass. He goes into his sister's house, and in his brother's house; he eats a bit in this place and a bit in another place, but he has no home for himself; like an old jackass straying on the rocks."

Synge left Inishmore on October 7th. He stepped off the steamer in Galway in the dark of evening but found the city celebrating the eighth anniversary of the death of Charles Stuart Parnell. The train for Dublin left at midnight from a platform crowded with intoxicated people. The revelry continued all night in the adjacent compartment, but a young girl who sat beside him lost her shyness and they struck up a conversation while he pointed out the sights to her through the grey of early dawn. "This presence at my side," he wrote, "contrasted curiously with the brutality that shook the barrier behind us. The whole spirit of the west of Ireland, with its strange wildness and reserve, seemed moving in this single train to pay a last homage to the dead statesman of the east."

Seven

PARIS. IRELAND AND QUEEN VICTORIA. THIRD
AND FOURTH VISITS TO ARAN. FIRST PLAY

> *Queens of Sheba, Meath, and Connaught,*
> *Coifed with crown, or gaudy bonnet;*
> *Queens whose finger once did stir men,*
> *Queens were eaten of fleas and vermin,*
> *Queens men drew like Mona Lisa,*
> *Or slew with drugs in Rome and Pisa.*

Shortly after Synge left for Paris on November 3rd, the founders of the Irish Literary Theatre began making preparations for their second series of performances during the week of February 19, 1900. Once again English actors were to be used, but instead of the Antient Concert Rooms Yeats hired one of Dublin's best commercial theatres, the Gaiety, which seated more than a thousand people and was used mostly by touring English companies doing drawing-room plays. The major offering was George Moore's adaptation of Edward Martyn's *The Tale of a Town*, entitled *The Bending of the Bough*. In addition two shorter pieces were to be given—*The Last Feast of the Fianna* by Alice Milligan and *Maeve* by Edward Martyn. *Maeve* drew some of its inspiration and one of its characters from Irish heroic legend, but Miss Milligan's play was the first heroic drama based directly on Irish saga material to be offered. Yeats wrote in *Beltaine*, "We have brought the 'literary drama' to Ireland, and it has become a reality."

During the week of the performances a luncheon was given to the members of the Irish Literary Theatre by the parent organization, the

Irish National Literary Society. George Moore, who was one of the speakers, announced that the next offering of the theatre would include Yeats' *The Land of Heart's Desire* in an Irish translation by Douglas Hyde. The language "was slipping into the grave," he said, and if a great national effort were not made to save it, it would take with it "the character and genius of the Celt." But none of the founders of the Irish Literary Theatre except Lady Gregory knew any Irish, and she had yet to write her first play in any language. Susan Mitchell, one of Dublin's sharpest satirists for whom Moore was a favorite target, wrote a poem entitled "George Moore Comes to Ireland."

> We have reformed the Drama, myself and Yeats allied;
> For I took small stock in Martyn, and less in Douglas Hyde;
> To bow the knee to rare AE was too much for my pride.
>
> But W. B. was the boy for me—he of the dim, wan clothes;
> And—don't let on I said it—not above a bit of a pose;
> And they call his writing literature, as everybody knows.[54]

If the second appearance of the Irish Literary Theatre evoked no response from Nationalist quarters, the visit of Queen Victoria in April, 1900, did. Since the writs of ejectment under which thousands of Irish farmers had been evicted from their homes were issued over the queen's name and resounding titles, she had become a living symbol of oppression. When she and her party came ashore at Dún Laoghaire and proceeded to Dublin by carriage, many among the crowd who watched her from the roadside cheered and waved, but as many more looked on in brooding resentment. Mrs. Synge wrote to her son Samuel: "There were four carriages and she was in the last. I saw no one but her in that carriage. She looks so small and sad. She bowed first to one side and then to the other, but did not raise her eyes."

In the Phoenix Park thousands of children gathered to be reviewed by the queen, but Maud Gonne staged an opposition demonstration of children led by young men of the Celtic Literary Society and the Gaelic Athletic Association. Yeats wrote a letter to the newspapers in which he referred to the queen as a "woman of eighty-one, to whom all labours must be weariness, without good reason, and the reason is national hatred. . . ."[55] In another letter which appeared the day before her arrival he described her as "the official head and symbol of an empire that is robbing the South African Republics of their liberty, as it robbed Ireland of theirs. Whoever stands by the roadway cheering for Queen Victoria cheers for that Empire, dishonours Ireland, and condones a crime."[56]

When Lecky withdrew his support from the Irish Literary Theatre to protest Yeats' letters, Yeats wrote to Lady Gregory that "he had nothing to resign as his guarantee had not been removed. I think this will greatly irritate him and, may be, lead to controversy about the Queen in the *Express* which would make both Moore and myself quite happy. I did another 'Queen Letter,' by the by, which I will send you if I can find a copy and Moore is at the moment doing another."[57] But the last word on the queen's visit was written by Percy French, whose songs and sketches entertained a whole generation of Irish people. In a lampoon entitled "The Queen's After-Dinner Speech (As overheard and cut into lengths of poetry by James Murphy, Deputy-Assistant Waiter at the Viceregal Lodge)," French wrote:

> "And that other wan," sez she
> "That Maud Gonne," sez she
> "Dhressin' in black," sez she
> "To welcome me back," sez she
> "Though I don't care," sez she
> "What they wear," sez she
> "An' all that gammon," sez she
> "About me bringin' famine," sez she
> "Now Maud will write," sez she
> "That I brought the blight," sez she
> "Or altered the saysons," sez she
> "For some private raysons," sez she
> "An' I think there's a slate," sez she
> "Off Willie Yeats," sez she
> "He should be at home," sez she
> "French polishin' a poem," sez she
> "An' not writin' letters," sez she
> "About his betters," sez she
> "Paradin' me crimes," sez she
> "In the Irish Times," sez she. . . .[58]

When Synge returned to Dublin in the last week of May, the excitement was all over. His mother had invited two young ladies interested in church work to join her at Castle Kevin for the summer. When he complained of their presence to MacKenna, who was still in Paris, MacKenna sent him a copy of Omar Khayyám and followed it with some doggerel reminding Synge that listening to the talk of missionaries was a small price for the accommodations at Castle Kevin. In July MacKenna wrote a sixteen-page letter. He was moving in the best circles, but his fortunes remained at their lowest ebb:

. . . Your last letter distinctly states the damning desire of "a breath of the wickedness of Paris." Oh, my friend! Oh! I will not hide from you that I have often been pained to find in you a certain worldly spirit. It has sometimes seemed to me as we reeled home from a *gargote* of the Boul' Mich., or as we strolled in the hush of evening or in the *clair* of the moon through the quiet streets after dining hermetically on a crust of bread and a Maryland cigarette, that you were not as given to holy things as I could desire. Perhaps I ought to have spoken out more strongly the thought that was in me, striving to lift you to higher thoughts. Perhaps, perhaps, I might have done more than I did, might have given you the word your soul needed, might have helped my erring brother more steadily homeward; but what will you? Man is but as a reed, as the smoke of a cigarette he floateth, and stability is not always in him, and he drinketh of strange drinks that trouble his soul so that he sees not always clearly and his feet not always tread the straight path. Now however I will speak, fasting. I will warn you. Give not yourself up to the gorging of the flesh; look not on mutton when it is boiled, nor on beef when it's red. Avail yourself in a weak and humble spirit of the improving conversation that is round you; feast on the word; fill your soul with the sweetness of saintliness; many would be glad of the crumbs that fall from the table where you sit calmly, naturally, unconcerned. . . .

I was interested in the odd scraps of Dublin you threw out in your last letter. . . . I do not despise Dublin, tho' it is very provincial; its provinciality is not like the provinciality of Manchester; it is a province not of England but of dreamland. One feels lost causes in the air, and the stir of new hopes; the material side of the hopes is not inspiring. I detest committees and committee intrigues; but, letting others do the work, one feels a certain big life in the hopes, sometimes even in results. I wish, though, that these things were being done in and from Cork. Cork is a delightful city, the Celtic center; if it hadn't such a ridiculous name it would be an ideal place to live in, work in and make a literary and artistic capital in. . . .

But answer me about Best and peace be with you. My peace I give unto you. The trouble about you heretics is that your Bible doesn't correspond with the one true and unclassic version of us; and when one uses a text to point a moral or adorn a tale, often the allusion is lost; ye know not Joseph when his words come *via* Douai. For which as is well known you will all be damned—God help ye.   MacKenna.

Synge's third visit to Aran lasted a month, from the middle of September. Except for a few days on Inishere he spent it on Inishmaan. The McDonoughs welcomed him warmly. "In the cottage everything was as usual; but Michael's presence has brought back the old woman's humour and contentment. As I sat down on my stool and lit my pipe with the corner of a sod, I could have cried out with the feeling of festivity that this return procured me."[59] He had a new set of gymnastic tricks to show the people, and wrote: "As I pulled their limbs about in my effort to teach them, I felt that the ease and beauty of their movements has made me think them lighter than they really are. Seen in their curaghs between cliffs and the Atlantic, they appear lithe and small, but if they were dressed as we are and seen in an ordinary room, many of them would seem heavily and powerfully made."[60]

A man's body had been found floating off the coast of Donegal, and some of his clothes were sent to Inishmaan where the people debated for three days about whether they belonged to a local man recently lost or to one from the south island. All the islanders of course wore the same kind of clothing, made of the local flannel and woven on Inishmore. As Synge sat in the McDonough cottage listening to the mother of the dead man from Inishmaan slowly keening to herself, he noted the ease with which the people not related to the drowned man could accept his death as an ordinary occurrence. "The loss of one man seems a slight catastrophe to all except the immediate relatives. Often when an accident happens a father is lost with his two eldest sons, or in some other way all the active men of a household die together."[61] Out of the incident came *Riders to the Sea*.

Although he was deeply moved by the elemental struggle between the fishermen and the sea, it did not strike him—and indeed *Riders to the Sea* does not strike us—as being the kind of material a modern dramatist would find varied or meaningful enough for visualization on a stage. He was reading Keating's *History of Ireland*—that curious seventeenth century compilation, half-fable, half-history, of Ireland's hedge-master Herodotus—a story which seemed to him much more adaptable to dramatic projection. Recounting a legendary story of the first inhabitants of Ireland, Keating writes, "Some others say that it is three fishermen who were driven by a storm of wind from Spain unwillingly; and as the island pleased them that they returned for their wives to Spain; and having come back to Ireland again, the deluge was showered upon them at Tuaigh Innbhir, so that they were drowned. Capa, Laighne and Luasad, their names."[62]

Fishermen from the Continent are frequent visitors to Aran because they fish the waters off the west coast of Ireland, and Synge may have seen in Keating's crude story some archetypal pattern of island life. At any rate it was this rather than the contemporary struggle with the sea on Inishmaan that suggested itself to him as a theme. He made preliminary sketches and wrote some dialogue. In 1902 he returned briefly to it again, but all that survives is a long passage of verse dialogue in a notebook. As he worked it out, Luasmad, Capa and Laine and their wives sit on a rock in Ireland and watch the Deluge swallow the world around them. Luasmad's wife dies while giving birth, and her child is then killed by a falling stone. Then Capa, Laine and Capa's wife are washed off the rock and only Luasmad and Laine's wife are left. Finally Luasmad makes love to Laine's wife in order to defy the powers of death that threaten them. They are both finally washed away like the others.

On a wild day when he had been on Inishmaan for about a fortnight, he crossed Gregory Sound in a *curragh* to stay for a few days on Inishere. He returned to Inishmaan then for the rest of his time, and as it drew to a close wrote in his notebook: "Another visit is over. This year I have learned little but Gaelic and nearer understanding of the people." On October 14th, another wild day, he took the steamer over to Kilronan, but she shipped water on the way and the captain decided not to try to get across Galway Bay with her. Synge went ashore for the night and took a room at the Atlantic Hotel. After dark he walked down to the pier and found an old man in the watchman's shelter near the pier who told him that he had been taken to the house of a Mr. Synge in Dublin when he first sailed there as a cabin boy. He had met his Uncle Alec's cabin boy. The next day the steamer reached Galway safely, though a terrible sea was still running and several times the engines stopped, she lost headway and drifted helplessly towards the grey mass of Black Head. He stayed two nights in Galway before leaving for home.

Best was in Dublin, and they talked about the book he was planning to write about Aran. Best advised him to buy a typewriter, and selected one for him. It was a Blickensdorfer, apparently of German design but carrying on its name plate the words "Newcastle-on-Tyne" and "Made in the U.S.A."*

Synge's seventh season in Paris lasted from November 1, 1900, to May 6, 1901. Through Yeats he met R. Barry O'Brien, the biographer of Parnell, who was editor of *The Speaker,* a sixpenny London weekly later known as *The Nation.* Synge's review of Father Mac-Erlean's edition of the poems of Geoffrey Keating appeared in the December 8th issue, and over the next four years he wrote five more reviews for *The Speaker.* He wrote his second piece about Aran for *The Gael,* a New York monthly, in April. He also began to put his Aran notes together into a connected narrative, and before he went back to Ireland in May he had the first three parts in nearly final form. He also began working on a play which he had sketched out during the summer months at Castle Kevin.

The hero of it is a young Irish writer of the Ascendancy class who has been brought home from Paris by a telegram announcing the illness of his uncle. Sister Eileen, a nun in a nursing order who has been taking care of the dead man, is the writer's distant cousin and

---

* It is a curious machine, mounted in a wooden carrying case and much smaller and simpler in construction than a modern portable typewriter. The keyboard, which is not standard, works according to the same principle as the toy typewriters made for children today. Its type is mounted on a small circular drum which rotates when the keyboard is struck to the proper letter and then dips to the paper, inking itself on the way by striking against a tiny pad mounted on a roller suspended above the paper. The inking pad is replaceable, and to change the type one has merely to remove the small drum on which it is mounted and substitute another with different type. From this time on he used the machine steadily, doing all his writing on it except his personal letters and the rough, preliminary drafts and passages of dialogue which he still continued to write in his notebooks. He must have been one of the first writers, except for working journalists, who composed directly onto a typewriter.

the companion of his childhood. The uncle dies, the writer is wounded by a shotgun blast from the half-mad brother of a woman the uncle had wronged, and the nun stays at the estate for three more months to nurse her wounded cousin. The central incident in the play is a love scene in which the writer woos the nun and persuades her to renounce her life of celibacy. She finally doffs her white habit for a green dress which is found in the dead man's trunk, and the play ends with the two lovers in each other's arms.

Three women had contributed to the making of the heroine— Florence Ross, whom he had played with as a child in the woods of Rathfarnham demesne; Cherry Matheson, whose religion had defeated him; and Margaret Hardon, whom he referred to in his diary as *La Robe Verte*. Like all his early work the play is full of a deep and haunting sense of death, and no matter how eloquently the hero preaches his doctrine of the joyful life, the atmosphere of death, madness and decay which saturates the action is never dispelled. The important speeches Synge drew from observations he had written in his notebooks long before he had any thought of using them in a play. One of these is in a passage which Sister Eileen reads from one of the writer's manuscripts:

Every life is a symphony; and the translation of this sequence into music and from music again, for those who are not musicians, into literature, or painting or sculpture, is the real effort of the artist. The emotions which pass through us have neither end nor beginning, are a part of eternal sensations, and it is this almost cosmic element in the person which gives all personal art a share in the dignity of the world. Biography, even autobiography, cannot give this revelation, for the deeds of a man's lifetime are impersonal and concrete, might have been done by anyone, while art is the expression of the abstract beauty of the person.

The hero's attack on traditional attitudes and his ridicule of the nun's belief in God and the virtue of self-denial is also a reflection of the utterances Synge had shocked his mother with:

No one pretends to ignore the bitterness of disease and death. It is an immense, infinite horror; and the more we learn to set the real value on the vitality of life the more we dread death. Yet any horror is better than the stagnation of belief. . . . The people who rebel from the law of God are not those who linger in the aisles droning their withered chants with senile intonation. . . . In the Christian synthesis each separate faculty has been dying of atrophy. . . . The only truth a wave knows is that it is going to break. The only truth we know is that we are a flood of magnificent life, the fruit of some frenzy of the earth.

When she replies, "It is simpler to believe in God," he answers, "I will believe in millions of them if you like, but I have no doubt they care as little for us as we care for the sorrows of an ant-hill." In a letter to a friend which he dictates to her he says: "The old-fashioned Irish conservatism and morality seemed to have evolved a melancholy degeneration worse than anything in Paris. Every one seemed to be taking his friends to the asylum or bringing them back from it."

Like Joyce's *Exiles* the play has too much emotion and too much meaning for its slight and poorly constructed framework to support. It is the work of a man of genius who does not yet understand the dramatic form and takes the easy way out by talking his play to its conclusion. The most remarkable thing about it Yeats and Lady Gregory noticed at once. The peasant characters, though they play a minor part, are more effectively realized than the principals. And they speak in the dialect Synge was beginning to master from his life with the Aran people. "It's a grand night now, Sister Eileen, and the people is in great spirits and joy with the smell of the things growing and the breaking up of the drought." One of them distinctly echoes Martin McDonough's words about his brother's tragedy— "I'm destroyed crying; but what good is in it? We must be satisfied and what man at all can be living forever."

With all its imperfections it carried the seed which would come to flower as soon as Synge could learn to plant it in different soil. The language of his hero is didactic and vapid, but some of the richness and the reality which he called for in the preface to *The Playboy* are to be found in the words of the servant girl. Yeats and Lady Gregory realized this when they rejected the play and urged him to stick with his peasants and forget life in the Big House. Perhaps they wanted plays about peasants so badly that they would have pushed Synge in that direction anyway, even if they had not sensed the particular attraction it had for him. But if it had been the best play Synge ever wrote, they could hardly have attempted to play it before Catholic audiences in Dublin, where the mere suggestion of heresy in *The Countess Cathleen* had nearly crushed their theatre at birth. This was a problem they were to face more than once with Synge. Long before the explosion over *The Playboy* they refused to produce *The Tinker's Wedding*, in which a priest is beaten up and thrown into a sack, as being unsuitable for Dublin audiences. Yeats was fond of telling how Synge once innocently suggested writing a play in which a Protestant woman faces certain rape from a band of soldiers in preference to staying in the company of a Catholic woman she is hiding with.[63]

When Synge returned to Dublin in May of 1901 he had the two published reviews to show his mother and the first three parts of his book on Aran. His most significant achievement—his play—he did not show her. She would have been scandalized by it, and he probably felt that she already had had enough to be alarmed about. He was now thirty years old and in her eyes was living a life without belief, ambition or purpose. She was also beginning to be concerned again about his neck. When he came back from Aran the previous October she had noticed "one very large gland on his neck just above his collar," though he looked well otherwise. He had written her from Paris in February that the swollen gland had become even more enlarged. His friend Dr. Cree had given him an ointment, but it seemed only to irritate the swelling. She wrote to Samuel: "He fears this is a bad time to begin treatment, after a winter of such hard work and poor living. I am very sorry for him poor fellow. He prefers poor living away from home to good living at home. I shall try to persuade him to come home in April and give up the attic." Then on April 25th she wrote to Samuel again:

I had a letter from Johnnie yesterday, a sad one. He says he met a Russian doctor, a friend of his, and he strongly advised him to have the glands removed at once, before the summer holidays, and then to take quantities of cod liver oil to try and remove the tendency and get strong before he went away again. Johnnie thinks that this is good advice, but he says his heart is so flighty he does not know if the doctor would give him ether in his present state of health. Poor fellow, how sad, he has let himself run down dreadfully and I can't get him home. He has always some excuse; he says he would rather wait till this house is empty as he is "worn and weary and disfigured" and he does not want to come home until they are all gone! Poor boy, "worn and weary and sad," if he would only come to Jesus, He would make him glad, so my heart is full of thoughts and prayer for him, more than ever since I got that letter. He has written an article for some American magazine which has been accepted, and now he wants to stay in Paris till he is paid for it. It will leave such a short time here, and he will have to recoup before he goes in for the operation, I fear, so I don't know how things will be settled. I am putting all into my Father's hands. . . .

In Dublin Synge's doctor gave him some medication and advised another operation in September. But he did not submit to another operation until 1907, and for the next six years he was plagued by the swelling in his neck. He had no pain from it, and except for his concern over its being malignant his only worry was the disfigurement.

He spent the entire summer of 1901 at Castle Kevin where his mother had two more young ladies interested in church work. MacKenna wrote him early in the summer about "the risk you suffer of becoming irretrievably holy, a thing enskied and sainted." Within a week of his return to Dublin from Castle Kevin in September he wrote to Lady Gregory and asked her if he could stop off on his way to Aran and show her his play and the three parts of the Aran book. She wired an invitation, and he left on September 14th for Gort. In the account which she gave in *Our Irish Theatre* she confused her recollections of his first visit to Coole in 1898 with his second in 1901: "At the time of his first visit to Coole he had written some poems, not very good for the most part, and a play which was not good at all. I read it again after his death when, according to his written wish, helping Mr. Yeats in sorting out the work to be published or set aside, and again it seemed but of slight merit."[64]

He left Coole on the 20th, stayed one night in Galway and took the boat the next morning for Aran. This time he stayed only nineteen days, dividing his time equally between Inishmaan and Inishere. Martin McDonough was upset about seeing one of his letters in Synge's article "The Last Fortress of the Celt," which had appeared in April in *The Gael*. Synge's mother wrote to Samuel:

John intended to have gone to Inishmaan, one of the Aran Islands, to stay there for a fortnight, but he wrote to say he did not think he would go to Inishmaan this year, as he heard Martin McDonough, his chief

friend on the island, son of the old woman he lodges with, is offended
with him because he put a version of a letter he got from McDonough
in an article he sent to an American paper. John thought that he would
be quite safe, but someone sent Martin the paper and he is offended.
The letter was written in Irish to John and he put in a free translation
I fancy. I am very thankful John heard of it before he went to the islands,
as it might have been very unpleasant to have found himself among an
angry set of islanders quite at their mercy.

But Synge went directly to Inishmaan, patched up his differences
with Martin, and their friendship remained as sound as ever. He must
also have obtained Martin's permission to use the five letters which
eventually appeared in *The Aran Islands*. Until his death in 1940,
Martin McDonough was pleased to be known as Synge's friend. Like
the pile of stones on the cliff overlooking Gregory's Sound, which is
always pointed out to visitors as "Synge's Seat," he was part of the
legend.

On this fourth visit Synge brought his violin with him and played
for a large gathering in McDonough's kitchen. The islanders preferred jigs and reels and popular airs they could dance to. As a serious
musician he had been terrified at the prospect of ever having to play
before an audience, but his only concern here was that his fingers,
stiff from lack of practice, might not keep up with the speed of the
dancers. "The lightness of the pampooties," he wrote, "seems to make
the dancing on this island lighter and swifter than anything I have
seen on the mainland, and the simplicity of the men enables them
to throw a naïve extravagance into their steps that is impossible in
places where the people are self-conscious."[65]

The islands were just recovering from a typhus epidemic when he
arrived, and he saw much more of death and the stoic attitude of the
people than he had seen before. He was particularly moved by an
incident which he describes in his notebooks in more detail than in
his book:

Norah, the girl who was spinning in this house last year, is very ill and
some of the people say she is dying. A *curragh* went off this evening,
faster than I thought possible, for the doctor and the priest, and I can
see the sail now on the return journey through the rain that has begun
to fall. I did not realize till tonight how fond I am of these people. This

sudden illness has put a gloom over every one, and the thick fog that has come down separates us from the world. Another event of the day has increased the feeling of depression. Last week a young man was drowned, and they have just found his remains and carried him up to his home while they are making the coffin. In bad weather the rocks are desolate enough without this actual death, which has made the whole island as mournful as a room where a dead person is laid.

He stood on Dún Conor listening to the man below him making the coffin for the drowned man out of boards that had been borrowed from another man who had saved them for two years to make a coffin for his aged mother. Later he heard from a young boy the full account of how the dead man had met his death in a *curragh* while trying to bring some horses across the sound to the south island. There had been portents. "Before he went out on the sea that day his dog came up and sat beside him on the rocks, and began crying. When the horses were coming down to the slip an old woman saw her son, that was drowned a while ago, riding on one of them. She didn't say what she was after seeing, and this man caught the horse, he caught his own horse first, and then he caught this one, and after that he went out and was drowned."[66]

All of these incidents—the old women he had heard keening, the man washed ashore in Donegal and identified by his clothing, the borrowed coffin boards and the woman with her prevision of death —were the materials for his first tragedy, *Riders to the Sea*. Some critics have complained that the play lacks dramatic action and embodies an attitude of passive acceptance of death, foreign to modern sensibilities. But to Synge it was a direct translation of a life that had come to its own hard terms with the realities it faced, even if those terms seemed incomprehensible to an audience for whom life and death had other meanings.

Before he left the islands Lady Gregory wrote to Synge that she had been reading the manuscript of his book aloud to Yeats and that they both liked it:

It is extraordinarily vivid and gives an imaginative and at the same time convincing impression of the people and of their life, and it ought, we think, to be very successful. I have called Mr. Yeats in to say what he thinks—that I may speak with his authority—and he thinks, and I agree with him, that the book being so solid and detailed, as it is, would lose nothing but would rather gain by the actual names of the islands and of Galway not being given. Borrow always left his localities vague in this way, which gives a curious dreaminess to his work. It would be sufficient to say that they are islands off the west of Ireland. Leave the three islands distinct as they are—in fact maybe no change except leaving out the names—and I would say also Michael's English letters. The book would be greatly improved by the addition of some more fairy belief, and if you could give some of the words of the keens, and of the cradle songs you allude to, however few, the passages in which you touch on them would be greatly improved—as an important section of your readers will be students of these things. . . .

Synge did not take the advice. Yeats and Lady Gregory were interested in the Celtic twilight, and he was interested in flesh-and-blood people—"a particular time and locality and the life that is in it."

When he got back to Dublin on October 9th he gave his mother an account of the typhus he had seen on Aran, and she wrote to Samuel:

The priest told Johnnie they use no care or precaution, so it spreads. It was in the other end of the island from Johnnie, but I am sure he went down there, though not into houses where the illness was; but he is wonderfully fearless. He lodged in the house where it had been in the spring and of course no disinfectants were used, so he has been preserved by Our God's mighty love and care. . . . On the south island he also found some illness, he did not know exactly what. He lodged in a pub called an hotel and paid 4/- a day. They had nurses out on Inishmaan in the summer attending the sick people, but now there is no one there, neither nurse nor doctor. One girl very nearly died, but struggled and got well. Johnnie was wise enough not to wear any of the clothes he had washed on Inishmaan, as he was afraid they might have been put in some infected drawer or press, so he brought them all home and Kate is having a great washing today with Life Buoy soap. . . .

Edward Stephens, his nephew, who was fond of slipping quietly into the Synge house through the door which connected it with his own, wrote:

Usually I found him in his cycling knickerbockers and thick, knitted stockings, sitting in a large arm-chair that was covered in black horse hair, beside a pile of books most of which were in paper covers. Sometimes he had kicked off his rough slippers, and was sitting with one foot on the mantelpiece and one on the fender. . . . As he talked he often spun his folding scissors on his finger, or rolled a cigarette of light tobacco, and I noticed the quick action of his sensitive hands. Sometimes for my amusement when the shoe was off, he would grip the shining steel poker with his toes and put it into the fire. He took a child-like pleasure in this feat.

During the last week of October, 1901, the Irish Literary Theatre gave its third and final program at the Gaiety Theatre. For the first three days a company of amateur Irish actors under the direction of Willie Fay gave Douglas Hyde's Gaelic play *The Twisting of the Rope,* while F. R. Benson's Company of English professionals performed *Diarmuid and Grania* by Yeats and Moore and followed it up with *King Lear* during the last three days of the week. *Diarmuid and Grania* was the result of a collaboration between Yeats and Moore. As Moore described it in *Hail and Farewell,* he was to write the play in French, Lady Gregory would translate it into English, Taidgh O'Donoghue would turn it into Irish, and Lady Gregory would then produce a literal English translation from O'Donoghue's Irish version, which would be "racy of the soil."[67] Needless to say the plan was abandoned and the play, which had to wait until 1951 to be published in *The Dublin Magazine,*[68] was put on as it was written—in the aboriginal English of Yeats and Moore.

Eight

THE FAYS OF THE ABBEY THEATRE. PARIS.
THE IRISH NATIONAL THEATRE SOCIETY. LAST
VISIT TO ARAN. LONDON: NEW FRIENDS.
FAREWELL TO PARIS. COUNTY KERRY

*For I've heard tell there are lands beyond in Cahir Iveraghig and the
Reeks of Cork with warm sun in them, and fine light in the sky.*

One wonders if there could have been an Irish dramatic movement without Willie and Frank Fay. It is customary to speak of them
as though they were amateurs whose achievements were either ac-
cidental or the result of spontaneous genius. But in 1901 only Frank,
who earned his living as a shorthand writer, could accurately be
described as an amateur. Willie had spent some years with professional
travelling companies, first as advance agent and then as actor. He had
toured the country towns of England and Ireland doing "spectacular
Irish dramas" and had once acted in *Uncle Tom's Cabin* with an
American all-Negro company. George Moore described him as "a
clerk in some gas-works,"[69] but the fact is that he had been a foreman
electrician. Frank wrote articles and reviews for Arthur Griffith's *The
United Irishman,* and it was as a result of his review of *The Land of
Heart's Desire* that he began to correspond with Yeats.

In a series of articles in 1901 Frank Fay developed his theory of
what a national theatre should be and asked for the establishment of
a company made up exclusively of Irish actors who could be taught

a fresh style of acting free of the mannerisms of the English professional stage. He and his brother believed that they had the nucleus
of such a company in the group they had trained to perform Hyde's
play in Gaelic. All they needed was more plays about Irish life. When
AE gave them his play *Deirdre* the following April, Yeats contributed
Cathleen Ni Houlihan to round out the bill. It was the beginning of
what came to be known as the Abbey Theatre Company. Yeats wrote:
"Mr. W. Fay is the founder of the society, and from the outset he
and I were so agreed about first principles that no written or spoken
word of mine is likely to have influenced him much. I, on the other
hand, have learned much from him and from his brother, who knows
more than any man I have ever known about the history of speech
upon the stage."[70]

Synge saw the performances at the Gaiety Theatre in October, 1901,
and was most struck by the Gaelic play in which Hyde himself acted.
Five years later he wrote that it was "in some ways the most important
of all those produced by the Irish Literary Theatre" because it "gave
a new direction and impulse to Irish drama, a direction towards which,
it should be added, the thoughts of Mr. W. B. Yeats, Lady Gregory
and others were already tending." The play was crude, and the actors'
skill must have been as uncertain as their command of Gaelic, but it
was entirely a local enterprise and interesting enough to be encouraged.

On his way to Paris in November Synge stopped off in London to
leave the manuscript of *The Aran Islands* with Grant Richards, as
Yeats had suggested. But Richards told him that it was too limited
in appeal, and returned the manuscript. It is no wonder that he was
discouraged. He now had on his hands an unacceptable play, an un-
publishable book, and a number of rejected shorter pieces. At the age
of thirty, and after more than six years of effort, he had published
exactly six articles, two of which were book reviews. He decided to
continue writing topographical pieces about Ireland, and he was encouraged when the editor of *L'Européen* agreed to accept them.

In January he began his diary again, after a lapse of two years, and
it is possible to see from it what he worked at from his brief daily
entries. On January 21st he noted that a second publisher, Fisher
Unwin, had returned the Aran manuscript to him. On the same day
his mother wrote to Samuel: "He is very anxious to remain in Paris
as he has been asked to write for some French paper and, though the

pay is small, it may bring him into notice. He is to write on Irish literature." Then after an account of Grant Richards' rejection of the Aran manuscript she added:

Poor Johnnie! We could all have told him that, but then men like Yeats and the rest get round him and make him think Irish literature and the Celtic language and all these things that they are trying to revive are very important, and, I am sorry to say, Johnnie seems to believe all they tell him. Now perhaps his eyes are beginning to be opened in that direction, as he says he wants to keep in with French literature, as after a time he may be able to write for some of the big English papers and that is the only hope of his making any money, and if he comes over and lives in Ireland he will be always a pauper, as there is no chance of getting on in Ireland commercially.

Poor Johnnie's eyes were not being opened on the subject of the Gaelic language, as Mrs. Synge hoped, for on February 14th he enrolled in Jubainville's course in Old Irish at the Sorbonne. He was apparently the only student present, at times, to hear Jubainville's lectures,[71] but as anyone who teaches Old Irish even today realizes, this fact is not so strange. Jubainville, if one can gather correctly from Synge's notes, was fond of drawing parallels between Old Irish verb and noun forms and those of other Celtic languages like Breton. Classes were held twice a week, and Synge faithfully attended them all. Whether the professor was grateful to him for his attendance or whether it was customary politeness, he had Synge to his home for lunch on April 19th. Synge paid tribute to Jubainville in his article *La Vieille Littérature Irlandaise*, which appeared in *L'Européen* in March. It was a lucid account of the literature of the medieval Celt and reveals a not inconsiderable knowledge. The modern literature of Ireland, Synge pointed out, was now being "written by young writers completely ignorant of their native tongue."

Synge's French must have been adequate, even though he asked Thérèse Beydon to check it for him. He was taking a sensible precaution that any writer would take, especially an unestablished one eager to convince an editor of his competence. The impression which had some currency after his death that his ability to read and speak French was surprisingly slight was due to the statement made by MacKenna in 1912 at a meeting of the National Literary Society to

the effect that Synge knew nothing of French literature, had no
natural ability at learning languages, spoke French imperfectly and
had no touch with French life. MacKenna was something of a genius
with languages and would have disparaged Synge's ability in any
case. But when he spoke he was defending his friend against charges
made in Dublin that Synge was a Parisian *flâneur* whose culture was
more French than Irish and who was libelling his own country with
Irish peasant plays which were European in their origin and flavour.

Actually, Synge's indebtedness to French literature is negligible.
As we will see later he derived the idea for the plot of *The Well of the
Saints* from an early French farce he had become acquainted with
through his course in medieval French literature with Petit de Julleville in 1895. A list of modern French authors whom he either reviewed or mentioned in his notebooks, includes Baudelaire, Mallarmé,
Zola, Huysmans, Pierre Loti, Anatole France and Maeterlinck. But
demonstrating the influence of any of these upon his work would
be difficult. Despite the remark made to Best about his wishing to
emulate Loti's achievements, Synge found fault with Loti's treatment
of primitive people. Some critics have attributed the combination of
the tragic and the grotesque in Synge's work to the influence of
Baudelaire, but there is little evidence in the notebooks that he had
done more than read Baudelaire. In the preface to *The Tinker's
Wedding* he repudiated Baudelaire because of his morbidity.

The myth of his lifelong devotion to Racine is due mostly to the
evidence of Masefield and Yeats. Yeats was responsible for the story
that Synge had projected a critical work on the French dramatist.
But Synge nowhere mentions Racine, and the incongruity of any
analogy between the French neoclassical dramatist and the author
of *The Playboy* discourages any consideration of it. As for the de-
pendability of Yeats' testimony, one inclines in this instance to the
opinion of Moore that "Yeats' stories that Synge read the classics and
was a close student of Racine is a piece of Yeats' own academic
mind."[72] Moore was quite right too in pointing out that Synge's
translations into Anglo-Irish of the French poets Villon, Marot, Colin
Musset, like his translations into dialect of Petrarch, Leopardi and
von der Vogelweide, were merely exercises, made at the time when
he was experimenting with peasant dialect to see if it was adaptable
to different material.

Unlike Yeats, who read his Mallarmé by way of Arthur Symons, Synge spurned the European naturalists and symbolists alike—Zola and Ibsen, somewhat unjustly or at least inaccurately, for their "joyless and pallid words," Mallarmé and Huysmans for their detachment from "the profound and common interests of life."[73] His own theory of language was radically different from either the symbolists or the naturalists.

During the spring of 1902 he worked hard, though one wonders how he managed to keep going in view of the difficulties he had getting anything into print. Two of his Wicklow pieces, which later appeared in *The Manchester Guardian* and *The Shanachie*, were rejected by *The Gael* and *The Cornhill Magazine*.[74] His Aran manuscript he sent off to Yeats in March for advice about where to turn next with it. He also worked at his verse play based on Keating and at another which he referred to as his Vernal Play, a pastoral drama. In it characters with exotic names which suggest Irish legendary personages recite a lament:

Etain. All young girls must yield to rage.
      All firm youth must end in age.
Boinn. I call the lambs that browse with fright,
      To mourn the man who died tonight.
Niave. Every eye must fade and blear,
      Every bone bleach bare and clear.
Boinn. All must rise from earth and clay.
      All must end in green decay. . . .

On May 31st *L'Européen* printed his article on the intellectual movement in Ireland, in which he stated for French readers with skill and clarity the fact that the beginnings in Ireland in the seventeenth century of a literature in English coincided with the virtual disappearance of the Irish language, but that it was not until the Irish themselves had assimilated the new tongue sufficiently to produce a William Carleton in the middle of the nineteenth century that the literature in English took on characteristics that entitle it to be described accurately as an Irish literature. Since Carleton's day the most significant development had been the dramatic movement and the emergence of W. B. Yeats, who writes verse with a "curiously learned simplicity."

In Dublin meanwhile the Fays' performance on April 2, 3, and 4 of AE's *Deirdre* and Yeats' *Cathleen Ni Houlihan*, with Maud Gonne in the title role of Yeats' play, had excited everyone. Miss Gonne was not a professional actress but she made full use of her own personality and depended on the image of herself which her political activity had created in the imagination of young Ireland to compensate for her lack of acting skill. If one Dublin critic was disenchanted by her performance and referred to her as a Nationalist agitator speaking directly to her audience as she might address a mob in Beresford Place or the Phoenix Park, others were quick to see that mere acting in her case was superfluous. In being herself—the young girl with the walk of a queen who had inspired the young men of Ireland—she was Cathleen Ni Houlihan in the flesh.

The rest of the little company, who were to be the nucleus of the Abbey Theatre, were equally inspiring. An editorial in *The United Irishman* on April 12th saluted their success in creating an Irish Theatre "where the heroic past of Ireland can be made to live again for us and give us inspiration and aspiration." Yeats hailed their performances as the beginning of a truly native style. "It was the first performance I had seen since I understood these things," he wrote, "in which the actors kept still enough to give poetical writing its full effect upon the stage. I had imagined such acting, though I had not seen it, and had once asked a dramatic company to let me rehearse them in barrels that they might forget gesture and have their minds free to think of speech for a while. The barrels, I thought, might be on castors, so that I might shove them about with a pole when the action required it. The other day I saw Sara Bernhardt and Der Max in *Phèdre* and understood where Mr. Fay . . . had gone for his model."[75]

The result of the Fays' success was that Yeats, Maud Gonne and Douglas Hyde formed the Irish National Theatre Society, and it was this organization that was to survive until Yeats forced its reorganization in the autumn of 1905. By that time Maud Gonne and Douglas Hyde had been replaced by Synge and Lady Gregory as codirectors with Yeats, and the little company of amateurs whom the Fays had developed were no longer amateurs and their style of acting and production had grown to maturity.

The summer of 1902 was to mark Synge's beginning as a dramatist.

His mother had hired a small house in Wicklow, known as the Tomrilands House, and during his summer there Synge wrote *In the Shadow of the Glen* and *Riders to the Sea* and produced the first draft of *The Tinker's Wedding*, which he later rewrote and enlarged from one act to two. In June his review of Lady Gregory's *Cuchulain and Muirthemne* appeared in *The Speaker*. Lady Gregory's book was a retelling of the stories from medieval Irish legend and saga centring upon the hero Cuchulain and was written in the Anglo-Irish dialect which later came to be known as Kiltartan after a village in Galway near Coole Park. Synge complimented her for her skill in handling dialect, but he disagreed with the claim made by Yeats in his introduction to the book that she had been the first to use it. Credit for this, he thought, should go to Douglas Hyde, who "used a very similar language in his translations of the *Love Songs of Connacht*," and in any case since the whole intellectual movement in Ireland for the past twenty years had been moving towards an appreciation of the country people and their language both Hyde's and Lady Gregory's efforts were the result of an evolution rather than a personal idea. Lady Gregory later said of Synge's language: "I wrote in it before Synge did. He said he was amazed to find in my *Cuchulain of Muirthemne* his desired dialect."[76] There is no reason for doubting that Synge paid her the compliment or that he learned a good deal from her.

Tomrilands House, which is much smaller than Castle Kevin, is the "old Wicklow house" Synge referred to in the preface to *The Playboy*, where he made the unfortunate statement about listening through a chink in the floor to what was being said by the servant girls in the kitchen. He meant of course to bolster his claim that the language of *The Playboy* was not the product of his imagination but that of country people whom he had carefully observed. The statement was to anger more people than it was intended to placate because it made him appear an eavesdropper, a gentleman eager to learn about peasants without accepting the indignity of associating with them. On Aran he had lived as close to the people as it was possible for an outsider, but in Wicklow his mother would not for a moment have tolerated his associating with the servant girls in her own house. Synge never realized the reaction which the patronizing attitude in his statement would evoke.

In his essay "The Old and the New in Ireland," which appeared in September in *The Academy and Literature*, he stated the whole problem of the Gaelic language revival and the creation of a modern Irish literature based upon native tradition. The trouble with writing in Ireland in the centuries following the disappearance of Gaelic was that writers who had sprung from the people found themselves in an atmosphere of linguistic uncertainty. They had lost their native language, and yet they could not "reach the finer cadences of English." Writers who sprang from the Ascendancy stock on the other hand so permeated themselves with English thought that they never succeeded in producing anything but a garrison-class literature. Now, however, when Ireland had developed a crop of native writers who, without losing their roots, had thoroughly assimilated the English language and were beginning to produce in it a literature which was distinctively Irish, the old roots in Munster and the west of Ireland were beginning to put out a new growth and Gaelic was flourishing again. Would Gaelic stifle English once more, or would the writers realize that in an Ireland standing precariously between England and America to abandon English would be as disastrous as to ignore the native tradition?

English is likely to remain the language of Ireland; and no one, I think, need regret the likelihood. If Gaelic came back strongly from the west, the feeling for English which the present generation has attained would be lost again, and in the best circumstances it is probable that Leinster and Ulster would take several centuries to assimilate Irish perfectly enough to make it a fit mode of expression for the finer emotions which now occupy literature. In the meantime, the opening culture of Ireland would be thrown back indefinitely and there would perhaps be little gain to make up for this certain loss. Modern peasant Gaelic is full of rareness and beauty, but if it was sophisticated by journalists and translators . . . it would lose all its freshness; and then limits, which now make its charm, would tend to prevent all further development.

The Gaelic League, he argued, should not attempt to do any more than "keep the cruder powers of the Irish mind occupied" till the influence of an Irish literature written in English had become more definite in Irish life.[77]

He was not only defending his own use of an English idiom based directly on native sources but also formulating what could be called the rationale of the Irish Literary Revival. If he had lived to see the Ireland of fifty years later, where the number of native speakers in the *Gaeltacht* is declining annually and English is still the language of the country, despite the government's attempts to force the use of Irish, he might have felt that his prophecy had been confirmed.*

When Synge arrived at Coole on October 8th, 1902, on his way to Aran for the last time, he had with him the finished texts of *In the Shadow of the Glen* and *Riders to the Sea*. The birth of a new playwright could not have been more opportune. The Fays were at the moment rehearsing, for performance in October, Yeats' slight farce *The Pot of Broth*, a Gaelic play *Eilis and the Beggar Woman* by P. T. McGinley and plays by Fred Ryan and James Cousins. Ryan, who was secretary of the Irish National Theatre Society, was no dramatist, and Yeats had written to Willie Fay that Cousins was "hopeless," that if they had to depend on him for plays it would be better to do foreign masterpieces.[78]

For his last visit to Aran, Synge stayed twenty-five days and spent all of them on Inishere. He probably stayed at Michael Costello's public house, which served as an inn. He returned to Dublin on November 9th, and when on December 4th the Fays repeated the performances they had given in October at the Antient Concert Rooms in a smaller theatre on Camden Street, Synge saw the company for the first time. It could not have been very impressive. Enthusiasm, even among the actors, was beginning to run at a lower pitch. Willie Fay wrote: "The hall was cold and so was the audience, if you can call the few that turned up an audience. The roof leaked. The stage was so small that you couldn't swing a kitten let alone a cat."[79] The Irish dramatic movement was in the doldrums, and the arrival of a new dramatist of power and originality was the only hope of saving it.

---

* A sizeable number of young Irish writers today, encouraged by government subsidy and motivated by a genuine desire to identify themselves with the native tradition even more closely than Yeats and his contemporaries had, are now writing in Irish. Mr. Liam O'Flaherty, to mention only one of Ireland's best known writers, has recently begun to write stories in the language he spoke as a boy on the Aran islands after a lifetime of writing in English. But since the number of people in Ireland who can read Irish is still very small, and of those who buy books even smaller, Mr. O'Flaherty has had to translate his stories into English in order to have them read.

Synge had decided to give up his room in Paris. He was at work on another play about Irish peasant life, and both Lady Gregory and Yeats were convinced that he had at last found his *métier*. But he was still unpublished, and there was nothing for it but to go to London where he might deal directly with the publishers and editors whom Yeats could introduce him to. Lady Gregory wrote of him at this period, "He was anxious to publish his book on Aran and these two plays and have something to add to that '£40 a year and a new suit when I am too shabby,' he used with a laugh to put down as his income."[80] He left Dublin for London on January 9th, 1903, and except for one week in March when he returned to Paris to close up his apartment in the rue d'Assas, he remained in London until March 18th. Since he kept his diary faithfully and wrote two long letters to his mother, it is possible to see how he was beginning for the first time to move in literary circles and make the kind of impression that Masefield, whom he met at this time, described afterwards. "My first impression of him was of a dark, grave face, with a great deal in it. . . . The hair was worn neither short nor long. The moustache was rather thick and heavy. The lower jaw, otherwise clean-shaven, was made remarkable by a tuft of hair, too small to be called a goatee, upon the lower lip. . . . The eyes were at once smoky and kind. . . . His voice, very guttural and quick, with a kind of lively bitterness in it, was of a kind of Irish voice new to me at that time. . . ."[81]

He wrote to his mother on January 17th about his lodgings—a rooming house at 4 Handel Street, Brunswick Square—asking her to send money. "My landlady seems inclined to be suspicious so I suppose I will have to pay her in advance for a while, so I would be obliged if you could send me some money before Wednesday, but I think you had better not send a cheque as I would certainly have all sorts of bother about it. I was with Yeats on Monday evening and I met a good many writers and artists. . . ." He wrote again a week later to say that he had been with Yeats again and was not getting much sleep because of his social life. "I have several more editors to see on the papers I have written for already, but I could not go to them last week as I was uncertain about my address. This week Joyce —on his way back to Paris—is going to them all so I will not go round for a few days as it is better not to have too many Irishmen turning up at once."

Lady Gregory was staying in London, and both she and Yeats, anxious to show Synge off, asked him to read his plays aloud to audiences consisting of Masefield, Chesterton, Arthur Symons, Maud Gonne and others. Three of these readings took place in Lady Gregory's rooms and one at Yeats', and the reception was encouraging. Arthur Symons wanted to publish *Riders to the Sea* in *The Fortnightly Review* but returned the manuscript a month later. The publisher R. Brinsley Johnson was apparently present at one of the readings and asked if he might publish it, but he too returned the manuscript with regrets. When Synge came back to Dublin in the middle of March he had nothing to show for his time in London but encouragement from more successful writers. But that was a good deal, and he had needed it badly.

During the week he spent in Paris, from March 6th to 13th, he disposed of the few pieces of furniture in his room in the rue d'Assas, and packed his knife, fork and frying pan to take back with him to Dublin. He found few friends to say goodbye to. MacKenna was in Dublin, Cree had left Paris because of ill health, Arthur Lynch was in prison as the result of having joined the Boer army in the South African war, and Margaret Hardon had gone back to America to get married. Thérèse Beydon was the only one left, but he did not see her. The only fellow countryman he met was James Joyce, who had arrived in Paris from London. There is no record of their having met before, but they saw a good deal of each other during the week. Joyce was inaccurate in his later recollection when he dated their first meeting in Paris to 1902.[82] Synge showed him the manuscript of *Riders to the Sea*, but Joyce, who later admired the play and translated it into Italian, pronounced it un-Aristotelian. Synge was annoyed, they spent the rest of the time arguing, and Synge's "harsh gargoyle face" was subsequently enshrined in *Ulysses*. Joyce was twenty years old at the time, only six months out of college, and his prospects were far grimmer than Synge's. They saw more of each other after Joyce returned to Dublin in April, though Synge records in his diary only one other meeting, on September 21, 1903.

While Synge was in London the Fays opened on March 14th with Yeats' *The Hour-Glass* and Lady Gregory's first play, *Twenty-Five*, in the Molesworth Hall on Molesworth Street. During the intermission Yeats told the audience that he and his colleagues were going to restore beautiful speech in the theatre, simplify acting by eliminating needless gestures and stage business, and dramatize types of heroic manhood out of Irish legends. Synge arrived on the 18th and was impressed by the company. Willie Fay wrote afterwards that the improved acting and the move to a better hall had evoked respect, if not sympathy with their new method, from the Dublin press. Most critics thought it presumptuous if not futile for an inexperienced company to develop an art that had little appeal to the man in the street. But such ambition, they conceded, deserved to be taken seriously.

While Synge was in London, J. L. Hammond, who had succeeded R. Barry O'Brien as editor of *The Speaker,* agreed to accept occasional articles from him. Synge's review of Loti's *L'Inde sans les Anglais,* Huysmans' *L'Oblat,* and Anatole France's *Monsieur Bergeret à Paris* appeared in *The Speaker* on April 18th, but he did not write for Hammond again until a year later when he reviewed Best's translation of De Jubainville's *The Irish Mythological Cycle.* Meanwhile he started work on his next play, *The Well of the Saints.*

The Well of the Saints is about two blind beggars who have their sight miraculously restored by a saint, only to discover that their happiness as man and wife is destroyed. Synge borrowed the central idea from a fifteenth century French farce entitled *Moralité de l'Aveugle et du Boiteux* by a Burgundian writer, Andrieu de la Vigne. He may not actually have read De la Vigne's play, but he was familiar with it through an account which Petit de Julleville—whose lectures in medieval literature he had attended in 1896—gives in the second chapter of his *Histoire du Théâtre en France.* According to his diary for 1903 he was reading *Théâtre en France,* and the notebook he was using at the time contains notes on De la Vigne's play, a simple plot summary and short passages of dialogue, all of which he may have transcribed from De Julleville.*

The French play is based on a story familiar to students of folklore. A blind man agrees to carry a crippled man on his back so that each can compensate for the other. The arrangement is completely success-

* Knowing only Synge's remark to Padraic Colum that his play had been inspired by an early French farce, and having no access to Synge's papers, the late Professor Gertrude Schoepperle identified the source in 1921. "John Synge and His Old French Farce," *North American Review,* CCXIV (October, 1921), 503-513.

ful until they are both cured by passing a procession in which the remains of St. Martin are displayed. The blind man is delighted, but the cripple curses the saint for destroying an easy life on the back of his companion. But in Synge's play both of the beggars are blind and they urge the saint who cures them to revoke his miracle so that they can return to an existence of happy illusion. Except for his indebtedness to the central idea—the unhappiness that can be produced by a miracle—Synge's play is entirely his own. Ireland is full of sacred wells where people have prayed for cures and left gift offerings, rosary beads and pieces of clothing as tokens of their faith. The well in this instance is the one Martin Coneely had shown Synge on Inishmore, near *Teampall an Ceatrair Alainn*—the Church of the Four Beautiful Persons—as is clear from the question Timmy the Smith asks Martin Doul: "Did you ever hear tell of a place across a bit of the sea, where there is an island, and the grave of the four beautiful saints?"

In May of this year the Fays, who had told Lady Gregory that they would like to produce *In the Shadow of the Glen* in the autumn, made their first appearance outside Ireland. Stephen Gwynn, president of the Irish Literary Society in London, who had seen the Fays perform the previous October, arranged matinee and evening performances for them on May 2nd in the Queen's Gate Hall in Kensington. They gave five plays—*The Hour-Glass*, *Cathleen Ni Houlihan* and *The Pot of Broth* by Yeats, Lady Gregory's *Twenty-Five*, and Fred Ryan's *The Laying of the Foundations*. Their success was something they had not expected. Sir James Barrie and Henry James were in the audience, and if it had not been for a first-night performance of George Bancroft's *The Little Countess* at the Avenue Theatre, most of the London critics who had seen the matinee would also have seen the evening performance. A. B. Walkley wrote to Yeats that he was vexed that a "stupid theatre elsewhere" had prevented his seeing the evening performances.

The London critics were not entirely unprepared for what they saw. Stephen Gwynn had written an article on the Fays in *The Fortnightly Review* called "An Uncommercial Theatre," and of course Yeats' work was now known in London. Most of the critics noted that what they saw was inspired playing by amateur actors, but the critic of the *Daily News* saw the beginnings of a "peculiar and native convention in dramatic art" and pointed out that "in Dublin the theater is beginning to be what it has not been for hundreds of years in England—the expression of the aspirations, the emotions, the essential spirit and movement of the people, both in the sense in which it is so in France . . . but also in the sense in which it expresses the idealism and poetry of the national sentiment."

William Archer of *The Manchester Guardian* praised the acting, and the critic for the *Star* wrote that the Fays "acting a parochial drama and a drama of the soil with such talent as they have gathered from their surroundings . . . dramatically represent Ireland to a greater extent than any fashionable drama being acted today within our sacred half-mile radius of Charing Cross can possibly be said to represent England." But the most enthusiastic praise was from A. B. Walkley of *The Times*. The acting had "a touch of affectation," he noted, but this was to be expected since "all new movements in art are self-conscious, abound in little exaggerations and affectations. Is there not an Irish precept, 'be aisy; and if ye can't be aisy, be as aisy as ye can'?" He went on to define the peculiar style the Fays were evolving with their inexperienced actors. "As a rule they stand stock-still. The speaker of the moment is the only one who is allowed a little gesture. . . . When they do move it is without premeditation, at hap-hazard, even with a little natural clumsiness, as of people who are not conscious of being stared at in public." The players came back to Dublin by the Sunday boat-train and next day were overwhelmed to read that they had been seriously reviewed by the foremost drama critics in London.

It was not until June that the company heard the work of their newest playwright. In her rooms at the Nassau Hotel in Dublin, Lady Gregory read *In the Shadow of the Glen* to the entire group. Maire Nic Shiublaigh, who was present and who was to play Nora Burke, wrote in her autobiography that Synge's play struck her and her fellow actors by its novelty. Synge, she recollected, sat in the background as his play was being read and was gentle, shy and quiet. "His bulky figure and heavy black moustache gave him a rather austere appearance—an impression quickly dispelled when he spoke. His voice was mellow, low; he seldom raised it. . . ." She remembered him during rehearsals later quietly rolling cigarettes. "At the first opportunity he would lever his huge frame out of the chair and come up onto the stage, a half-rolled cigarette in each hand. Then he would look enquiringly round and thrust the little paper cylinders forward towards whoever was going to smoke them. In later years he became the terror of fire-conscious Abbey Stage-managers. He used to sit timidly in the wings during plays, rolling cigarettes and handing them to the players as they made their exits."[83]

Synge had spent five seasons in Aran, living with Irishmen whose way of life was as different from that of other Irishmen as one could imagine. In Wicklow he had noticed how the people of the hills had been so isolated from the life outside their narrow glens that they spoke with a unique accent. Ireland is a small country, but in the west especially this sharp differentiation between people of neighbouring localities has enabled much of the native tradition to survive and makes for sharp differences in custom, dialect and even outlook between the Galway man, the Kerry man and the Mayo man. The thought was beginning to take hold of him that if he was to be an interpreter of Irish peasant life he had better widen his knowledge. The man of Aran was only one variety of Irishman, and being an islander he was probably as different from his countrymen on the mainland as the Wicklow peasant was different from the western peasant. Synge had not accompanied his mother to Tomrilands House for the summer of 1903 because his asthma, which always became acute in Wicklow, had begun to bother him again. When his brother Robert returned from a fishing expedition to Kerry in August, he was able to give Synge the name of a family in Kerry with whom he could stay.

County Kerry, in the southwest of Ireland, is a hilly country, and for centuries it has been one of the beauty spots of Ireland. Like Clare to the north, and Galway to the north of Clare, it is part of the *Gaeltacht* or Irish-speaking district. Despite the flood of tourists who for generations have visited its Lakes of Killarney and made the circuit of its southern peninsula known as the Ring of Kerry, it has managed to retain the characteristics which stamp it as a piece of old Ireland. In addition to the picture-postcard beauty of its natural scenery and the unique life that one can still see in the hill farms of west Kerry, the Dingle or northern peninsula offers rich evidence of the archaeological past.

Synge was to spend parts of four summers in Kerry and came to

know not only the Kerry mainland but also the Blasket islands off
the Dingle peninsula, which have been written about almost as
much as Aran. Today the Blaskets stand unoccupied except for grazing
cattle in the summertime because the government, recognizing the
plight of an island people no longer able to earn a living on their
isolated island, has moved them to the mainland and built homes for
them which look down from the heights of Slea Head across the
bay to the slanting green fields their fathers and grandfathers tilled
before them. On the southern peninsula Synge stayed at Mountain
Stage, near Glenbeigh, in the house of a man named Philly Harris,
perched on the top of a hill from which he could look across the bay.
"I was singularly pleased," he wrote, "when I turned up the boreen
at last to this cottage where I lodge, and looked down through a
narrow gully to Dingle Bay. The people bade me welcome when I
came in, the old woman kissing my hand."[84] There was no village
near the cottage, but there were farms scattered about on the hills
near it, and since the Harrises were important people in the neighbourhood many men and women looked in "to talk or tell stories, or to
buy a few pennyworth of sugar or starch." Because the house was only
a short distance from the main road the cottage was also "well known
to the race of local tramps who move from one family to another."
Life in Kerry has changed so little that Philly Harris's house still looks
as it did in Synge's day except that its thatched roof has given way to
the corrugated metal that has begun to disfigure many of the cottages
of the west of Ireland. Patrick Harris, the son of Philly Harris, still
lives in the cottage, and he remembers Synge coughing with his
asthma and the "nonsensical" stories his father told Synge about
Oisin and the Fenian heroes and Tir-na-nog, the Celtic Valhalla,
which was reputed to have been located across the bay on the Dingle
peninsula.

    Philly Harris and his brother Denis, whose cottage was nearby,
were both storytellers. The notebooks Synge filled during his visits
to Mountain Stage contain scores of anecdotes, local history and folk
tales which he carefully recorded as they were told to him. Kerry
people were completely bilingual, and English was more likely to
be the language of the day than Irish. But it was a colourful English,
full of the kind of vigour and natural charm that a rural people would
endow it with quite naturally. On Aran Synge jotted down the Irish

idioms he heard and translated them into English. But at Mountain Stage the idioms and coinages he heard were in English. He began to realize that here, even more than in Aran, he was listening to the dialect of his plays.

In his notebooks he wrote down placenames like The Stooks of the Dead Woman and later used them in *The Playboy* or phrases like "naked as an ash-tree in the moon of March," which is the language Christy Mahon uses to describe his drunken father. He recorded a story Philly Harris told him about a woman from Cahirciveen who suckled a lamb at her own breast, and the doctor to whom she later served it as a meal "detected the elements of a Christian" in it. Pegeen Mike reviled the Widow Quin with the words, "Doesn't the world know you reared a black ram at your own breast, so that the Lord Bishop of Connaught felt the elements of a Christian, and he eating it after in a kidney stew?"

The Widow Quin was also notorious for having shaved "the foxy skipper from France for a threepenny-bit and a sop of grass tobacco would ring the liver from a mountain goat you'd meet leaping the hills." Synge learned in Dingle that French fishermen from Fécamp were fond of putting into Kerry, and one man he talked with on the north peninsula told him that the Irish were fond of the "grass tobacco" which the French seamen gave them in exchange for some of their plug tobacco. Synge's Kerry notebooks, as well as his Aran notebooks, are the record of the raw materials he transformed into his plays. He did not exaggerate when he wrote in the preface to *The Playboy* that he had used only one or two words that he had not actually heard spoken, and it must have angered him when his Dublin critics accused him of foisting an outlandish vocabulary upon the peasants of the west of Ireland.

Some of Synge's poems also came directly out of his experiences in Kerry. "Beg-Innish" is a Kerry poem, its title from the name of an island in the Blasket group. "On an Island" is a description of the dancing he had seen in the house of his host on the Great Blasket. "The 'Mergency Man" was based on a story he had heard in Kerry. Another poem entitled "In Kerry" is an interesting example of how he was able to transform an unsuccessful love lyric by endowing it with a grotesque element he had heard in Kerry. The first version of the poem was an uninspired piece in which the speaker asks the rhetorical question of why his love for his mistress has enhanced for him the beauties of nature. Not until he remembered a story he had heard in Kerry, and used in *The Playboy*, was Synge able to transform the lyric into something more characteristic of his own personality. As the story appears in *The Playboy*, one of the minor characters tells how "there was a graveyard beyond the house with the remnants of a man who had thighs as long as your arm. He was a horrid man, I'm telling you, and there was many a fine Sunday I'd put him together for fun, and he with shiny bones you wouldn't meet the like of these days in the cities of the world." The same story provided the concluding couplet of an otherwise conventional love lyric.

> We heard the thrushes by the shore and sea,
> And saw the golden stars' nativity,
> Then round we went the lane by Thomas Flynn,
> Across the church where bones lie out and in;
> And there I asked beneath a lonely cloud
> Of strange delight, with one bird singing loud,
> What change you'd wrought in graveyard, rock and sea,
> This new wild paradise to wake for me. . . .
> Yet knew no more than knew those merry sins
> Had built this stack of thigh-bones, jaws and shins.

Synge's conviction that poetry must contain a grotesque element may well have come to him from the Continent, but critics who are tempted to see the influence of Baudelaire in this identification of sex and the anatomy of death are wrong. It came to him out of the mouths of Kerry peasants. He was able to see in it potentialities for comedy besides the more serious business of love.

Synge was in Kerry from August 28th to September 19th. Just before he left Dublin, or shortly thereafter, he began to make preliminary sketches and to write sample passages of dialogue for *The Playboy*, although his major energy was devoted to *The Well of the Saints*. His first working title for *The Playboy* was *The Fool of Farnham* and later *Murder Will Out* before he hit upon the final flamboyant title. *Playboy* is possibly the translation of a Gaelic phrase used in hurling,[85] or it may be the English word *play-boy*, a hoaxer. The Widow Quin, who dubs Christy with the full title, seems to use it with that meaning when she turns upon him after seeing the man he had boasted of killing, still very much alive. "Well, you're the walking Playboy of the Western World, and that's the poor man you had divided to his breeches belt." But when Christy wins in the races the epithet takes on a different meaning and he is now "the champion Playboy of the Western World." In a discarded passage from an earlier draft Pegeen uses the word with a similar sense of hoaxer when she says, "There's no decent girl would take a little sweaty play-boy has played fool upon the earth world. Ah, isn't love a mighty madness, and I'm hard set to think it's the same man you are I'm after squeezing to my bosom this half an hour gone by."

The "Western World" is a phrase Synge may never have heard an Irish countryman use, though he puts it and its counterpart, "eastern world," into the mouths of several of his characters in the play. But he was undoubtedly aware that it occurs frequently in early Irish texts as an epithet for a champion. For example, a tenth century poem reads:

> Where is the chief of the western world?
> Where the sun of every clash of arms?
>
> *Caiti mail iarthair betha*
> *Caiti grian cech airm greatha.*[86]

While Synge was in Kerry, Willie Fay wrote to him that *In the Shadow of the Glen* would shortly go into rehearsal but that *Riders to the Sea* "wanted more speed towards the end, after the body is brought in." Yeats had decided to publish *Riders to the Sea* however in *Samhain*, the "occasional review" he had begun in October of 1901 as an organ of the Irish Literary Theatre. Only two numbers had appeared, and the third, which was published in September, 1903, contained Synge's play and a play in Irish by Douglas Hyde with English translation. Yeats contributed a commentary in which he described Synge as "a new writer and a creation of our movement" and praised his play as "the finest piece of tragic work done in Ireland in late years." The whole number was reviewed in *The Manchester Guardian* on October 27th. Synge, who had yet to see his first play on the stage, was praised for having written "the most poignant piece of tragic drama that we have seen written in English since Mr. Phillips's *Paolo and Francesca*." The reviewer praised its simplicity of construction, its rhythmic speech and its insight into the minds of the Irish peasants. It was Synge's first appearance in print with a work of his own imagination since his poem in a college magazine ten years before.

When he returned from Kerry the Fays had already put *In the Shadow of the Glen* into rehearsal, in a rented hall on Camden Street which Synge described as a "little ramshackle hall where the rain came in through the roof on wet nights and drunken wanderers used sometimes to be found asleep in the long passages when it was time to go home." When he went to see the rehearsal the hall was "half-filled with scenery and costumes and at one end a carpenter was hammering a movable platform and fit-up while at the other end the actors were rehearsing the elaborate verses of Mr. Yeats." Willie Fay remembered the effect Synge's language had upon actors accustomed to hearing the stage Irish of Boucicault and O'Keefe, Lever and Lover.

Nine

IN THE SHADOW OF THE GLEN.
RIDERS TO THE SEA

It's making game of me you'd be, and putting a fool's head on me in the face of the world. . . .

The performances of *In the Shadow of the Glen* were to call forth opinions that neither Synge nor Yeats had anticipated. Five Dublin newspapers were to play an important part in moulding, or reporting, Dublin opinion towards Synge in the years to come. *The Irish Times* was the paper of the Ascendancy and catered to the tastes of a people uninterested in any nationalist movement, but its editor, John Healy, was a classical scholar and his paper tempered its political prejudice with a regard for the development of the arts. William Martin Murphy, who controlled *The Irish Independent,* was a prosperous Roman Catholic businessman who supported Parliamentary nationalism. In fact his paper had been founded to support Parnell at the time of the schism in the nationalist party and therefore maintained some independence of clerical interference in politics. Murphy, who later became the villain who broke the great Dublin strike of 1913, was interested in the Irish stage only to the extent of preventing it from falling into the hands of extreme nationalists like Maud Gonne or labor leaders like James Connolly.

The Freeman's Journal was a Parnellite paper which had deserted Parnell in his moment of crisis. It continued to support Parliamentary nationalism, guided by the Roman Catholic hierarchy. Its editor,

William Brayden, did not see anything dangerous in the dramatic movement and, subject to his personal tastes, was willing to give it support. Lord Ardilaun, the head of the Guinness family of brewing fame, had bought a controlling interest in *The Daily Express* in order to quell the liberal ideas the paper had been spreading under the influence of Sir Horace Plunkett, the founder of the cooperative movement in Ireland. Its former editor T. P. Gill, who had made the paper the organ of a social reconstruction policy, had become secretary of the new Department of Agriculture, but *The Daily Express* remained friendly to the literary movement.

The least influential of all Dublin papers, because it was nothing more than the strident voice of extreme nationalist opinion, was *The United Irishman*, a weekly. Its editor, a stocky little man named Arthur Griffith, was to have a profound effect upon the political future of Ireland. He had been educated at the Christian Brothers' schools and apprenticed to a compositor in a Dublin newspaper office. In 1896 he gave up printing for the diamond mines of South Africa but soon took up journalism in Johannesburg. In Paris Maud Gonne had introduced him in nationalist circles, and he returned to Dublin to become editor of the weekly newspaper which made its first appearance on March 4, 1899. Believing neither in violence nor in the establishment of a republic, Griffith preached abstention from Westminster and the establishment of a dual monarchy after the pattern of Hungary, and founded the political party Sinn Fein to further his objectives. Ironically enough, Sinn Fein was taken over by less squeamish compatriots and committed to the expulsion of English rule by force, if necessary, and the establishment of a republic. Griffith's moderation was a steadying influence during the bitter days of arbitration after the Anglo-Irish war of 1918–1921 and the setting up of the Free State, when he became its president; but he is one of that triumvirate of controversial figures in the history of modern Ireland, along with Michael Collins and Eamon De Valera. Conservatives have extolled him as the real strong man of Irish politics. Republicans, on the other hand, have begrudged him their praise and charged that his timidity was responsible for the betrayal of the ideals of Pearse and the heroes who died fighting for the republic which he bargained away as head of the delegation which negotiated the treaty of 1921.

On October 8th, 1903, hours before his first play had a chance to be heard, an editorial in *The Irish Independent* pounced upon Synge,

. . . who, an overfriendly preliminary notice informs us, lives his life between the gaiety of Paris and the homes of the fisher-folk on the Aran Islands. Mr. Synge did not derive his inspiration from the Western Isles. We do not for a moment think that all the members of the Irish National Theater Society can be held accountable for the eccentricities and extravagances of Mr. Yeats and his friends. But once they are made acquainted with what is being done in their name, we hold that those who ambition the uprise of a dramatic art that shall be true, pure and National, should make their voices heard against the perversion of the Society's avowed aims by men who, however great their gifts, will never consent to serve save on terms that never could or should be concealed.

The writer went on to describe the plays about to be presented as "unwholesome productions."

Coming as it did before the plays had even had a hearing, the attack was disconcerting to the company engaged in last-minute preparations for the opening that night. It is easy enough now from the vantage point of time to see that the realism of Synge's play and the independent attitude of Yeats towards what he regarded as philistinism would not escape attack in an atmosphere so charged with political feeling. But Yeats and Fay were soon to be disabused of their complacent attitudes by an incident which happened innocently enough but later created bitter criticism. The society had now identified itself so closely with the nationalist movement that it had lost the patronage of those wealthy people of the Ascendancy who had supported the founding of the theatre. To his surprise Fay received a request from George Wyndham, Chief Secretary of Ireland, to reserve six seats for him and his party at the Molesworth Hall for the opening-night performances. Fay hastily collected and arranged in front of the other seats six armchairs, of which the one assigned to the Chief Secretary chanced to be covered in red. Wyndham was a man of letters and, like his kinsman Lord Dunraven, interested in social reconstruction in Ireland. Fay welcomed him and his party as an important addition to the audience, but he was to regret it.

The United Irishman, which did not strike until the play had been performed, came out on the day of the performance with a friendly notice on the plays and an article by J. B. Yeats, the poet's father, praising the play by the new dramatist and describing it as an attack on "our Irish institution, the loveless marriage." He attributed to Synge "the true Irish heart—he lives in Aran, speaks Irish and knows the people. He is, besides, a man of insight and sincerity, that is to say, a man of genius. Such men are the salt of Ireland."

The Molesworth Hall, on the street of the same name, which the society used as its home until they acquired the Abbey Theatre a year later, is still in use. The small group of people who walked up the wide stone staircase to its auditorium were probably the same people who had come to the earlier productions of the society. Seats were priced at one, two, and three shillings, and a small printed program containing the names of the officers of the society was for sale. In the audience was an Englishwoman, Miss A. E. F. Horniman, who was soon to offer her generosity to the society and procure for them the hall which later became known as the Abbey Theatre.

The program opened with *The King's Threshold*. When the curtain fell there were shouts for the author, and Yeats appeared on the stage and bowed to the applause. *In the Shadow of the Glen* followed with George Roberts as Dan Burke, the beautiful Maire Nic Shiublaigh as Nora Burke, Willie Fay as the tramp and P. J. Kelly as Michael Dara. When Nora Burke walked out with the tramp at the end of the play with his melodic speech still ringing in the ears of the audience there were hisses and boos from a large number of the spectators. There was also applause, and when Synge appeared on the stage nervously bowing he could hear a part of the audience still booing him. But the displeasure was on the whole minor, and when the program concluded with the patriotic *Cathleen Ni Houlihan* the audience went out quite happily.

When Mrs. Synge came down to breakfast the next morning she was more perplexed than pleased by the review of her son's play which she read in *The Irish Times*. The reviewer spoke of a "schism" which the play had caused among the members of the Irish National Theatre Society, expressed no sympathy with the section of the audience which had hissed the play but agreed that the play was "excessively distasteful."

A mean and odious old man "lettin' on to be dead" in bed while his pretty young wife provides refreshments for stray tramps, and is asked to arrange an immediate marriage with a young suitor with whom she absconds when her husband comes to life, seems to us an extraordinary choice of subject for a society that claims to have a higher and purer standard than ordinarily accepted in things dramatic. Mr. Synge has distinct power, both in irony and in dialogue, but surely he could display them better in showing in some other way—the way that should above all cast no slur on Irish womanhood—the wrong of mercenary marriage.

The reviewer was inaccurate when he described Nora as absconding with her young suitor—she was thrown out by her husband and went off with the tramp after her lover had abandoned her. But his reference to a schism among the players had some basis in fact. Fay's most competent actor, Dudley Digges, expressed disapproval of the play before it went into rehearsal, refused to play in it, and resigned from the company, taking with him one of the company's best actresses, Maire Quinn, who later became his wife.

Mrs. Synge had not read her son's play—no member of the family was to see a play of his performed during his lifetime—and she had no way of knowing how inaccurate the reviewer's account was. But she was puzzled at her son's being accused of writing unflattering things about Irish country people when, with his political sympathies, he would be much more likely to do just the opposite. The only favorable press comments were from the reviewer for *The Daily Express*, who wrote that Synge's play was "the gem of the evening," denied that it had any polemical significance and called it "most agreeable fooling," with a "convincing ring of truth" in its characterization.

Arthur Griffith spoke a week later. A statement of Yeats', made the week before in Griffith's paper, that the Irish National Theatre Society would produce no propaganda but that of good art was undoubtedly meant as a warning to a number of people who were already beginning to think of the society as a useful appendage of the political movement. In his editorial of October 17th Griffith took issue with Yeats for his independent attitude which he claimed was pandering to "the feelings of the servants of the Englishmen who are among us." Yeats was wrong, Griffith wrote, to reprint in *Samhain* commendatory notices of the company's acting from the English press and wrong in taking the company to England in the first place. "We are willing if need be to sit at the feet of the Frank, the Teuton, the Slav, and learn from them—to accept reproof, to accept praise—we shall accept neither from the Anglo-Saxon."

As for Synge's "In a Wicklow Glen" (sic) it was no more Irish than the Decameron. "It is a staging of a corrupt version of that old-world libel on womankind—the 'Widow of Ephesus,' which was made current in Ireland by the hedge-school master," and derives its inspiration from "the decadent cynicism that passes current in the Latin Quartier and the London salon." Synge may have spoken Irish and lived on Aran but he was "as utterly a stranger to the Irish character as any Englishman who has yet dissected us for the enlightenment of his countrymen. His Wicklow tramp who addresses an Irish peasant-woman as 'Lady of the house,' and his Wicklow farmer's wife who addresses the man who has craved his hospitality as 'stranger,' never existed in the flesh in Wicklow nor in any other of the thirty-two counties."

Griffith printed Yeats' reply a week later. Yeats charged that "under the influence of a violent contemporary paper, and other influences more difficult to follow," nationalist politics seem to be in the process of uniting themselves to a hatred of ideas. The Irish National Theatre Society had three sorts of ignorance to contend with—first, from the more ignorant sort of Gaelic propagandist, who would have nothing said or thought that is not in country Gaelic; second, from the kind of priest who would deny "all ideas that might perplex a parish of farmers"; and third, from the kind of politician, "not always of the more ignorant sort, who would reject every idea which is not of immediate service to his cause." He was more concerned about the "discipline of his squad than with the most beautiful or the most profound thought." Griffith lashed back in the same issue. Irishwomen were the most virtuous in the world, and the wife in Synge's play was the widow of Ephesus, not an Irishwoman. A theatre which would produce good art but not propaganda had not the right to call itself either Irish or National.

The whole question of the relationship which the Irish National Theatre Society should have to the political movement was discussed in two articles in the same issue, and they seconded Griffith's charges. To the writer of one of the articles, James Connolly, who later gave his life in the rising of 1916, there was no doubt that the theatre should support "the forces of virile Nationalism" in their fight against "the widespread spirit of decadence," instead of undermining them. Since the spirit of nationalism was not yet free and untrammelled in Ireland, foreign ideas were only likely to be a detriment to the cause. "At present we need a National Theatre, not for the purpose of enlarging our national vanity, but of restoring our proper national pride." Mr. Yeats is talking nonsense, "somewhat pettishly as though he were speaking to naughty children." The author of the other article was Maud Gonne, and like Connolly she expressed herself in generalities. But her reference to writers who in describing scenes of peasant life in the Aran Islands allow "foreign thoughts and philosophies to creep in and distort their heroes and heroines" made it clear that Synge was her target. Yeats was wrong in asking for freedom from "patriotic captivity."

A week later, J. B. Yeats, who had inadvertently created some of the suspicion of Synge, returned to his defence in *The United Irishman* on October 31st:

The outcry against Mr. Synge's play seems to be largely dishonest, the real objection not being that it misrepresents Irishwomen, but that it is a very effective attack on loveless marriages—the most miserable institution so dear to our thrifty elders among the peasants and among their betters, by whom anything like impulse or passion is discredited, human nature coerced at every point and sincerity banished from the land. . . . My complaint of Mr. Synge's play is that it did not go far enough. . . .

Griffith's editorial comment was, "It remained for a member of the Society who spends most of his time away from Ireland, and under the operation of foreign influences, to represent, in good faith no doubt, adultery as a feature of Irish rural life, and to exhibit his utter ignorance of the Irish character by treating women's frailty as a subject for laughter." With this the controversy came to a temporary halt. It was renewed a little more than a year later when the play was revived and Griffith repeated his charges.

Synge's reaction to the flurry he had caused is something we have no record of. He did not discuss it with his mother, who like most Dubliners was hardly aware of the existence of Griffith's paper and little interested in the opinions of a handful of nationalists. The last entry Synge made in his diary for 1903—he kept no diaries after that year—was made five days before *In the Shadow of the Glen* was

performed. The short note he sent to Griffith slightly more than a
year later, when the controversy was renewed, was his only public
pronouncement. But out of his anger, and perhaps amusement, came
a short piece entitled "National Drama: A Farce," which exists in
two rough drafts, little more than summaries with patches of dialogue.

Fogarty, a "country upper-class Catholic with strong patriotic
principles and a considerable thirst," and Murphy, who has lived in
London and "learned to talk of the three styles of Rossetti," are
awaiting other members in a national club room, on the wall of which
hangs a map of Ireland and of Hungary. Fogarty reads aloud the
titles of the books on a bookshelf:

The Whole History of Hungary for Beginners, by an Eminent Writer.
The Afforestation of the Sea-Shore. The Five Parts of Father O'Growney,
being the complete Irish course needed for a patriot. How to be a Genius,
by a Gaelic Leaguer. The Pedigree of the Widow of Ephesus. The Com-
plete Works of Petronius and Bocaccio, Unabridged. Plays for An Irish
Theater, Abridged and Expurgated by a Catholic Critic. Controversial
Ethics for the Use of Editors, by a Doctor of Louvain. Fairy Tales for All
Ages. The Dawn of the Twilight, and the Autumn of the Spring. The
Encyclopedia Celtica. A Brief Statement of Facts of the Universe for
Irishmen, being very useful for all who are awaiting the foundation of a
University of Orthodox Science and Art.

Presently the other members arrive, the chairman calls the meeting
to order and announces, "The subject for debate this evening is the
possibility, origin, and future of an Irish National Drama, but before
beginning the debate two motions are to be carried unanimously
calling on the National Bank and the National Gallery and the
National Merit Society to leave off sailing under false pretences."
Mr. Murphy then rises and defines an Irish national drama as one
"that embodies in a finished form the pageant of Irish life and shines
throughout with the soft light of the ideal impulses of the Gaels."
When he asks rhetorically if Molière were not a national dramatist
someone replies, "Not a bit of him. Wasn't he always making fun of
his own country, till the holy bishop wouldn't take his corpse when
he was dead?" The debate which follows brings out the fact that
Shakespeare is "infected with the plague-spot of sex," that Ibsen's
delineation of "the livid realities of the north can be only a harmful

influence," and that in fact there has never been a national drama "in our sense of the word" that can serve as a model for Irish dramatists.

In the other draft of the farce one member dissents from the majority and advances what could be called Synge's position. "An Irish drama," he argues, "that is written in Ireland about Irish people, and not on a foreign model, will and must be national in so far as it exists at all. . . . If you do not like a work that is passing itself off as national art, you had better show that it is not art. If it is good art it is vain for you to try and show that it is not national."

In ridiculing the futile attempt to formulate a definition of an art that would be "national" and therefore congenial to the political environment which nourished it, Synge saw the weakness of the position Yeats had put himself into in the very beginning. The National Bank and the National Gallery could call themselves national because nobody ever expected them to play a part in the political movement. But the word *national* in the title of Yeats' theatre immediately called attention to the fact that willy nilly it was playing a part in the unfolding destiny of Ireland herself. Yeats was willing to harness his theatre to the nationalists' bandwagon when he needed their help, but now that Miss Horniman was waiting with a purse full of English pounds he could not be blamed for wanting to save himself and his theatre for what any artist would call a higher destiny than that of writing propaganda for revolutionaries.

What Griffith, Connolly and Maud Gonne meant by a national drama was one which would aid them in moulding public sentiment against England and preparing it for the day of revolution. But they were hard put to define their terms. One is reminded of Joyce's satire on the ambiguous meaning of the word *nation* when an embattled Leopold Bloom in Barney Kiernan's pub responds to the anti-Semitic barbs of the Citizen with the statement that a nation is "a group of people living in the same place."

It may also have been while he was smarting from attack that Synge conceived the idea of writing the play which he described to an incredulous Yeats. Yeats' recollection was that "one night when we were still producing plays in a little hall, Synge brought around a scenario which read like a chapter of Rabelais." According to Yeats it was about two women—one Protestant, one Catholic—who take refuge in a cave during the insurrection of 1798. When they start to quarrel about religion, one of them chooses rape by the soldiers or rebels to staying in such company.[87] Only a fragment of a scenario and some dialogue in a notebook remain, and they may actually be all that Synge ever wrote on the subject. If so, one can only conclude that Yeats' account of the plot was a little too bald, but it was strong stuff no doubt and would have drawn a violent reaction from a Dublin audience of 1903. The Catholic woman asks, "I'm axing if it's myself or you [had] the biggest escape." Her companion answers, "It'd be hard to have a biggest than me, and I with two cads calling at my heels, 'Come here, you heretic!'" And when the Catholic asks, "Heretic? What made them call you a heretic?" the Protestant answers, "What is it they call any good Christian Protestant but a heretic now?"

The argument is disrupted when a wounded rebel, the son of the Catholic woman, runs in and collapses. The despair of the mother moves the other woman, who helps her carry the wounded man into the woods nearby and then comes back to put the soldiers off the track, standing up to their abuse and saving the boy's life. Synge had in mind the kind of woman Sean O'Casey was later to portray as Bessie Burgess in *The Plough and the Stars*—a Protestant woman of the tenements who waves the Union Jack and reviles the Catholic rebels of 1916 but in the end gives her life for one of them.

In the Shadow of the Glen seems innocent enough today, but one can see why audiences of 1903 could find it objectionable. It is based upon a motif familiar to students of folklore—the jealous husband who feigns death to test the fidelity of his spouse.[88] The same story has been recorded in other countries and cultures far removed in time and distance from the McDonough cottage on Inishmaan, where Synge heard it. It must have been current in the west of Ireland because collectors of the Irish Folklore Commission have recorded four different versions of the story, three of them in County Galway and one on the Dingle peninsula, County Kerry.[89] Like all folk tales it was international in origin and must have depended for its existence on the fact that it was a good story and dealt with emotions and attitudes close to the universal conscience. Synge of course adapted it to his own purposes and gave it an application to its Irish setting which the folk tale did not have.

In making Nora Burke a young girl married not only to a jealous husband but an old one "the like of a sick sheep close to your ear," Synge was indeed, as J. B. Yeats said, making a pertinent observation on an Irish institution—the loveless marriage. Rural Ireland sees many marriages like Nora Burke's because of a peculiar fact of Irish life— the inability, or unwillingness, of men to marry until their youth has left them. One can cite many Irish writers, from the author of *The Midnight Court* in the eighteenth century to the author of "The Great Hunger" in the twentieth—both of them bachelors incidentally —who have dramatized this tragic fact.[90] In a country where more than 80 per cent of the men between twenty-five and thirty years of age, and more than 63 per cent of those between thirty and thirty-five, are unmarried, one can find many Nora Burkes whose marriages were motivated by little more than the desire to take the only man that offered and who, like Dan Burke, had "a bit of a farm with cows on it, and sheep on the back hills." For an imaginative girl like Nora Burke, in whom the blood ran strong, such a life would have been frustrating enough. Synge transplanted his play to Glenmalure where the wildness and isolation of the setting and the sweeping fogs which blot out the rugged landscape would intensify her loneliness and exaggerate her desperate need for the companionship of a man more nearly her own age. It was the very truth of Synge's observation, aided no doubt by Maire Nic Shiublaigh's interpretation of Nora, that infuriated people in the audiences of 1903. Molly Allgood, who later played Nora, toned down the heroine's sexual ebullience and emphasized her simple humanity. The bitter truth of the play still remained, but it was etched a little more sharply by the sympathy which a superb actress could elicit for a lonely and desperate woman.

Synge also effected another transformation in the simple folk tale. Pat Dirane's story concludes with the enraged husband attacking his rival with a stick so that "the blood out of him leapt up and hit the gallery." In the play the wife, deprived of her brief vision of the life a widow's money can buy for her, expelled from her home in disgrace and deserted by her cowardly lover, is suddenly saved by the tramp. "Come along with me now, lady of the house, and it's not my blather you'll be hearing only, but you'll be hearing the herons crying out over the black lakes, and you'll be hearing the grouse and the owls with them, and the larks and the big thrushes when the days are warm. . . ." She goes out with him, like the Playboy and his father, to go "romancing through a romping lifetime," and we are given the final ironic contrast of the husband and lover consoling themselves over a glass of whisky. Nora does not go willingly, but she goes with dignity. For Synge the tramp was a perfect representation of the imaginative life, because he suggested romance and liberation from the gnawing frustration of the life on the land—"the dancer that dances in the heart of men."

Whatever Synge's family thought of his activities and the controversy they had aroused, there is no indication that his relations with them changed. He had sent a copy of *Samhain*, containing *Riders to the Sea*, to Valeska von Eiken and another to MacKenna, who was now in Berlin. *In the Shadow of the Glen* had not yet been published, but he wrote to MacKenna about the flurry it had caused. MacKenna replied: "I feel that your hour has begun to strike and I am very glad of it, very. . . . I think Yeats' estimate is very true . . . the play* is somewhat Gaelic-Greek of the kind I always thought should come out of Ireland." Both Lady Gregory and Yeats were also of the same opinion. Lady Gregory wrote to Synge from London in December to tell him an unhappy story about how she and Yeats had been trying to interest publishers in *The Aran Islands*. "Mr. Yeats took it to Bullen who promised to read it at once. After three weeks I went to ask him about it, and he had not yet looked at it, and didn't seem inclined to—so I carried it off. Then I asked Masefield to read it and enclose you his opinion. . . . It would be a great thing if he could get your plays brought out this spring, especially if you think one, about the blind man† is ready."

Masefield thought that Synge's manuscript was among the five best of the 150 books he had read for publishers during the year, but he thought also that "one or two modifications" would be necessary before it could get published. "I am afraid its publication will send scores of tweeded beasts to the islands, but that cannot be helped." He had interested Elkin Mathews, he thought, in publishing not only the book on Aran but possibly also the two plays. Masefield wrote again on December 18th, "After Christmas sometime will you send me a fair copy of the plays that I may give to Mathews. By all

* *Riders to the Sea.*
† *The Well of the Saints.*

means add the abortive wedding play.* If you come to London we
will have a big feast together and go through the Aran book, doctoring
the doggerel." But Synge was to wait three and a half more years
for Mathews to publish *The Aran Islands* and two and half years
for *Riders to the Sea* and *In the Shadow of the Glen.*

A bad cold in November of 1903 had put Synge in bed for several
days. He wrote to MacKenna telling him of a suspicion that he might
have tuberculosis. As the year drew to a close MacKenna replied:

To us in remote Berlin you are still in the ante-spat-upon stage; we
want to see the fun, to see it beginning and to see it end; let you send
it us—the papers. We will return 'em. . . . My son, I do not believe a
fine-built, hardy, sportiose boy like yourself has tuberculosis. I am sincerely—though if you like, ignorantly—unanxious on that point. But I
wish you would not delay to let me know, let us know, what grave thing
drove you to doctors and what, by now, was the verdict. I hope these
damp Gaelic huts have not been permeating your bones or your morale
and pulling down the outer man while they feed the fires of the spirit. . . .

Synge did not have tuberculosis, but he was never entirely free of
the suspicion that he had. Among his papers is a physician's report
of a test—results of which were negative—for tubercular bacilli made
on him in May of 1907. Even afterwards the fear remained. According to Lily Yeats, the poet's sister, Synge told Molly Allgood during
his last illness that he could not see her for fear of infecting her with
the consumption he suspected he had.[91]

In December the Fays had performed a new play entitled *Broken
Soil* by a young dramatist named Padraic Colum, and as the new year
began they were rehearsing Yeats' *The Shadowy Waters*, Lady Gregory's *Twenty-Five*, which she had rewritten, and Seamus MacManus'
The Townland of Tamney. Miss Horniman was in Dublin helping
the company with the making of costumes, and she had already made
her mind up to provide them with a new theatre of their own. Synge
was present at the opening performances in the Molesworth Hall on
January 14th, but he was disappointed at the staging and the reception of Yeats' play, which he described in his notebook as "tenuous
and delicately toned as Cylvaine and Silysette." But the press notices
at least were friendly, and even Griffith had words of praise.

* *The Tinker's Wedding.*

Synge had sent MacKenna the press notices of *In the Shadow of the Glen* and the discussion in *The United Irishman* over the kinds of plays which a nationalist society should or should not produce. The failure of *The Shadowy Waters* had apparently provoked him into remarking that the only alternative his critics seemed to allow him was writing innocently bloodless plays about ancient Irish legendary figures. MacKenna replied:

My dear child I do not know which of yez is in the right. A blessing on both your houses. You should be free as artist, *penseur*. Whether you should be played I do not know. I think art has many mansions. . . . I mean vaguely that I like the phillistine idea of a purely fantastic unmodern—forgive me if I borrow "unIbsenified"—ideal, breezy-spring-dayish Cuchullainoid *etc.* national theater. Of course there is a great deal of nonsense in what the Phillistine says but much more in the way it is said, and the fundament I think is sound enough. I confess I believe in the ripeness and unripeness of nations and class Ireland blessedly unripe. Modern problems even in peasant robes I do not like to see made public property in Ireland yet. Give us our own literary nationhood first, then let us rise to our frieze-clad Ibsens. (I know, of course, you hate the word Ibsen. I speak as one less wise, for brevity's sweet sake and indolence's.)

I would like to see your play in book form, not on boards, I think, nor for myself, but for the people, I mean. The stage might regenerate Ireland, used Cuchulainly. Otherwise I like it not till we have a stomach of our own, to digest to our own substance all ideas on land and sea. It appears I do not know what I think after all. I fear I am a phillistine. Do forgive me.

The letter Synge wrote in reply on January 28th is now in the New York Public Library, but a preliminary draft of it is among his papers. The fact that he took the trouble to rewrite it and in the process delete some of the stronger statements before sending it on to his friend indicates how upset he must have been by MacKenna's views and how determined he was to state his position exactly. His first draft reads,

Dear MacKenna, It is hardly possible to thrash out a critical question like the one—rather perhaps the score—you raise, by slinging crystals at each other from Dublin to Berlin, but all the same I'm going to give you a volley.

You say we should not deal with modern matters on the stage in Ireland because Ireland is "blessedly unripe." *Bon!* Do you think that the peasantry—the people—of Norway are less blessed, or greatly less blessed than the Irish? Do you think that if they are as innocent as the Irish, that Ibsen should not have been played in Norway, and, therefore, have never become an efficient dramatist? Do you think that because the people I have met in the valleys of Wurzburg and the Rhine are as unripe as those of Kerry and Galway that Suderman and Hauptman should be driven from the boards of Berlin? The Dublin audiences who see Mlle. Rejane in Ibsen, Mrs. P. Campbell in Suderman, Miss Olga Netherstock in *Sapho etc. etc.* are hardly blessedly unripe. They want to suck smut every evening and to rise up every morning and say "Behold! We are the most virtuous nation in Europe. Thank God we are not as other men!"

Heaven forbid that we should have morbid, sex-obsessed drama in Ireland, not because we have any peculiar sanctity, which I utterly deny— blessed unripeness is sometimes akin to damned rottenness, see percentage of lunatics in Ireland and causes thereof—but because it is bad as drama and is played out. On [the] French stage you get sex without its balancing elements. On [the] Irish stage you [get] the other elements without sex. I restored sex and the people were so surprised they saw the sex only.

I do not believe in the possibility of "a purely fantastic, unmodern, ideal, breezy, springdayish, Cuchulainoid National Theater." We had *The Shadowy Waters* on the stage last week, and it was the most *distressing* failure the mind can imagine—a half-empty room, with growling men and tittering females. Of course it is possible to write drama that fills your description and yet it is fitter for the stage than *The Shadowy Waters*, but no drama can grow out of anything other than the fundamental realities of life which are never fantastic, are neither modern nor unmodern and, as I see them, rarely spring-dayish, or breezy or Cuchulainoid.

The stage, even if it agreed to all your adjectives, would not regenerate —or for that matter unregenerate—Ireland any more than the symphonies of Beethoven can regenerate Germany. . . .

When I deny Ireland's peculiar sanctity, I do so as compared with other potato-fed, thinly populated lands of same latitude. I have as you know perambulated a good deal of Ireland in my thirty [years] and if I were [to] tell, which Heaven forbid, all the sex horrors I have seen I could a tale unfold that would wither up your blood. I think of course that single plays may and should be spring-dayish *etc.* But while life is what it is and men are what they are, I do not think any group of writers will write such work chiefly unless they do so with a wilful insincerity of joy that would make their work useless, and destroy the power of their souls.

I think squeamishness is a disease, and that Ireland will gain if Irish writers deal manfully, directly and decently with the entire reality of life. I think the law-maker and the law-breaker are both needful in society—as the lively and volcanic forces are needed to make earth's crust habitable—and I think the law-maker is tending to reduce Ireland, or parts of Ireland, to a dismal, morbid hypocrisy that is not a blessed unripeness. On the other hand I feel of course the infinitely sweet and healthy piety of a great deal of Irish life. I will use it gladly in my work, and meanwhile it is perfectly safe from any fear of contamination from my evil words. . . .

The road Yeats had charted—"histories and romances of the great Gaelic men of the past"—was not for him. He had no interest in

> All the rare and royal names
> Wormy sheepskin yet retains:
> Etain, Helen, Maeve and Fand . . .

He preferred to

> . . . search in Red Dan Sally's ditch,
> And drink in Tubber fair,
> Or poach with Red Dan Philly's bitch
> The badger and the hare.

He would deal with the "entire reality" of contemporary Irish life, and the richness of that life and the vitality of its idiom would save him from the drabness that vitiated the work of so many European writers. When he did turn to Irish legendary material in his last play, *Deirdre of the Sorrows*, it was not to create a *spring-dayish Cuchulainoid* drama but to change the rare and royal names of wormy sheepskin into western peasants.

Whatever changes Willie Fay had asked for in *Riders to the Sea* were apparently made, and the play went into rehearsal for performance on February 25th with AE's *Deirdre*. Synge wrote to Michael Costello, the innkeeper on Inishere, for samples of Aran flannel and some pairs of pampooties so that Fay could costume the actors appropriately. The company was made up mostly of Dublin men and women to whom the garb of an islander from the west was almost as exotic as it would have been to foreigners.

The audience which saw *Riders to the Sea* was a small but enthusiastic one. Synge and AE were both called before the curtain to be applauded, but the press was remarkably subdued in its praise of what has come to be considered the most perfect one-act play in the English language. One critic called it a trifle, another "something like a wake," and Griffith's paper a week later conceded that its "tragic beauty powerfully affected the audience," but described the use of a drowned man's body on the stage as "a cheap trick of the Transpontine dramatists." Padraic Colum wrote Synge, who stayed home with a toothache after the opening night, "The more I think of the play the more it seems—to my imperfect vision—perfect, and I cannot offer to criticise as to construction or dialogue. I can only say that the long speeches of Maurya beginning 'Bartley will be lost now' and the next one cannot be given by any actresses I know."

In answer to Synge's letter MacKenna replied from Berlin, restating his position. Then, describing his own work, he wrote:

Plotinus progresses. I have the whole First Ennead—there are six of them (of nine naturally) done, all in the rough, a great part nearly ready and all get-readyable in a week or two, I think. I hope Magee will use one book of the accomplished nine in *Dana*. He has the TSS. That publication I think will help me perhaps to a publisher. When I think that this noble stuff doesn't exist in English yet and must surely some day, I long to devote all my laborious day to it for a bare living wage. I wish if you saw Yeats in London you would find an artful way to touch the matter, just to see whether he could be interested in it later when I should perhaps, renewing relations with him, try to get through him entry to a publisher's parlor. I hate using these people; yet it seems the way. And if I got in touch with Yeats again, there is no man I would think more worthy of helping Plotinus to talk English. . . .

I see of late much in the New York *Nation* and in the *Athenaeum* of Irish things—Lady Gregory and Douglas Hyde upon Raftery among the rest. I wish Plotinus had been a bare-legged Irish tramp. But indeed Raftery seems to have had a quaint and powerful soul. If he had not existed, he would have had to be invented. He makes things plausible. Did he exist?

Ten

MISS HORNIMAN AND THE ABBEY THEATRE. LONDON PERFORMANCES. *THE WELL OF THE SAINTS*. RENEWAL OF THE CONTROVERSY OVER *IN THE SHADOW OF THE GLEN*

. . . you'd find a radiant lady with droves of bullocks on the plains of Meath, and herself bedizened in the diamond jewelleries of Pharaoh's ma.

Miss Horniman's plans for providing the society with its own theatre were maturing. A small building known as the People's Music Hall, built as part of the Mechanics Institute on Abbey Street, had been closed by the municipal authorities because it no longer complied with safety regulations. Willie Fay examined it carefully, talked to a Dublin architect named Joseph Holloway, who was a regular member of the society's audiences, and told Miss Horniman that if she could acquire the Music Hall and an adjoining building which had originally been a bank and then a morgue Holloway could make a theatre out of them which would meet the safety requirements of the Dublin Corporation.

Miss Horniman immediately set about acquiring the two properties through Lady Gregory's solicitors and appeased the other Dublin theatre owners by promising that she would not place her theatre in competition with them. She took a lease on both buildings for ninety-nine years, to extend from May of 1904, and in a formal letter to Yeats offered the theatre rent free to him and to the society, stipulating only that she reserved the right to rent it to other groups when it was not in use by the society. Her offer was accepted on May 11th in a letter signed by the directors and members of the company. It soon became clear that Miss Horniman's generosity was prompted more by her interest in Yeats' career than in the future of an enterprise identified, however loosely, with Irish Nationalism. But her generosity was a fact.

Until it was gutted by fire in the summer of 1951, the Abbey Theatre, as it was named, was the centre of the dramatic movement in Ireland. It seated fewer than six hundred people and its stage was almost impossibly shallow, measuring only sixteen feet from curtain line to back wall. Once action had begun onstage, passing from one wing to the other was possible only by a catwalk overhead or from the public lane behind the theatre. Many an actor over the years has wondered which alternative to take as he awaited his cue.

On Saturday, March 26th, the company made its second London appearance at the Royalty Theatre with a performance of Synge's two plays and *The King's Threshold* for the matinée and *Broken Soil* and *The Pot of Broth* in the evening. The house was filled for both performances. One critic described *Riders to the Sea* as "a singularly beautiful and pathetic piece of hopeless fatalism." Another found it "intensely pathetic and, in a sense, supremely human." William Archer and Max Beerbohm both praised it elaborately. *In the Shadow of the Glen* did not attract much attention, but it too was praised.

The acting was also appreciated. The critic for *The Times Literary Supplement*, however, warned that "premature success" might be a real misfortune for so talented but so immature a company. But the warning was unnecessary, and a letter from Frank Fay to Synge reveals more than anything else why there was little danger of complacency or a false sense of accomplishment:

Have we not had an extraordinary triumph? I am not prone to use words lightly but I can call it nothing less. As usual you had to go out of your own country to be appreciated. Some of our local oracles must feel disturbed when they recollect how they wrote about *Riders to the Sea*. . . . Archer . . . says we either do not seek for or else despise accomplishment. Well accomplishment means the cultivation of individuality rather than of ensemble and I hope we shall always prefer the latter; but we shall have no chance of acquiring the former until we are playing constantly. Constant practice is what we must have; it will give us all the qualities which Archer says and I feel we (with the exception of the brother) lack. I don't know how we are to get this constant practice. Twelve or sixteen appearances in a season are not worth much and we shall only have had about that number when we close in May. I think we could have done a couple more shows in London and drawn, especially after the notices we got.

Curiously the crowd was much less nervous on the theater stage than we were in Queen's Gate Hall, or even the Molesworth Hall. The theater has one immense advantage. You are so far from the audience that you do not feel them influencing you. You know how awkward it is rehearsing with people a few feet from you; well, in a hall there is something of the same embarrassment.

I should like to know in what way you think the acting could be improved all round. You have seen enough of us now to be able to give a helpful criticism.

A few weeks later he had more to say about acting, and wrote:

Archer says what I always thought, that except the brother we are not strong in facial expression. Max* talks about our "blank" faces. Others however (as in *Today*) say that I and others have "wonderful" eyes. Miss Horniman says that I have expression but not always. I aim at what Symons says about Coquelin and Duse at not giving facial expression from moment to moment but as summarizing.

Tarpey says in a letter, "your players do actually seem to listen to, hear, and apprehend, each other before replying. This is a truth to nature, which the professional actor rarely achieves; he generally gabbles his words on the cue; set in motion, as he is, by the cue and the cue alone." Now that absolutely contradicts Max and Archer and Miss Horniman (the latter has seen much and the best) and it puzzles me because Tarpey is a dramatist and as he says has seen many rehearsals he knows how the strings are pulled and this is one of the points that would strike him. And yet I feel that the others are right.

Miss H. spoke to me of our "tentativeness." She instanced it by saying that if we found a box was difficult to open we would fumble at it instead of putting our whole strength into the operation; that we would open a door a quarter of the way in coming into a room instead of the whole way, that in short there is hesitation. I think however that is a part of

* Beerbohm.

Irish character and if so we must preserve it on the stage; but she says (and surely with truth) that we must do so by means of art. Tarpey is strong against our paying any attention to words like "sophistication," "freedom," *etc.* and he denies that we "slip about the stage like a sick room." But as I have said we undoubtedly want worst of all continual public practice.

Synge had become acquainted with Miss Horniman through Yeats, and they talked about astrology. At the end of May she wrote to him from London, casting his horoscope and telling him that he learned languages easily, enjoyed a healthy pugnacity, was attracted by gloomy ideas and tragic stories and had an imaginative faculty of a disturbing nature to other people. "Comparing your planets with those in Mr. Yeats' nativity I find it clear that his influence has been excellent for both of you . . . and you will add to the prosperity of his theatrical schemes." She was not far wrong.

MacKenna, who had moved to London, wrote complaining about the first number of *Dana*, the new magazine founded by W. K. Magee (John Eglinton) and Fred Ryan, which had come out in May:

I have seen Dana. I am damnably disappointed—some of it seems to be blatant and some of it silly, and the only thing I cared for was Eglinton's self, whose article I thought really of the first excellence for thought and in the main for expression. I like George Moore from the evenings I saw and heard him, but I think his article was not fit to wrap ham in. I am amazed that Eglinton should print it. The idol of the name? The presentation foreward or whatever they called the manifesto seemed to me crude and clumsy and illiterate. I hope Maud Gonne whom I greatly esteem had nothing to do with it save to blush for it.

Synge replied:

I spent last winter with my ten toes in the grave, and now I'm riding my seventy miles in the day with a few mountain ranges thrown in, doing more and doing it more easily than ever before. Next month maybe I'll be down again. Breathe, eat, sleep, smoke not too much, and you'll be fine.

I haven't seen the spring quite so intimately this year as last—I've been too busy at my play—but not the less I've seen many wonders. I miss my talks with you at Cintra* infinitely, but when I'm out pilgrimaging on the hills it's a kind of relief to know you aren't there any more shut up in your cellar . . . I have just got my new play† off my hands; it was read to the company on Friday and goes into rehearsal at once. It is a much bigger affair than the others and is in three acts. We hope to begin our new season in October in our new theater. Everything is settled now I believe except patent, an important point, so we are still keeping the whole affair out of papers—no paragraphs. Miss Horniman (*entre nous*) is coming out heroically.

MacKenna preserved an undated fragment which was either part of this letter or of another one written at approximately the same time, but he mutilated it as he did the rest of Synge's letters. In it Synge gave more details about the construction of the Abbey Theatre, referred to Miss Horniman's horoscope, which he found bizarre, vague, interesting but not convincing, and commented on the efforts of Vera Esposito, a member of the company, to translate *Riders to the Sea* into Russian and French. Then, in an apparent reference to John Eglinton—the name is scissored out—he writes, "He was too refined and too cultured to have any of our enthusiasms, or to take part in any of our movements, and now he has come to admire the drivel of George Moore. . . . His own article, however, as you say, is alright. After all it is better to rave after the sun and moon as Yeats does than to be sane as [he]."

Miss Horniman was indeed emerging as a heroine. On July 1, 1904, she signed a petition prepared for her by her solicitors, addressed to the Lord Lieutenant General and General Governor of Ireland and asking that she be granted a patent to produce plays in her new theatre. On August 4th a public hearing was held in Dublin Castle at which testimony was heard and witnesses cross-examined. Yeats wrote to Lady Gregory on the day of the hearing:

Final decision is postponed until Monday but the battle is won to all intents and purposes. . . . I think I was a bad witness. Counsel did not examine me but asked me to make a statement. The result was, having expected questions and feeling myself left to wander through an immense subject, I said very little. I was disappointed at being hardly cross-examined

* MacKenna's last house in Dublin.
† *The Well of the Saints.*

at all—by that time I got excited and was thirsting for everybody's blood. One barrister . . . asked if the Irish National Theatre Society had not produced a play which was an attack on the institution of marriage. Somebody asked him what was the name of the play. He said it didn't matter and dropped the subject. He had evidently heard some vague rumours about [In]The Shadow of the Glen.[92]

Since neither Miss Horniman nor Yeats was a legal resident of Ireland, Lady Gregory agreed to be patentee. On August 20th the result of the hearing was made public. The law advisors of the crown recommended the granting of the patent, subject to certain limitations, and only the formalities were left. The Abbey Theatre was a fact.

Synge missed all the excitement over the granting of the patent because he was in Kerry for the entire month of August. After finishing The Well of the Saints and turning it over to Willie Fay, he left Dublin for Coole on July 16th. Yeats had arrived ahead of him, and they were joined later by AE. Lady Gregory asked Synge to help her with her new play Kincora, which she hoped would be ready by the fall, but the main subject of conversation was the coming hearing over the patent. Yeats wrote to Charles Ricketts on the 26th, "Synge and AE the poet are staying here, and though they have come to their task from the opposite sides of the heavens they are both stirring the same pot—something of a witch's cauldron, I think."[93] Synge left for Philly Harris' cottage at Mountain Stage around the first of August, and the only news he had of the patent was what Lady Gregory relayed to him from Yeats. She wrote on August 7th. Two weeks later Yeats, who had returned to Coole after the hearings, dictated a letter to Lady Gregory about the rehearsals of The Well of the Saints:

One or two criticisms occurred to me. There is a place where you make the saint say that some one of the characters has a low voice or should have a low voice, and that this is a good thing in women. This suggests that he has been reading King Lear, where Cordelia's voice is described as low, "an excellent thing in woman." I think this is a wrong association in the mind. I do not object to another passage about the spells of smiths and women which suggests that he has been reading St. Patrick's hymn.*

* The "Lorica of St. Patrick," or the "Deer's Cry" as it is more commonly called, is a seventh or eighth century composition in Old Irish which the saint, according to the tradition, chanted as a protective charm against his enemies.

He might naturally have done so. This point is not however very important. But I do think it of some importance that you should cross out a number of the Almighty Gods. I do not object to them on the ground that they are likely to shock people but because the phrase occurs so often that it may weary and irritate the ear. I remember the disastrous effect of the repetition of the word *beauty* in the last act of Edward Martyn's *Maeve*. I daresay the people do repeat the word very often, but unhappily the stage has its laws which are not those of life. Fay told me that you gave him leave to cross out what he will, but though he is very anxious to reduce the number of the God Almightys he does not like to do it of himself. He wants you to do it. We have not your MS here, as Roberts wrote to ask for it. . . .

I forgot to say that I think William Fay will be as fine as possible in your play if I can judge by the first act. Frank Fay will be good as the saint. I like the women rather less. Miss Allgood has some objectionable trick of voice, certain sounds that she gets wrong. I could not define it though I tried again and again. Miss Esposito is not without cleverness, but she does not seem to me to have a right ideal.

One of our difficulties is that women of the class of Miss Garvey and Miss Walker* have not sensitive bodies. They have a bad instrument to work with, but they have great simplicity of feeling, a readiness to accept high ideals, a certain capacity for noble feeling. Women of our own class on the other hand have far more sensitive instruments, are far more teachable in all that belongs to expression, but they lack simplicity of feeling, their minds are too full of trivial ideals, and they seldom seem capable of really noble feeling. . . . Miss Horniman is staying here now with a lady who acts as chorus. The theatre is not to open till December. . . . This is as far as W. B. Y. goes.

He took the Horniman party out fishing yesterday, and they got ten, mixed pike and perch. I hope your asthma is better. Yesterday was fine, and now we have drizzle again, and the hay is not yet saved. Moore has written an article for *Dana* in which he says the one thing the company requires is a stage manager. He tried to induce Gogarty to sign it, but he backed out, and I fancy Moore has toned down the writing since then. But it won't make the Fays love him.

After a month in Kerry, Synge was back in Dublin by the first of September. He had intended to go to Aran, and Martin McDonough had written that he was welcome and expected. But he suddenly changed his mind and on September 17th went to North Mayo, a

* Maire Nic Shiublaigh.

part of Ireland he had never seen before. He stayed in Sligo for a few days—he had his bicycle with him—and then continued westwards by taking the boat which ran from Sligo town to Belmullet, a small town at the entrance to the bleak and windswept slice of land known as the Mullet.

North Mayo has its share of natural beauty, particularly the cliff scenery on the north coast which Synge could see from the deck of the tiny steamer, especially when she came in close to shore to deliver a load of salt or timber to the *curraghs* which came out to her. But the Mullet itself is a treeless stretch of sand and bog, fifteen miles long, connected to the mainland by a narrow isthmus between Broadhaven Bay on the north and Blacksod Bay on the south. Since the isthmus is bisected by a small canal, used by the coastal steamers and fishing boats, the Mullet is an island, and the bleakness and isolation of the scenery must have reminded Synge of Aran. This was part of the Congested Districts area, so designated because it was literally a wilderness lacking the fertility to support its rather heavy population. A year later he was to travel through the same area again with Jack Yeats, the poet's brother, on commission by *The Manchester Guardian* to write a series of articles which it was hoped might dramatize the plight of a people badly in need of help.

Like other remote parts of the west, Mayo had seen more than its share of violence. The French under General Humbert had sailed into Killala Bay in 1798 and landed a force which got as far as Ballinamuck in County Longford before it ran into superior British forces. It was in Mayo also that one of the most sensational demonstrations of the Land Wars took place in 1880, when Captain Charles Boycott, the agent for Lord Erne, was shunned by his tenants and subsequently gave his name to the English language. The tradition of rebellion was strong in Mayo because the tenants were impoverished and the landlords a long way from the centre of authority. The potentiality for violence which Synge must have sensed in the people he met and in their stories found a response in his own love of violence. Eight months earlier he had written to MacKenna that "the law-maker and law-breaker are both needful in society." His ballad "Danny," which Elizabeth Yeats refused to include in the Cuala Press edition of Synge's poems because of its brutality, is based on a story Synge heard in Mayo:

. . . But seven tripped him up behind
And seven kicked before,
And seven squeezed around his throat
Till Danny kicked no more.

Then some destroyed him with their heels,
Some tramped him in the mud,
Some stole his purse and timber pipe,
And some washed off his blood.

And when you're walking out the way
From Bangor to Belmullet,
You'll see a flat cross on a stone
Where men choked Danny's gullet.

When Synge came to write his play about a man glorified by a whole community for having murdered his own father, he selected Mayo as its setting rather than Connemara, where the actual murder took place, or Inishmaan where he had first heard the story. In a notebook he kept on this trip he wrote:

In Mayo one cannot forget that in spite of the beauty of the scenery the people in it are debased and nearly demoralized by bad housing and lodging and the endless misery of the rain. . . .

About sunset I went out some distance on the Mullet and saw the evening coming down over Blacksod Bay filled with searching loveliness with low mists from the bogs and rose and purple colors on the sea. Here and there I passed a girl in the usual dress—a short red petticoat over bare feet and legs, a faded uncertain bodice and a white or blue rag swathing the head—who was looking after a few shadowy cattle on bringing them home from the bogs.

For a passer through it is not easy to be just to the belated towns of Ireland. Belmullet in the evening is squalid and noisy, lonely and crowded at the same time and without any appeal to the imagination. So at least one says for a moment. When one has passed six times up and down hearing a gramophone in one house, a fiddle in the next, then an accordion and a fragment of some traditional lullaby with many crying babies, pigs and donkeys, and noisy girls and young men justling one in the darkness the effect is not indistinct. All the light comes crossways from doors or windows of shops or "the North East" the flaring doorway of the forge so that the moving people are now dark outlines only then for an instant lit up from the east or west.

When he returned to Dublin he found a letter from MacKenna asking him to criticize a passage of his translation of Plotinus. "Any comment you'd make would be valued, but even an idle pencil dab under an offensive word or phrase would interest me. Don't say yes unless you could return it within a few weeks. *The London Contemporary* rejected it: I think of trying *The Monthly Review.* You can be frank if you prefer not to see the thing. I too have been frank." Synge replied, describing himself as "lonesome and uncanny, wandering like an unserviceable ghost," and apparently informing MacKenna that he had revived his interest in occult phenomena. MacKenna replied in surprise:

It is queer, but I who am the dogmatist have only on these things a sympathetically open mind. You, the lean and hungry sceptic, admit "their reality." Of course I see that your "so called" is meant to annihilate any spiritualistic or other-worldish deductions from the "so called occult phenomena," but any proven occult phenomena—so called or not— would fit excellently well into *my* theoretic scheme of the universe. The grossest theorist of us all would gladly prop himself at times against a solid rock of empiric observation, knowledge.

By "occult phenomena," by the way, I do not mean the mere facts of hypnotism or telepathy; though, naturally, any sound inferences from more facts—the philosophy of them tending towards a proof of soul separable and enduring and powerful—would have the highest value. I am like those Hebrews that crave a sign; when I ask for bread most often I get a cod. That doesn't mean that I doubt my soul, its real existence and consequent survival. It means only that I would like to know something of the law of it, its action. I would like a foretaste of its quality, too—to enjoy it a little now so that I may be fitter to know it and play with it when it alone is all the me. And of course there is a certain gain of certainty by the mere handling of many proofs. I know much more truly that there were Greeks of B.C. 400 than that there were Ethiopians of B.C. 3000. I don't feel as if I had said quite what I wanted to bring out. It doesn't matter. Give me an occasional idea of your researches.

One can only guess at the "researches" Synge apparently told MacKenna he was doing. There is certainly no evidence beyond his correspondence with MacKenna that he had ever really been interested in the subject which took up so much of Yeats' interest. One is tempted to conclude that he was not the kind of man to take anything but the world of the senses very seriously, but many Dubliners of his day dabbled in occult studies, joined the Hermetic Society or the Theosophical Society, both founded by Charles Johnston, a schoolmate of Yeats; and not all of them were, like Yeats and AE, driven by temperament and inclination to such studies. The first historian of the Irish Literary Revival, Ernest Boyd, went so far as to describe the Dublin lodge of the Theosophical Society as a vital factor in the evolution of Anglo-Irish literature, which seems now to be an extravagant claim for an activity which brought together some young Dublin intellectuals who would have met each other anyway.[94] Yeats, of course, with his lifelong interest in the subject is a special case, but this is one side of his genius which seems to have had no influence on the literary movement he founded.

Synge was, as he wrote to MacKenna, "lonesome and uncanny" when he came back from Mayo. His brother Samuel, returned from China with a wife and baby, and his cousin Stewart Ross, and his son, were staying in the Synge house at Crosthwaite Park. He decided to take a room of his own at 15 Maxwell Road, Rathmines, and moved into it on October 10th. He was within a mile of his old home at Orwell Park, on a quiet road along which were rows of small red-brick houses and some empty lots. He was also within a fifteen-minute tram ride of the center of Dublin and the new theatre.

Preparations for the production of *The Well of the Saints* were under way, and Jack Yeats was to design the scenery for it. Yeats wrote from London:

Of course I do not know how my brother's designing will turn out. It won't make any difference to you, as if his design is not quite right, I shall get young [Robert] Gregory to work over it. He is enthusiastic about decorative scenery and Ricketts has told him that some great painter or other advised a favorite pupil to make scenery. I am nearly wild over the difficulties of getting a new tree-wing however. If I can get a morning in the British Museum Print Room over the Japanese prints, I may find out something.

I am delighted about your new play. That's the best thing that could have happened to us. I know that you will be an upholder of my musical theories 'ere long; they follow logically from certain principles which we have all accepted. One must have a complete aestheticism when one is dealing with a synthetic art like that of the stage.

Yeats, as is well known, was tone deaf and without any formal training in music. Whatever his musical theories were—they would have stemmed from his theory of chanted verse and from experiments of reading verse to the accompaniment of a psaltery—they had apparently not appealed to Synge, who had a great deal of musical training. The picture of Yeats consulting Japanese prints for a clue to guide his brother Jack in designing sets for *The Well of the Saints* strikes one, as it must have struck Synge, as a trifle eccentric. No two men could have differed more in their conception of theatre.

In the middle of December, Masefield wrote from Manchester offering Synge the chance to write occasional pieces and book reviews for *The Manchester Guardian*. Synge's first contribution, published on January 24th, was a passage from his Aran manuscript entitled "An Impression of Aran." This was followed three weeks later by an article on Wicklow which *The Gael* had rejected three years before, entitled "The Oppression of the Hills." The relationship with the *Guardian* continued until Synge's death. A few months after his first articles appeared the editor commissioned him and Jack Yeats to travel through the poverty-stricken parts of Galway and Mayo to do a series of illustrated articles. It was an ideal assignment. The twelve articles with Jack Yeats' illustrations appeared in the *Guardian* during June and July of 1905. Two years later C. P. Scott, the editor of the *Guardian*, asked him to do another series on "various 'types' of Irishmen, which need not be entirely imaginary but could be reinforced by personal touches and anecdote." Synge found the assignment attractive, asked Scott if Jack Yeats could work with him again as illustrator, but apparently never got to work on it because more than a year later Scott was still asking him not to give up the idea.

The Abbey Theatre was to open the 1904–1905 season at the end of December, and to celebrate the occasion Yeats published the fourth number of *Samhain*, the most ambitious issue yet. It contained over thirty pages of comment by Yeats, full texts of Lady Gregory's *The Rising of the Moon* and Synge's *In the Shadow of the Glen*, and drawings by J. B. Yeats, unsigned, of Synge and of Frank Fay in the costume of Cuchulain. To protect Synge's American copyright, an American lawyer named John Quinn published *In the Shadow of the Glen* simultaneously at his own expense in New York. J. B. Yeats' drawing of Synge was one of several portraits. The next spring Synge

sat to him for an oil, commissioned by Hugh Lane, which now hangs
in the Dublin Municipal Gallery. But the most striking, and certainly
the best known, impression of Synge is the pencil sketch entitled
"Synge at Rehearsal" which J. B. Yeats drew in 1907 showing Synge
huddled under his black cape, black Stetson on the back of his head,
sitting in the back of the Abbey Theatre listening to the players
rehearsing. Sara Allgood once said that for her this was the impression
of Synge most indelibly stamped on her memory.

The new theatre opened on December 27th with two new plays—
Yeats' *On Baile's Strand* and Lady Gregory's *Spreading the News*—
and two old ones—*Cathleen Ni Houlihan* and *In the Shadow of the
Glen*. Lady Gregory was ill and unable to attend the opening night,
and Miss Horniman was in London. The audience was large and
friendly, the new plays were well received, and Yeats made a curtain
speech to great applause. When Synge's mother read the account of
the opening in the newspapers of the next morning she was astounded
to learn that an Englishwoman had financed the establishment of a
theatre describing itself as an Irish Nationalist Theatre. "She must be
a little mad," was her comment.

Miss Horniman might well have felt uncomfortable about the attitude of people like Mrs. Synge, but her chief discomfiture came from
a different source. Before her theatre had even opened, Arthur Griffith
and others had taken issue with her decision to establish a minimum
admission price of one shilling for any performance in the new theatre,
whether it was given by the Irish National Theatre Society or any
other group which might lease the building. Miss Horniman's motive,
as it was made clear in the letter she wrote in April to the society
offering it a free theatre, was "to prevent cheap entertainments from
being given, which would lower the letting value of the Hall." This
letter was reproduced in the issue of *Samhain* published to coincide
with the theatre's opening in December, and it immediately drew
comments to the effect that no theatre could call itself a part of the
Nationalist movement if it did not offer at least some sixpenny seats
for the common people of Ireland. It should be conceded, especially
for readers accustomed to a commercial theatre where an admission
price is generally determined by what the public will bear, that
Griffith had a point. The Abbey Theatre may have been privately
owned and operated, but as Miss Horniman and Yeats clearly ad-

mitted, it was created for the use of a society committed to the Nationalist cause. One can see the effect of Miss Horniman's decision upon the theatre's potential audiences when one realizes that even today an admission price of two or three shillings is not uncommon in Dublin and the theatre is not a luxury reserved to people of means. But, as later events were to prove, Griffith's opposition to Miss Horniman and to the direction the theatre was taking had very little to do with admission prices. His real objection was that Yeats' insistence upon freedom for the dramatists to write as they saw fit would eventually deprive his movement of a valuable form of propaganda. In this his suspicions were sound.

The press notices of opening night were enthusiastic. Perhaps the most significant of all was written by Masefield for *The Manchester Guardian*. He praised the plays and complimented Miss Horniman on her vision and her generosity. Of the company he wrote, "With an art of gesture admirably disciplined and a strange delicacy of enunciation they perform the best drama of our time in the method of a lovely ritual. . . . Their art is unlike any to be seen in England. It is never common, it is never derivative. One thinks of it as a thing of beauty, as a part of life, as the only modern dramatic art springing from the life of a people."

Standing on the stage of the new theatre on opening night, speaking to an audience of six hundred people, Yeats might have felt that he was standing on the threshold of the most considerable achievement of his career. The dramatic movement in Ireland had been his doing more than any other's, and the new theatre was the tangible embodiment of his vision. He had conceived the idea as a patriotic undertaking, but he had not hesitated to alienate it from the environment which gave it its meaning when he felt that that environment threatened to stultify it. He had discovered both Lady Gregory and Synge and directed their undeveloped talents. If he had not discovered the Fays, they at least had discovered him. He was ruthless in getting his own way. He had eliminated Edward Martyn and George Moore as soon as the price of living with them had become too high. He had survived the defection of two of his best actors. A theatre had been created for his use, and it was beyond the influence of anyone except Miss Horniman. His plays and his players had created an audience and impressed English audiences and critics. Nobody now will deny that he had been right in proclaiming that the only real service an artist can render his country is in producing good art.

When his brother's designs for the stage set of *The Well of the Saints* did not materialize, Yeats turned to an Englishwoman named Pamela Coleman Smith. The finished script of the play had been in the company's hands since the previous July. But Willie Fay had some reservations about it, and it would appear that they were strong enough to discourage Yeats and Lady Gregory from offering it as part of the first program of the new theatre. Fay objected to the speech in the second act where Timmy says, "And she after going by with her head turned the way you'd see a priest going where there'd be a drunken man in the side ditch talking with a girl," on the grounds that no priest in Ireland would turn his head away from such a thing. Synge's explanation was:

What put the simile into my head was a scene I saw not long ago in Galway where I saw a young man behaving most indecently to a girl on the roadside while two priests sat near by on a seat looking out to sea and pretending not to see what was going on. The girl, of course, was perfectly well able to take care of herself and stoned the unfortunate man half a mile into Galway. The way the two priests sat stolidly looking out to sea with this screaming row going on at their elbows tickled my fancy and seemed to me rather typical of many attitudes of the Irish Church party.* Further, though it is true, I am sorry to say that priests do beat their parishioners—the man (in my play) may have been a tinker or tramp, sailor, cattle drover—God knows what—types with which no priest would dream of interfering. Tell Miss G.—† or whoever it may be—that what I write of Irish country life I know to be true, and I most emphatically will not change a syllable of it because A, B, or C may think they know better than I do. . . .‡ I am quite ready to avoid hurting people's feelings needlessly, but I will not falsify what I believe to be true for anybody.[95]

Years afterwards Fay wrote: "I realized that every character in the play from the Saint to Timmy the Smith was bad-tempered right

---

* That is, the Protestant, Church of Ireland.
† Miss Garvey, one of the actresses in the company.
‡ Synge nevertheless did change it—in the acting text only—to, "see a sainted body going where there'd be drunken people in the side ditch singing to themselves."

through the play, hence, as I pointed out to Synge, all this bad temper would inevitably infect the audience and make them bad-tempered too. I suggested that the Saint anyway might be made into a good-natured, easy-going man, or that Molly Byrne might be made a love-able young girl, but Synge would not budge. He said he wanted to write 'like a monochrome painting, all in shades of one color.' "96

Willie Fay's fears were groundless—at least as far as the audience's reaction was concerned. But before the company could find out what reception the new play was to incur, Arthur Griffith renewed his attack on *In the Shadow of the Glen*. "Mr. Synge's adaptation of the old Greek libel on womankind—'The Widow of Ephesus'—" he wrote in an editorial on January 7th, "has no more title to be called Irish than a Chinaman would have if he printed 'Patrick O'Brien' on his visiting card. . . . If *In the Shadow of the Glen* had been allowed to go unchallenged, there was no reason why its author should not have constructed fifty 'Irish' plays out of the *Decameron*, and the cry of 'Obscurantist' be raised by a literary man with a chorus against any who protested they were libels on the women of Ireland."

The charge that Synge was palming off on the ingenuous Irish a corrupt version of a story out of Petronius drew only one response from Synge—a letter which Griffith slyly neglected to print until Yeats forced him into acknowledging it. Synge wrote, "Sir, I beg to enclose the story of an unfaithful wife which was told to me by an old man on the middle island of Aran in 1898, and which I have since used in a modified form in *The Shadow of the Glen*. It differs essentially from any version of the story of the Widow of Ephesus with which I am acquainted. As you will see, it was told to me in the first person, as not infrequently happens in folktales of this class."

Synge's letter was factually too chaste to be vulnerable and Griffith's real target was Yeats, who rose to the challenge. In a letter to the editor, which Griffith published on January 28th, Yeats pointed out that the story might well have originated in a place remote from Ireland in time and space but that the source of Synge's play was a folk tale told by an Aran islander—which Synge was shortly to publish in book form—and that if, like all folk tales, it had been altered to fit the native environment the alterations had been made not by Synge but by the Irish *shanachie** who had first told it:

* Storyteller.

You yourself once suggested that it was imported by the hedge school-masters. I do not, myself, see any evidence to prove what country it first arose in, or whether it may not have had an independent origin in half-a-dozen countries. The version of the Widow of Ephesus that I know differs from Mr. Synge's plot, and also from the Irish folk-story on which he has founded his play. I would be very much obliged if you would give me the reference to the story referred to by you. . . . There is certainly nothing in the account that travellers give of medieval Ireland or in Old Irish or Middle Irish literature to show that Ireland had a different sexual morality from the rest of Europe. And I can remember several Irish poems and stories in which the husband feigns death for precisely the reason that the husband does in Mr. Synge's play. . . .

Griffith ignored Yeats' demand for a specific reference and re-peated the charge that the story of Synge's play

. . . is a stock one in the *Quartier Latin*, and [one] which he could have purchased in the Palais Royal. . . . It is a story invented by the wits of decadent Greece and introduced, with amendments, into Latin literature by the most infamous of Roman writers, Petronius Arbiter, the pander of Nero. . . . Mr. Synge's Nora Burke is not an Irish Nora Burke, his play is not a work of genius—Irish or otherwise—it is a foul echo from degenerate Greece. . . . Mr. Yeats never heard an Irish tramp in Wicklow or elsewhere address a peasant-woman as "lady of the house," nor did he, Mr. Synge or any other human being, ever meet in Ireland a peasant-woman of the type of Nora Burke, a woman void of all conception of morality, decency and religion. She is a Greek, a Greek of Greece's most debased period, and to dress her in an Irish costume and call her Irish is not only not art, but it is an insult to the women of Ireland.

Yeats replied a week later, repeating his request for specific refer-ences. It was an effective counterattack because it succeeded, for one thing, in forcing Griffith into shifting his attack onto Yeats himself. Yeats, at any rate, was not going to allow him to continue repeating it. He wrote to John Quinn: "the story that Synge had taken a plot from Petronius and pretended that it was Irish was calculated to do a deal of mischief."[97] In his letter to Griffith, Yeats wrote:

You have wasted some of my time. There is no such story in Petronius, and I must again ask you for your reference. He does indeed tell the well-known story of the Ephesian widow. You will find a rather full paraphrase of his version in chapter five of Jeremy Taylor's *Holy Living*. It is an admirable fable . . . but it is not Mr. Synge's story nor the story of your paragraph. . . . Ireland may, I think, claim all the glory of Mr. Synge's not less admirable tale. The only parallels I can remember at this moment to the husband who pretends to be dead that he may catch his wife and his wife's lover are Irish parallels. One is in a ballad at the end of *The Love Songs of Connacht*. . . . In everything but the end of the play Mr. Synge has followed very closely the Aran story, which he has, I believe, sent to you; but it is precisely the end of the play that puts him at once among the men of genius. For this there is no parallel in any story that I know of. The sitting down together of the husband and the lover is certainly "the perfection of ironic humour."

Griffith's rejoinder was a sneer at Yeats for his ignorance of Petronius and his opinions about Irish sexual morality—"we fear his imagination has carried him away in this matter as it did in America when he told his audiences the Castle* lived in fear of his theatre and sent forty baton-bearing myrmidons down to its each performance." Griffith then acknowledged receiving Synge's letter but printed neither it nor Pat Dirane's story which it contained. "Mr. Synge forwards us a tale he states he took down in Aran, which is essentially different to the play he insolently calls 'In a Wicklow Glen.' In the Aran story the wife appears as a callous woman—in Mr. Synge's play the wife is a strumpet."

Yeats then demanded the publication of Synge's letter. "I don't see how we can go on with the controversy about the origin of [In] *The Shadow of the Glen* until you have printed Mr. Synge's letter to you, with its enclosure giving the Irish original, and giving me a more definite reference than 'The Palais Royal'!" Yeats then turned to the attack on himself and the charge that he had boasted in America that the English lived in fear of his theatre. "This is as true as the statement made to me by an American journalist that you were paid by the British Government to abuse the Irish party. I described in many of my American lectures that attack made upon *The Countess Cathleen* by Mr. F. H. O'Donnell and *The Nation* newspaper. . . . I mentioned neither Dublin Castle nor politics of any kind."

* Dublin Castle, from which the English administered the government of Ireland.

The February 11th number of *The United Irishman* contained Yeats' letter and Synge's—though not Pat Dirane's tale—with Griffith's explanation that Yeats' reference to it was "the first intimation we had that Mr. Synge intended his letter for publication, and not for our personal enlightenment. Since we have erred, we subjoin it." With this the skirmish was over, and Griffith's hostility to Synge's first play was overshadowed by the much more impressive demonstrations over *The Playboy* two years later. Few Dubliners outside the small circle of extreme nationalists read *The United Irishman*, but it was from this quarter that opposition to Synge and to the theatre was to come later. Yeats realized that Griffith's influence, however small it might be in the community at large, was likely to cause as he said "a deal of mischief" if he were allowed to alienate Nationalist sympathy from Synge's work.

The second series of performances in the Abbey Theatre opened on Saturday, February 4th, 1905, with *The Well of the Saints*. A. H. Bullen, who had undertaken the publication of the play and proposed to issue it in December with an introduction by Yeats, had provided a small number of copies, without the introduction, for sale in the theatre. Yeats' epistolary war with Griffith was in progress, and for some people, at least, Synge's new play was an opportunity to take sides in the argument.

Press reaction to *The Well of the Saints* was more than cool, and since most of the Irish critics attacked it on the grounds of its "un-Irishness" one might conclude that if Griffith had not actually set the tune he had at least been the first to play it. The reviewer for *The Freeman's Journal* raised the question of whether a play was to be called Irish because it reflected the facts of Irish life, as they were commonly held to be, or merely because it was written in Ireland, performed on an Irish stage and used dialogue and characters described as Irish. "This is the third of Mr. Synge's contributions to the repertoire of the Irish National Theatre, and his point of view as a dramatist is pretty clearly defined. The point of view is not that of a writer in sympathetic touch with the people from whom he purports to draw his characters." The *Evening Herald* found the play unsatisfactory on the same grounds: the characters were all repulsive and therefore caricatures of Irish people. Arthur Griffith paused long

Photograph taken by Synge on a glass plate in Aran.
The figures have never been identified.

enough in his fight with Yeats to point out that the characters were not Irish and that the language they used was pure Whitechapel.

Implicit in these attitudes was the assumption that repulsive characters could not be Irish. Dedicated men and women believed not that they had a better understanding of Irish life than Synge but that he ought not to be allowed to paint grimaces on the face of a heroic and long-suffering Ireland. This was the work of the enemy. Yeats wrote to John Quinn the week after *The Well of the Saints* had closed: "We will have a hard fight in Ireland before we get the right for every man to see the world in his own way admitted. Synge is invaluable to us because he has that kind of intense narrow personality which necessarily raises the whole issue. It will be very curious to notice the effect of his new play. He will start next time with many enemies but with many admirers. It will be a fight like that over the first realistic plays of Ibsen."[98]

The Well of the Saints had, as Yeats said, its admirers. In a letter to the editor of *The Irish Times* on February 13th George Moore hailed it as an important event. "I would call attention to the abundance and the beauty of the dialogue, to the fact that one listens to it as one listens to music, charmed by the inevitableness of the words and the ease with which phrase is linked into phrase. At every moment the dialogue seems to lose itself, but it finds its way out. Mr. Synge has discovered great literature in barbarous idiom as gold is discovered in quartz, and to do such a thing is surely a rare literary achievement."

Moore's generous eulogy was particularly welcome in view of the cool reception the play was getting, but it puzzled both Yeats and Synge. Yeats wrote to Quinn: "I wonder what has converted him, for he abused the play when he saw an act of it in rehearsal some months ago. . . . I imagine that his dislike of our work was artificial and that he has gradually come to feel that he would make himself absurd. He is now unbounded in his enthusiasm, both in public and private, which makes Miss Horniman perfectly furious. She threatens us with all kinds of pains and penalties should we accept any help from him. That quarrel is just now the only little annoyance in a very promising state of things."[99]

The Well of the Saints has never been a popular play. Willie Fay was right about the unrelieved bad humour. More than that, it was Synge's first attempt at a full-length play and he had difficulty in keeping his lines from building up into lengthy speeches which the actors found difficult to manage. "They took a cruel lot of practice," Fay wrote, "before we could get them spoken at a reasonably good pace and without at the same time losing the lovely lilt of his idiom."[100] When the play was revived at the Abbey Theatre two years later, Synge rewrote the third act.

Except for the short, factual letter to Arthur Griffith Synge had nothing to say about either of his two unpopular plays. Living alone in Maxwell Road he was not under pressure to talk or avoid talking about the subject with his mother. But on February 15th he suddenly moved back to Crosthwaite Park. Now that his plays were being discussed in the newspapers his mother had begun to accept the fact of his being a professional playwright, whatever that might imply. She remarked to the Stephenses that if the hero of his latest play— which she had not read—could upset holy water from a saint's hands her son's associations with Nationalists had at least not brought him under the thumb of Rome. She had that much to be thankful for.

Eleven

THE TINKER'S WEDDING. EUROPEAN RECOGNITION.
CONNEMARA WITH JACK YEATS. COUNTY KERRY.
DIRECTOR OF THE ABBEY THEATRE. ACTORS'
SECESSION. MOLLY ALLGOOD

One time he and his woman went up to a priest in the hills and asked him would he wed them for half a sovereign, I think it was. The priest said it was a poor price, but he'd wed them surely if they'd make him a tin can along with it. "I will, faith," said the tinker, "and I'll come back when it's done." They went off then, and in three weeks they came back, and they asked the priest a second time would he wed them. "Have you the tin can?" said the priest. "We have not," said the tinker; "we had it made at the fall of night, but the ass gave it a kick this morning the way it isn't fit for you at all." "Go on now," says the priest. " It's a pair of rogues and schemers you are, and I won't wed you at all."

Elkin Mathews was planning to publish *Riders to the Sea* and *In the Shadow of the Glen* in May, 1905, and when he inquired about a third play Synge had shown him in the spring of 1904, Synge replied, "I would rather have the two plays you have brought out now together, and hold over the third, as a character in *The Tinker's Wedding* is likely to displease a good many of our Dublin friends, and would perhaps hinder the sale of the book in Ireland." The caution was well taken. If so mild a play as *The Well of the Saints* had drawn a hostile reaction, the publication of *The Tinker's Wedding*, with its central incident of a priest tossed into a sack, would certainly have precipitated demonstrations in the theatre at the next appearance of a Synge play. He had written *The Tinker's Wedding* in the summer of 1902 and subsequently expanded it from one act to two. But he continued rewriting it until December of 1907 and it was eventually published in January, 1908.

In writing a preface for it he apologized to the Irish clergy. "I do not think these country clergy, who have so much humour, and so much heroism when they face typhus or dangerous seas for the comfort of their people on the coasts of the west, will mind being laughed at for half an hour without malice, as the clergy in every Roman Catholic country were laughed at through the ages that had real religion." But apparently feeling that the apology really only begged the question, he crossed it out. Nevertheless the version of the play which he finally submitted for publication reflects quite clearly his suspicions that he had gone too far, even for the printed page. The earlier drafts have a violence which makes the published text look quite innocent. For example, Sarah Casey's speech, "Let you not be destroying us with your talk when I've as good a right to a decent marriage as any speckled female does be sleeping in the black hovels above would choke a mule," reads in an earlier version, "as good a right to a decent marriage as any speckled female bastard does be sleeping in the black hovels above would choke a rat."

The Tinker's Wedding, it must be emphasized, is not a play about the common people of Ireland. It is about tinkers, or vagrants as Synge called them, and one need only turn to the description of tinkers he had seen in Wicklow to realize that his play had come out of contemporary Irish life. The central incident has a parallel in Douglas Hyde's *Religious Songs of Connacht*:

> Sure if you were dead to-morrow morning
> And I were to bring you to a priest tied up in a bag
> He would not read a mass for you without hand-money.[101]

The source of Synge's play is in two of his Wicklow pieces—"The Vagrants of Wicklow" and "At a Wicklow Fair." In the first, a man "on the side of a mountain to the east of Aughavanna" discourses on the marriage customs of the tinkers when one of those gallous lads "would swap the woman he had with one from another man, with as much talk as if you'd be selling a cow." In the second, a herder in

Aughrim tells about a tinker and his woman who "went up to a priest in the hills and asked him would they wed them for half a sovereign, I think it was. The priest said it was a poor price, but he'd wed them surely if they'd make him a tin can along with it." When they came back three weeks later, the priest asked them if they had the can. " 'We have not,' said the tinker. 'We had it made at the fall of night, but the ass gave it a kick this morning the way it isn't fit for you at all.' 'Go on now,' says the priest. 'It's a pair of rogues and schemers you are, and I won't wed you at all.' They went off then, and they were never married to this day."

The priest, with his "long step on him and a trumpeting voice," sounds like an Irish country priest even if the portrait is not flattering. He is not without humanity. The life of the tinker "walking the world and hearing a power of queer things" has the same appeal for him that it had for Synge. "If it's starving you are itself," he tells the tinkers with a touch of envy, "I'm thinking it's well for the like of you that do be drinking when there's drouth on you, and lying down to sleep when your legs are stiff. (He sighs gloomily.) What would you do if it was the like of myself you were, saying Mass with your mouth dry, and running east and west for a sick call maybe, and hearing the rural people again and they saying their sins?"

Synge had sent MacKenna a typescript copy of *The Well of the Saints*. MacKenna, recently returned to London from Russia where he had been sent as correspondent of the New York *World*, replied on March 25th with enthusiastic praise:

I think then, in one foolish word, that you have written a beautiful thing beautifully and I admire you. I always did bet on you, you know. I always said, and say now with more conviction even than before, that (if you only have your health and get mere number of works on your side) you will be one of the two or three of your generation. I find your dialect by the way almost wholly admirable. Perhaps there is a slight abuse of that "itself" and I baulked at one word—which?—that I thought inappropriate to a peasant even so imaginative and deep-thinking a lustful brooder as blind Martin. I imagine your play will be better understood in France than in these dull lands. . . . Doul is a splendid name. . . .

In April, Hugh Lane, who was making a collection of modern Irish portraits for the proposed Dublin municipal gallery, commissioned

J. B. Yeats—the poet's father—to paint a number of Irish people, and Synge began sitting for the portrait which now hangs in Dublin and which W. B. Yeats described in a notable poem:

> And here's John Synge himself, that rooted man,
> "Forgetting human words," a grave deep face.

After the hostility aroused by *The Well of the Saints* in February, the Abbey Theatre quickly righted itself with successful productions of Lady Gregory's *Kincora*, a play about Brian Boru, in March; William Boyle's *The Building Fund* in April, and Padraic Colum's second play, *The Land*, in June. The success of Boyle's play was particularly fortunate because neither Lady Gregory nor Yeats felt that the theatre could go on without the work of new dramatists, and they had had reservations about Boyle's value.

Synge meanwhile discovered that his work was attracting attention outside Dublin and London, the only two cities which had seen it. In May he began a correspondence with a German named Max Meyerfeld, who asked for permission to translate *The Well of the Saints* for performance on the German stage. After asking Yeats' advice Synge agreed, and the play was performed at the Deutsches Theatre in Berlin on January 12, 1906, under the title *Der Heilige Brunnen*. Meyerfeld, who later published Synge's correspondence with him,[102] wrote that Synge's play, which "had no success at all," had to be withdrawn after some six or seven performances, but that he was able to send the author a small sum. Almost at the same time Synge received a proposal from a Bohemian named Pan Karel Musek to translate *In the Shadow of the Glen* into Bohemian. The play was performed at the Inchover Theatre, Prague, in February, 1906. Musek then went on to translate *Riders to the Sea* but was unable to interest the manager of the theatre in producing it. However unimpressive both of these ventures may have been, the effect of Synge's recognition in foreign countries at the very moment when the validity of his work was being questioned in his own country was not without its ironic value. Yeats wrote to John Quinn, "Synge's foreign success is worth more to us than would be the like success of any other of our people, for he has been the occasion of all the attacks upon us. I said in a speech some time ago that he would have a European reputation in five years, but his enemies have mocked the prophecy."[103]

Early in May of 1905 Robert Synge, who seems to have spent most of his life while in Ireland with a fishing rod in his hands, suggested a week's fishing in Donegal. He was a perfect companion because he never seemed to be much concerned about his brother's literary activities or political attitudes. When they were together they cycled along the country roads, not saying much to each other. Robert's diary for the trip, which lasted from May 4th to 11th and took them to a small hotel at Milford on the southernmost point of Mulroy Bay in Donegal, contains such entries as, "Rode with John to Lough Keel. Fished with Pat McGilligan. I got 5, John hooked a good one, but it got off."

A few days after Synge returned to Crosthwaite Park the offer came from Scott of the *Guardian* to do the series of articles on those impoverished areas of the west of Ireland, stretching approximately from the northeast corner of Donegal to the town of Tralee in Kerry, known as the Congested Districts. The land itself in the Congested Districts was far from fertile, and the difficulty was compounded by the fact that each man's holding was so small and uneconomical that it could support neither man nor beast. A Congested Districts Board, made up of distinguished Irishmen, had been set up by the Land Purchase Act of 1891 and empowered to enlarge small holdings by breaking up big estates, to move people out of one area to another where their chances would be improved, to establish or improve native industries and to promote any activity which could better the lot of the starving peasantry.

It was a formidable assignment, and Synge wrote immediately to the parliamentary representative of the district to get the information he needed before starting out on June 3rd. The trip lasted exactly a month and took him and Jack Yeats from Spiddal, an Irish-speaking town eleven miles from Galway city on the north shore of Galway Bay, through poverty-stricken hamlets to Gorumna Island at the head of the bay. Their road ran through barren fields black with turf mould. Occasionally they passed listless groups of men and women working on relief projects.

After several days on Gorumna, they took a ferry to Dinish Island, spent a day in the little village of Trewbawn, where people were collecting kelp, sailed from Gorumna in a hooker to Carna, a village at the end of a long peninsula, and then decided to head for a different part of the Congested Districts in north Mayo. From Ballina in Mayo they took the long car that used to start at four o'clock in the morning and rode it for forty miles over a rough road, stopping at intervals for a change of horses, to the town of Belmullet. It was a six-and-a-half-hour ride.

As he and Jack Yeats travelled through the Mullet he thought the poverty greater than any he had seen in the country west of Spiddal. The area around Erris, he wrote, was "the poorest in the whole of Ireland." But, he was able to note, the life of the people was not without its color and its integrity. "The impression one gets of the whole life is not a gloomy one," he wrote in one of his articles. "Last night was St. John's Eve, and bonfires—a relic of Druidical rites—were lighted all over the country, the largest of all being placed in the town square of Belmullet, where a crowd of small boys shrieked and cheered and threw up firebrands for hours together." In describing the same incident Jack Yeats remembered the "flaming sods of turf soaked in parrafine, hurled to the sky and caught and skied again and burning snakes of hayropes." Synge remembered it when he wrote the lines in which Christy Mahon described his drunken father "throwing clods against the visage of the stars."

The trip came to an end when they took the long car back to Ballina and stopped in the town of Swinford in East Mayo where Synge wrote two articles, "The Village Shop" and "The Small Town." Back at Crosthwaite Park on July 3rd he wrote the last of the series entitled "Possible Remedies." If it struck his readers as being pessimistic, with its reflections on the deep-seated prejudices of tradition-bound peasants and the contempt which the official workers felt for them, one should realize the difficulty of the task imposed on the Congested Districts Board. The attitudes deeply ingrained in a downtrodden people after generations of misrule and hardship could not be easily modified by trying to shuffle people from one small piece of unfertile soil to a slightly larger one. Frank Hugh O'Donnell once remarked, "The western peasantry will not move, and they cannot be moved, and there is nowhere to move them to."

Scott was enthusiastic about the articles. "You have done capitally for us, and with Mr. Yeats have helped to bring home to people here the life of those remote districts as it can hardly have been done before." A Dublin publisher named Whaley wanted to reprint the articles in book form, but Synge refused, feeling perhaps that they were not finished enough. W. B. Yeats apparently either felt the same way about them or knew of Synge's reservations because he refused to allow them to be included in the posthumous edition of Synge's works. When George Roberts, manager of Maunsel and Company, insisted on their being included and was supported by Synge's brother Edward, who found a note in Synge's hand among his papers apparently sanctioning it, Yeats withdrew his cooperation and published separately the introduction he had written for the edition under the title *Synge and the Ireland of His Time*.

Synge's attitude to the articles and to the assignment itself is indicated in a letter he wrote to MacKenna on July 13th:

I've just come home from the *Guardian* business. Jack Yeats and myself had a great time and I sent off three articles a week for four weeks running. Would you believe that? But he, being a wiser man than I, made a better bargain, and though I had much the heavier job the dirty skunks paid him more than they paid me, and that's a thorn in my dignity! I got £25.4.0 which is more than I've ever had yet and still I'm swearing and damning. However we had a wonderful journey, and as we had a purse to pull on we pushed into out-of-the-way corners in Mayo and Galway that were more strange and marvellous than anything I've dreamed of. Unluckily my commission was to write on the "distress" so I couldn't do anything like what I would have wished to do as an interpretation of the whole life. Besides, of course we had not time in a month's trip to get to the bottom of things anywhere. As soon as I recover from this cold affair I'm off again to spend my £25.4.0 on the same ground.

There are sides of all that western life, the groggy-patriot-publican-general-shopman who is married to the priest's half-sister and is second cousin once removed of the dispensary doctor, that are horrible and awful. This is the type that is running the present United Irish League anti-grazing campaign while they're swindling the people themselves in a dozen ways and then buying out their holdings and packing off whole families to America.

The subject is too big to go into here, but at best it's beastly. All that side of the matter of course I left untouched in my stuff. I sometimes wish to God I hadn't a soul and then I could give myself up to putting those lads on the stage. God, wouldn't they hop! In a way it is heart-rending, in one place the people are starving but wonderfully attractive and charming, and in another place when things are going well one has a rampant double-chinned vulgarity I haven't seen the like of.

Synge may have intended to spend his £25 in Connemara or may have merely been referring to the west of Ireland. At any rate he had been back in Dublin for just a month when he set off for Kerry, going this time not to Mountain Stage on the southern peninsula but to Ballyferriter on the northern peninsula where he stayed with a family named Long who took in visitors for three shillings sixpence a day. Ballyferriter is the tiny village which produced Kerry's famous Gaelic poet Pierce Ferriter, who was hanged by the English in Killarney in 1653 and whose subsequent fame is more legendary than real. From Ballyferriter Synge could walk to Smerwick on the north shore, where Lord Grey and Sir Walter Raleigh massacred a surrendered garrison of six hundred Spaniards and Irishmen in 1805 and where Brendan the Navigator is supposed to have started on his famous voyage. On the south shore, also within walking distance, near the town of Dingle, is Ventry Harbor, the scene of the quasi-historical battle described in an ancient Irish text between the Fianna of Ireland, under the fabulous Finn MacCumhaill, and Daire Donn, King of the World. He also could walk along the shore road from Ventry to the village of Dunquin on the tip of the peninsula, where the remains of an early Christian settlement of *clocháns* and pre-Christian megalithic remains testify to an impressive historic past. Off the tip of the peninsula are the Blasket Islands, and the stretch of water between them and the mainland marks the spot where four ships of the Spanish Armada took refuge and where two of them sank with all hands in sight of the shore.

The Great Blasket, Synge noted, was almost four miles long and one mile wide. He found only twenty-five families numbering 132 people living there and was told that since most of them had not paid their "rates" there were only two registered voters. For the sixteen days he was on the island he stayed in the house of the "King," whose hereditary title was no more shrouded in the mist of a forgotten past than some other native titles. The "King" is never identified in any of Synge's notes, but the great Celticist Robin Flower who first came to the Blaskets in 1910, five years after Synge, and who stayed in the cottage of the "King," identifies him as Pádraig O'Catháin. Flower's book about the Great Blasket, *The Western Island*, is the account of a man to whom it represented a fragment of the Gaelic past. He describes the prehistoric and early Christian remains on the mainland, listens to the legend of Pierce Ferriter and marvels at the persistence of some of the island's memories. But Synge's observations were those of an artist, not a historian. What interested him was a travelling circus which pitched its tent outside Dingle, or islanders dancing in a whirl of dust on the dirt floor of the cottage he stayed in. He was interested in the living present—his hostess, for example, "a young married woman of about twenty, who manages the house" and who is "a small, beautifully-formed woman, with brown hair and eyes" and "delicate feet and ankles." She was to be the prototype of Pegeen Mike in *The Playboy*, and he wrote a poem about her:

> You've plucked a curlew, drawn a hen,
> Washed the shirts of seven men,
> You've stuffed my pillow, stretched the sheet,
> And filled the pan to wash your feet,
> You've couped the pullets,* wound the clock,
> And rinsed the young men's drinking crock;
> And now we'll dance to jigs and reels,
> Nailed boots chasing girls' naked heels,
> Until your father'll start to snore,
> And Jude, now you're married, will stretch on the floor.

No one would ever describe Synge's narrative accounts of Kerry, Aran or Wicklow as guidebooks. They describe only the life of the people and their immediate relationship to the world around them. From "a long talk with a man who was sitting on the ditch waiting till it was time for Mass" he could walk off into the bog "with a smooth mountain on one side and the sea on the other, and Brandon in front of me, partly covered with clouds. As far as I could see there were little groups of people on their way to the chapel in Ballyferriter, the men in homespun and the women wearing blue cloaks, or, more often, black shawls twisted over their heads. This procession along

* Closed them up for the night in the lower compartment of the dresser.

the olive bogs, between the mountains and the sea, on this grey day of autumn, seemed to wring me with the pang of emotion one meets everywhere in Ireland—an emotion that is partly local and patriotic, and partly a share of the desolation that is mixed everywhere with the supreme beauty of the world." It was the point of view of the poet, for whom the world exists not for its own beauty but because it can wring, as he says, the pang of emotion and induce the vision which precedes poetic creation.

Synge returned to Ballyferriter for a few days before going to Mountain Stage for the final two weeks of his visit to Kerry. The Harrises were delighted to see him, and he felt that he was coming back among old friends. Both Denis and Philly Harris were full of stories and news of local happenings during the past year, and Synge jotted in his notebooks the "tall tales" and bits of gossip that struck his fancy.

"There is a glen there," he said, "called Gleanne nGall, where the people that were wrong in their heads in the old times used to go. Up there in the rocks there is a kind of a green stuff growing in the running waters that they would be eating till they would die off after a while. At one time the men who were working [there] used to see a boy back behind looking at them. So they thought maybe he was famishing and they left a little piece of bread after them when they came down."

"There was a woman down in a river washing or something and she never felt anything till a ram—a ram that was well known to her—came behind and had her tumbled down in the gullet. Then the ram was passing back and forward keeping a watch on her ever and always so that she was in dread she'd be the whole night in it if no one came to free her out of it. Then she saw that the ram was putting his foremost feet over the edge striving to get at her. In the course of a piece she got hold of one leg and then of another. And then what did she do but get on his back. He had wool a yard long and she got a great hold of it, and there wasn't a mule or a donkey in the country she wouldn't ride. So away with them up Barna. They passed over the tip and she was shrieking murder till the miller heard her and was before her in the road. Then he tumbled the ram and took her in."

He jotted in his notebook an "Idea for a Play," suggestive of *The Playboy*: "Island with population of wreckers, smugglers, poteen-makers *etc.* are startled by the arrival of a stranger and reform for dread of him. He is an escaped criminal and wants them to help him over to America, but he thinks that they are so virtuous he is afraid to confess his deeds for fear they should hand him over to the law that they are so apparently in awe of. At last all comes out and he is got off safely."

While Synge was in Kerry the Irish National Theatre Society was facing a crisis, this time from within. Miss Horniman's generous offer to guarantee salaries for the company up to £400 had brought to a head the problem of whether the society should continue to exist as an organization of amateurs. At the same time the method of deciding on plays to be produced, as well as authority in other matters, resting as it did upon the votes of the entire group of writers and actors, had become unwieldy and would prove to be even more impractical if the actors were to give up their jobs and become professionals. AE had suggested a revision of the constitution which would limit the liability of the society and make it, in effect, a corporation. W. G. Fay would become manager, and both he and the actors, who would now be salaried, would take their orders from a board of directors composed of Yeats, Lady Gregory and Synge. The reorganized society itself would be composed of only nine people. A meeting was scheduled for September 22nd to vote on the plan of reorganization. Yeats was pleased about the prospects. He wrote to John Quinn, "If all goes well, Synge and Lady Gregory and I will have everything in our hands; indeed, the only practical limitation to our authority will be caused by the necessity of some sort of a permanent business committee in Dublin."[104]

Meanwhile the weaknesses implicit in the old system of selecting plays were threatening a crisis over William Boyle's new play *The Eloquent Dempsey*. Yeats wrote to Synge from Coole on August 15th that both he and Lady Gregory thought it "impossibly vulgar" and that Padraic Colum should be sent to London to help Boyle revise it. But it was necessary that Synge vote with them. "I take a very serious view of the matter indeed, partly because I am not at all sure of the effect of a play of this kind on Miss Horniman who has spent £4,000 on us already. The only condition she makes is that we shall keep up the standard. I don't mind going against her where I know we are right, but if we produce this our position will be perfectly indefensible. When the revision of the constitution is through, those of us who know will be in authority."

The Fays had apprehensions about the projected organization. Frank wrote to Synge in Kerry: "I am glad that you will be here for the meeting. My brother is greatly disgusted at a rule which gives the final decision (in the case of a dispute between the stage manager and author, as to how a scene is to be acted) to a member of the Business Committee." But they were at one with Yeats about the players becoming professionals. The actors "must get it into their heads that this is going to be our life's work!"

Synge stopped at Coole for a few days before continuing on to Dublin, because Yeats had written to him again from Coole on September 9th:

If we get things through in the form in which Russell proposes them at present, I think we will have [a] quiet and workmanlike Society. To get them through it may be necessary for you and I and Lady Gregory and the Fays to stand together, having come to a previous agreement. Lady Gregory suggests you should if possible come here either Saturday next or Monday to talk things over, and you and I could go on to Dublin together. She will not be able to come. I hope you will be able to do this. Order in the Society is as essential to you as to me.

Bring if you can, or have sent to me, the MS of *The Tinkers*. I want to see if it would do for *Samhain*, if you don't object, and also to see whether we can discuss it for our winter session. We are rather hard up for new short pieces, and you have such a bad reputation now it can hardly do any harm. But we may find it too dangerous for the Theatre at present. Also bring the Satire on your enemies, and indeed anything you have.

At the meeting, which Lady Gregory could not attend, Yeats, Synge and the Fays held out for an absolute majority for the three directors. Fred Ryan, AE and Synge were then authorized to draw up rules for the new society to be voted on by the entire group. "The directors will be absolutely supreme in everything," Yeats wrote to Lady Gregory. "I think we will carry the thing through, but it was very doubtful last Saturday when we did not yet know how far Russell would go in his support of us."[105] A few days later the society became known as the Irish National Theatre Society, Limited, and Yeats, Lady Gregory and Synge were in control.

Synge and Yeats revised Boyle's play, since apparently their new authority made it unnecessary to send Colum to London as Yeats had suggested. "We have finished the first act and have crossed out quantities," Yeats wrote to Lady Gregory.[106] They also sat down with Willie Fay to consider "the tinker play with a view to performance and publication in *Samhain* but decided that it would be dangerous at present."[107] It was a discreet decision, now that the sole responsibility would have been the directors'. Another row over an unpopular play would only have increased the uncertainty which some of the members felt about relinquishing their votes in the selection of plays. There was already enough resentment over the new arrangement. Within a few months the second secession of actors took place, this one much more disastrous than the first since it included Maire Walker, probably the company's finest actress, and six others.

The explosion occurred when the company returned from a tour during the last ten days of November to Oxford, Cambridge and London. Critical reception had been generous and the receipts were large, but as soon as they returned to Dublin the actors who were most active in the Gaelic League and whose sympathies for the political movement were acute had decided that Yeats was taking the theatre completely away from the direction it had started out in. It is difficult today to visualize young actors with the critical plaudits of the London critics ringing in their ears being so willing to sacrifice their careers to the political movement. But that is exactly how a large number of them felt, and one can only assume that their attitude was coloured by their unawareness of what the future held for them as players.

In her autobiography, written fifty years later, Maire Walker recalled: "Although for most of us who took the course of secession, the action meant the finish of any progress we might have been making individually towards international distinction as Irish players —in my own case it virtually meant the end of a career on the stage which might or might not have taken me away from Dublin altogether in the years that followed—I doubt if many of us had any regrets at the time."[108]

Meanwhile the little company of talented amateurs just turned professional was decimated. Only the Fays, Sara Allgood and Arthur Sinclair remained. Willie Fay had to put together a new company, and he wrote to Yeats early in December that he could get two men for eighteen shillings a week. "They will of course be raw but anyone we get will be that. . . . I am glad in a way that we have at last seen the end of the emigrants and know what we have to do. I have Molly Allgood playing Cathleen in *Riders to the Sea* and she's not at all bad." Molly Allgood, who had had a walk-on part in *The Well of the Saints*, was then nineteen years old and was the younger sister of Sara Allgood. Her stage name was Maire O'Neill. She was to be Synge's last love.

From this point on Synge, who was the only one of the three directors to make his home in Dublin, was to play a more active role in the management of the theatre—Yeats actually suggested that he be made managing director. The first problem he faced was brought on when the seceders—who were to form their own company—announced that they were planning to produce Padraic Colum's *The Land*. Colum was torn by conflicting loyalties. As a member of Fay's original company before he had ever met Yeats, Lady Gregory or Synge, he had known Maire Walker and her brother Frank. He was active in the Gaelic League. Yeats felt that he should decide which side he was on, and wrote to Synge from London on January 6, 1906:

I have had a wire from Fay. "Enemy rehearsing *Land*. Author present. Letter tonight, Fay." I am delighted. This is far better than a vague feeling of irritation. Everything they do would only reveal the superiority of our work. *The Land* without the two Fays will be a miserable thing. If you see Colum be firm with him. He is with them now for all his works, and if he comes back to us he comes back with all his work. They will either collapse after a performance or two, or they will become more and more crudely propagandist, playing up to that element of the country.

Colum wrote to Yeats imploring him to reunite the company, but Lady Gregory was bitter over Colum's defection and maliciously argued, in a letter to Willie Fay, that his peace offering had come after he had seen his play in rehearsal and that he was merely attempting to get a better cast for it. To Colum himself she wrote a more diplomatic note, urging him to change his mind:

You may spare a few hours before making a decision that will I think affect your work and your life. I want you to sit down and read Mr. Yeats' notes in the two last numbers of *Samhain* and to ask yourself if the work he is doing is best worth helping or hindering. Remember, he has been for eight years working with his whole heart for the creation, the furtherance, the perfecting, of what he believes will be a great dramatic movement in Ireland. I am proud to think I have helped him all through, but we have lost many helpers on the way. Mr. Lecky who had served us well in getting the law passed that made all these dramatic experiments possible, publicly repudiated us because of Mr. Yeats' letter on the Queen's visit. Edward Martyn withdrew when we had to refuse the *Tale of a Town* which did not, as we thought, come up to the required standard. George Moore from a friend became an enemy. Then . . . others were lost for different reasons—Kelly and Digges and Miss Quinn and Mrs. MacBride, all of whom had been helpful in their time.* Now others are dropping off.

It is always sad to lose fellow workers, but the work must go on all the same. "No man putting his hand to the plough and looking back is fit for the Kingdom of God." He is going on with it. I am going on with it as long as life and strength are left to me. You who being younger ought to take some of the burden off our shoulders will not I think intentionally make it heavier.

There are two special reasons why you will not think it right to even consent to this performance of *The Land*. One is that your doing so at this moment would be looked upon as a corroboration of the most unjust and unworthy insinuations made in some papers that it had been intentionally given the worst place in the London program. The other is you cannot have forgotten the most generous and wholehearted help Mr. Yeats gave you on this very play, taking his best thought, his time and energy from his own work to do so. He has never alluded to this himself, and would not like you to feel under any debt, but I feel sure that you would not like to show a lesser generosity than his. I am sure you are having a good deal of worry. It is hard to hold one's own against those one is living amongst. . . .

When Colum answered her, urging conciliation, she replied: "I thought I might find in your letter what the complaint against us is, but I only find that we are becoming less and less a theatre of the people. I don't agree with you. . . . I was always against a 1/- pit, but it was decided to let Miss Horniman have her way about it for a year or so. I think we shall very soon be able to change it for a 6d one. What is wrong. . . . We refused and must still refuse the 'one

* P. J. Kelly, Dudley Digges, Maire Quinn and Maud Gonne.

man one vote' [an English Radical cry]. It gave too much power
to lookers on. Authors were given the chief power as directors."

On the same day she wrote to Synge, who was in the centre of
things in Dublin, that she would welcome Colum and Maire Walker
back but thought a reunion was unlikely. Synge, she thought, should
"find out if Colum has any possible scheme of a friendly reconstruction," but at the same time he should consult the theatre's
solicitors "about the most decent and effective way of getting a deed
of separation between the two societies, if it is necessary we should
have one."

When Colum on behalf of the seceders asked Miss Horniman for
the use of the Abbey Theatre in which to produce *The Land*, she in-
dignantly refused and wrote to Synge from Paris: "If anyone thinks
that 'Irish' or 'National' are anything to me beyond empty words
used to distinguish a society, merely a title for convenience, they
are much mistaken. . . . The theatre was given for the carrying out
of Mr. Yeats' artistic dramatic schemes and for no other reason. These
patriots are all jealous of *Art*; they want to keep the standard down
so as to shine themselves. . . . We are not in a 'political' side-show."

There is no record of what conciliatory measures Synge took. But
he did consult the theatre's solicitors because, as Lady Gregory suddenly discovered, she, Yeats and Synge were still in the minority and,
according to the rules of the society, "the enemy could vote all the
little Walkers in as V.P.s and thus swamp our voting power. . . . I am
afraid we are in a hole, if they choose to do their worst, and I wish
we could come to some terms before any more threats reach us. . . .
I agree with you that an ending of it would be worth anything." But
Yeats was opposed to conciliation and wrote to Synge from London:
"Today I got a letter from Colum asking what steps I was going to
take to reunite the company. I replied that a reunited company would
be 'four wild cats struggling in a bat,'* that all was going well and
I referred him to you. . . . I strongly advise you to concede nothing
—a rival theatre would only show the power of ours. Colum will be
chaos without us and his actors chaos without Fay. We have now
£400 a year to spend on salaries and a free theatre. All we have to
do is hold firm."

* *Bath*, in Dublinese.

The bitterness caused by the secession was not to subside very quickly. The seceders eventually organized themselves into a group called the Theatre of Ireland, with Edward Martyn as president, and Colum, Tom Kettle, Padraic Pearse and others on its governing board. The Theatre of Ireland lasted for six years and went out of existence, as Miss Walker writes, "only because its members were absorbed into the wider and, at the same time, more important work of the Irish Volunteer Movement."[109] Miss Horniman and the directors of the Abbey Theatre also relented on the question of letting the opposition use the Abbey Theatre, and for some time to come Dublin had two native companies describing themselves as Nationalist, whatever that meaningless term represented. One lasting result was the permanent hostility of the more extreme segment of Nationalist opinion to Yeats and his theatre.

There is little doubt that Synge was in complete agreement with Yeats and Lady Gregory on the subject of the secession, although he had been very friendly with Padraic Colum and was much closer to the actors, including the seceders, than either of his two co-directors. Yeats had been highhanded in dealing with Maire Walker's complaints about Willie Fay giving better parts to her rival Sara Allgood, and Lady Gregory had stooped to malice. If Synge were guilty of either of these offenses while personally negotiating with Colum and the seceders, there is no evidence of it from their recollections or from the letters which passed back and forth at the time. Perhaps his habit of silence saved him now as it was to save him in later controversies. But, though silent, Synge could speak out when he felt the urge. Mrs. Alfred North Whitehead, who had entertained the company only six weeks before in Cambridge when they were on tour, has testified to Synge's eloquence. "There was one young man, shabbily clad, who said almost nothing and coughed dreadfully. After lunch some one took them the rounds of the college, but this young man stayed behind with Alfred and me. And then! Three hours, he talked brilliantly. We hadn't got his name. But after they were gone, we told each other, 'No matter who he is, the man is extraordinary.' "[110]

While the controversy over the secession was at its height, Synge was trying to discharge his new duties. He was reading new plays submitted by young writers. Joseph Holloway, whose many-volumed diary is a valuable though biased record of rumor and gossip in the

theatre, recorded a criticism Synge sent to a new author named J. D.
Guinan. It is constructive and contains one characteristic comment:
"Once or twice you use expressions like 'I was never any great shakes
in a shindy,' which at least in their associations are not peasant dialect,
and spoil the sort of distinction one can get always by keeping really
close to the actual speech of the country people. On the whole, however, your dialect—is it not Kerry dialect?—is very good. If you write
any more plays we would be glad to see them."[111]

Synge had reason to feel that at last he had arrived. Two of his
plays had been performed on European stages and *Riders to the Sea*
had been successfully revived at the Abbey on January 20th, 1906, on
the same bill with William Boyle's *The Eloquent Dempsey*, which
he had helped revise. His publishing future also was encouraging.
Arrangements had been completed with Maunsel and Company,
Dublin, to publish *The Aran Islands* at long last, and Jack Yeats had
agreed to illustrate it. J. M. Hone, one of the owners of Maunsel and
Company, had discussed the possibility of publishing a collection of
his pieces on Wicklow and Kerry but first wanted to use some of
them in his magazine *The Shanachie*. Two other publishers—one
American and one English—had asked him to submit his work. Jack
Yeats wrote to him from Devon on February 4th that the illustrations
for *The Aran Islands* were in progress. "I have done several particularly bully ones I think—though I say it that shouldn't. . . . When
I finished reading your manuscript I was bothered to understand how
you could leave such people. . . . Masefield was here for a few days
in the New Year. We sailed cardboard boats to destruction on the
pond and on some flooded marshes." His letter contained a drawing of
the two cardboard ships he and Masefield had sailed, with the legend,
"This is the Reuben Rango sinking beneath the waves."

On February 6th Synge left his mother, who now had Samuel back
from China for a visit, for rooms that he had hired at 57 Rathgar
Road, Rathgar, in the Dublin suburbs. His new responsibilities at
the theatre made it necessary for him to be nearer the city, but he
may also have been influenced by the fact that he was seeing a good
deal of Molly Allgood. His rooms, which he kept until the end of
May, were a short distance from the Roman Catholic church of St.
Patrick, St. Bridget and St. Columkille, the three patron saints of
Ireland. One Sunday morning when he had a heavy cold and sat alone

in his room listening to the crowds going to mass, he wrote the poem
"Dread":

> Beside a chapel I'd a room looked down,
> Where all the women from the farms and town,
> On Holy-days and Sundays used to pass
> To marriages, and christenings, and to Mass.
>
> Then I sat lonely watching score and score,
> Till I turned jealous of the Lord next door. . . .

Two years later, when he was living in another set of rooms in Rathmines, and his affair with Molly had become the most important thing
in his life, he added the two final lines of the poem:

> Now by this window, where there's none can see,
> The Lord God's jealous of yourself and me.*

   Synge's first experience at managing a professional theatre could
not have taken him through a more crucial period. He had difficulty
keeping Yeats from feuding with AE, who was in sympathy with the
seceders. He helped the Fays to recruit and train new actors, and he
continued to read new manuscripts submitted to the directors. But
the only new play performed between January and October of 1906
was Lady Gregory's one-act *Hyacinth Halvey*, although she turned
her skills to work on a translation of Molière's *Le Médecin Malgré
Lui* into Irish dialect, and it was performed in April. The company
revived *Riders to the Sea* in January and *In the Shadow of the Glen*
in April, as well as plays by Yeats, Lady Gregory and William Boyle.
But the audiences began to drop away, partly because some of the
familiar faces were gone but mostly because nothing new was being
offered to them. On April 17th Joseph Holloway "found *In the
Shadow of the Glen* being rehearsed under the author's guidance,
who seated at the footlights with his back against the proscenium

* As Synge's literary executor Yeats commented: "It is psychologically very
interesting. No one need be shocked at it, for it is the expression of a violent
passing mood. The Catholic Church makes a distinction between devotional and
doctrinal literature, permitting to devotional literature (in which I suppose one
might put the Book of Job) statements which would, if they were not an expression of emotion, be objected to by devout souls."

pilaster followed the players closely, offering a suggestion here and there." That evening he saw the play in performance and noted sadly: "The pit alone was tenanted. A few occupied the balcony and stalls. Only for Lady Gregory, J. M. Synge, W. B. Yeats, P. Colum, R. Gregory and their friends the stalls were empty."

What kept up the spirits of the actors was the tours. They played a one-night stand in Wexford in February, went twice to Dundalk, once in March and again in May; to Longford in July, and made two overseas tours, the first in April when they played two-night stands in Manchester, Liverpool and Leeds, and the second in May for one-week stands in Glasgow, Aberdeen, Newcastle-on-Tyne, Edinburgh and Hull. Synge went with the company on all the tours.

Although he was trying to keep his affair with Molly as unobtrusive as possible, a member of the company named "Dossie" Wright—who appears to have also had an interest in her—later recalled that Synge's interest in Molly became apparent to the whole company during the trip to Wexford in February. She had now taken over the role of Nora Burke, and with her great natural talent showed promise of becoming a worthy successor to Maire Walker. Synge was now thirty-five and Molly was not yet twenty-one. She was slight in build, and large brown eyes gave her face a look of seriousness. She was not beautiful but had an actress's ability to make both her face and body interesting and expressive. She seems also to have had a special attraction for men, particularly older men, despite the fact that she had had only a grade-school education and no more sophistication than one would expect to find in a girl of her class. Her only experience before she went into the theatre was as a salesgirl in a department store on Grafton Street. Her father was a workingman, and she had three sisters and two brothers, one of whom is now a member of a religious order.

In the Ireland of fifty years ago the difference between them could hardly have been greater. He was fifteen years older, but his education and his class background provided a much more formidable barrier. For a long time he was unwilling to tell his mother or his family about her. His unorthodoxy in religion and politics was one thing, but falling in love with a Roman Catholic, an actress, a former department-store salesgirl, was something they would never have tolerated.

He had been in love before. But he was now a writer of increasing reputation, and co-director of a theatre in which she worked as a hired actress. His affair with Molly was to be a source of embarrassment to Yeats and to Lady Gregory, who felt that they could not interfere as they were later to do in other love affairs that developed between members of the company. "Dossie" Wright recalled years later that Lady Gregory was always hopeful that he would win Molly's affections away from Synge and save an awkward situation. Synge, on the other hand, found two great difficulties which constantly marred his relations with Molly—his intense jealousy over the attentions she paid not only to "Dossie" but to other young men, and his dissatisfaction at her inadequate education and her apparent unwillingness to improve it. In the many letters he wrote to her— unfortunately none of hers survive—he frequently scolded her on both counts and tried his best to remedy the situation by lecturing to her about her conduct and the necessity of improving herself.

The most unhappy aspect of their love was his constant complaining about his ordinary griefs and his not so ordinary fears about his health. He was haunted by the fact that compared to her he was old. In his last play of *Deirdre*, the young girl betrothed to an old man and in love with a young one, he was writing from the depths of his own consciousness as he had never written before. The sense of tragedy which motivates every line in that play, unrelieved by any humour, is not due to the thought of his own impending death as much as to forebodings about his marriage.

His very first letter to her was a complaint. At the end of the English tour in July of 1906 he had left Molly and the rest of the company in Hull with the understanding that she was going directly to Sligo for a short vacation. But she changed her plans and instead came back to Dublin and then went with other members of the company to Balbriggan, a seaside town twenty miles north of Dublin. "Dossie" Wright, whose brother lived in Balbriggan, had arranged lodgings for the group. When Synge learned of it from Frank Fay he wrote to Molly at once:

Dear Molly, I saw Frank Fay today and heard from him that you had gone to Balbriggan for a week. I have been wondering what had become of you. It seems strange that you would not send me a line to tell me where you were. If I had known you were in Dublin, I might have seen you on Saturday. I go down to Lady Gregory's tomorrow morning for a week and then come back here to meet the Bohemian,* who is to arrive on the 24th. I hope I shall see you then before I set off again. I hope you are enjoying yourselves. I have been dull enough these days here.

Molly's reaction was typical—she scribbled the word *idiotic* on his letter and answered it with a postcard. He wrote ten days later from Coole:

Why don't you write me? We have not seen each other for ten days and I've had nothing from you but a few wretched lines on a postcard. It makes me imagine all sorts of things when you are so queer and silent. I have a lot of things to tell you about my talks with Lady Gregory and Yeats, but will let that wait. Also a story about Wright which came out at a moment and in a way that was peculiarly painful and humiliating to me. Why—however I did not start this letter to scold you as I'm better again, though I have been more distressed about it than I can say.

I think I am going to stay about Dublin for the present and finish my play,† so I may see a good deal of you this next while, when you come back and the Bohemian goes. When my play is finished I'll go off myself for a while; I think to the Blasket Islands. I came up with Fay yesterday. . . . We have arranged the affairs of the company satisfactorily on a new basis, and everything is going to be much more regular and orderly than it has been so far. That is our only chance.

Friday morning. I have got your letter at last—and I am much better. I think about you a lot, indeed I'm nearly always thinking about you in one way or another, but my thoughts aren't always pleasant ones, as Cardiff and other incidents come up in spite of me—

I'm glad to hear that you are lonesome. It's very good for you. I wonder in the end if you will stay out there a week or a fortnight. . . . Is Wright at Balbriggan too, as he met you at the station. . . .

The meeting of the three directors at Coole for a week beginning July 10, 1906—they were joined by Willie Fay on the 14th—was to discuss measures for pulling the theatre out of the doldrums it had been in since the secession. Miss Horniman, who had seen the company perform in Scotland, precipitated it with a letter of complaint on July 4th. "I find that our present arrangements in regard to the

Abbey Theatre won't work," she wrote. "At Glasgow Mr. Fay spoke to me in a way which made my position very unpleasant. I have come to the conclusion that the whole power of the purse must be in the Directors' hands." In addition to Willie Fay's attitude, the work of the actors was slovenly. She proposed to remedy things by increasing her guarantee for actors' salaries to £500. But she wanted some action immediately.

The directors decided that a business secretary was needed to handle the practical affairs of the theatre and to relieve Willie Fay of the necessity of dealing with Miss Horniman on theatre business. Yeats then complained that for his own plays none of the actresses in the present company were adequate, and he suggested that an actress named Darragh from the English professional stage be hired on a permanent basis. Lady Gregory and Synge were not enthusiastic, but neither objected, at least very strongly. Lady Gregory did not want to interfere if Yeats felt that his work demanded a more sophisticated actress than the company presently had. She and Synge were quite willing to admit that for their own work such an actress might have to unlearn a great deal. They preferred to depend on native actors however inexperienced they might be. Willie Fay agreed to the proposals. The man Synge hired was W. A. Henderson, the secretary of the National Literary Society, and he took up his duties in the theatre on August 18th. Miss Darragh, whose real name was Letitia Marion Dallas, joined the company and played in Yeats' *Deirdre*, which opened on November 24th and in his *The Shadowy Waters*, which opened on December 8th. She was soon feuding with Willie Fay, however, and when she began to criticize Lady Gregory her days were numbered. She left the Abbey before the end of the year, but her short stay was to have repercussions.

Twelve

MARRIAGE DIFFICULTIES

Would you have him see you, and he a man would be jealous of a hawk would fly between her and the rising sun?

Synge gave up his flat in Rathgar at the end of May. His mother had moved from Crosthwaite Park to a suburban villa named Glendalough House, in Glenageary, to be near the Stephens family who had moved to another house on Silchester Road. Glendalough House was only a short walk from Crosthwaite Park and consequently just as far from the city as the old house had been. But his mother had reserved a large room for him upstairs at the back of the house where he could work without interruption. With the new business secretary he felt that his presence in town was no longer necessary every day, and he needed time to finish *The Playboy*.

He wrote to Molly on July 24th, telling her about Karel Musek, and asking her and her sister Sally to meet him for tea at the Abbey on the 26th. "He wants to hear the keen and see one of our Aran dresses *etc*. He brought me a most flattering letter from his director calling me *cher maître* (Dear Master) and telling me he is going to put on the *Shadow* next winter in their regular repertoire at the National Theatre, which will mean royalties! Musek himself is going to do Michael Dara. They have £12,000 from the government to play with and all scenery and light, so they can afford to do things well! Could you and Sally bring in means of making tea and cakes at my expense on Thursday?"[112]

The tea went off well, apparently, and he wrote to her the next day to thank her. "I liked your dress very much, but I'm not quite sure of the hat. It is very smart and becomes you, but I'm inclined to think it is just a shade too fly away. I'll make up my mind when I see it again. I wish you'd write me a line to keep me going till we meet." He was showing Musek Dublin and took him out to Bray to see the Dargle Glen where Musek took a photograph of him sitting on a boulder, in his best black suit and black Stetson, his face looking lean and sensitive over a stiff white collar. "I am fagged out with my efforts to amuse Musek all day. He goes away tomorrow. I like him very much, but it is hard to talk to him continuously as his English is so uncertain."

With Molly he spent most of his time walking. Their usual procedure on Sundays was to take the train to Bray and then head out over the hills, looking for a lonely place where they could lie in the heather, looking down on the fields and the sea and eating *fraughans*, the Irish equivalent of American blueberries. Molly called them "little purple grapes," because, being a city girl, she had never seen them before. Her phrase took on a private meaning for them, and he later used it in letters to her. In the evening he would put her on the train for home, and return to Glendalough House. Through the week he would work on his play every morning, bicycle after lunch, and write her a letter in the evening. When he was particularly lonesome, he would write two or even three letters a day, telling her that he could not wait until Sunday or the next holiday she would have from rehearsals. On such days, when he went into town for work at the theatre or to superintend rehearsals, he was careful not to make his feelings for her too conspicuous. They would go for a walk in the Phoenix Park, along shaded avenues, among old twisted hawthorn trees and across wide stretches of grass land, over which deer grazed peacefully except when they were startled by cavalry officers out for a canter.

He wrote her on Monday, July 30th: "I feel as if I could hardly wait till tomorrow, I am so eager to see you again. I have had a little ride round Bray. It was a most wonderful evening, and I never felt so happy between the memory of yesterday and the hope of tomorrow. What a joy to live in a place where the twilights are so glorious, and where I have such a little friend to share them with me. We'll make the old romance come to life again." If he didn't make the old romance come to life again he was at least writing the love scenes in *The Playboy* with a conviction which came out of his own love.

He wrote her on Tuesday, August 7th, having spent the previous Sunday with her on the hills around Bray:

Dear Changeling, I have just got your little note. I waited about in my sister's garden till it was near post hour, sitting on a dark seat by myself under a chestnut tree and feeling very lonesome. My sister was going about with her husband watering their flowers, and the nephews were doing other things and I wanted my changeling to keep me company and cheer me up. Then I came home here and presently the post came.

Changeling, do you think I can live on "little purple grapes?" If you want to write such little notes I must have them by the half dozen at least. What are those few lines for a very starving man? I wanted to hear how you got home, and how you supped, and how everybody's temper is, and what you did yesterday and what you read or didn't read and God knows what, and yet you're too lazy to tell me! What there was was very tasty so I won't scold you this time, but the next time I want a good fat letter with talk in it, that I can chew the cud with at my ease. I haven't taken any steps yet about going away, so I don't know when it'll come off. I have been hammering away at my play till I am dizzy, but it is too hot and I am not doing much good. My brother is to be here tomorrow morning I believe. I am rather amused at the prospect of our talk. I don't mind him a bit.

The talk with Samuel, however, did not materialize, and he wrote her the next day: "My brother has been [here], but it was something else he wanted to talk about that hadn't anything to do with you. I will write and tell him some day I think. I did not get a good opportunity or I would have told him today." He was biding his time before he broke the news to his family that he was seriously in love with a girl none of them had yet laid eyes on. Two days later, on Friday, August 10th, he wrote to complain about not receiving a letter from her and to tell her that the play was going well. "It is wonderful how the play begins to grow in one's mind when one gives one's whole time to it. After a few days of misery the ideas begin suddenly to come of themselves and then all is plain sailing. . . . Will you come down by the quarter to eleven train from Westland Row on Sunday and let us have a good walk."

How his family was going to react to the bombshell he intended dropping on them was worrying him. His brother Samuel was only one problem, and the least one, since he would be going back to China presently. His mother was away for the summer, so he didn't have to face her with it at the moment. But he was taking his meals with the Stephenses, and one day when he sat at dinner listening silently to a political discussion being led by Harry Stephens' sister, he realized the complete impossibility of ever reconciling them to his marriage. He wrote Molly that night:

Dearest Changeling, I'm very dejected tonight again. I don't know why except that I'm dead tired and that I was annoyed and bored to death at dinner by a foolish lady who was praising the English and abusing the French. I don't fit well into that family party somehow—they are so rich and I am poor, and they are religious and I'm as you know, and so on with everything. I used to feel very desolate at times, but now I don't so much mind as I've a changeling of my own to think about and write to.

I don't like hanging about their house as a poor relation, although I'm a paying guest, as I know that they, or most of them, in their hearts despise a man of letters. Success in life is what they aim for, and they understand no success that does not bring a nice house, and servants and good dinners. You're not like that are you?

I wish we could keep each other company all these evenings. It is miserable that we should both be lonesome and so much apart. I hope you'll read steadily when I'm away. I hate to preach at you or school-master you—I like you so perfectly as you are—but you must know that it will make life richer for both of us if you know literature and the arts, the things that are of most interest to me and my few personal friends, that you'll know one of these days.

Meanwhile Molly's sister Sally must have been aware of the danger signals. She pleaded with Molly to give up what appeared to be an impossible relationship, but Molly paid as little heed to her warnings as to her lover's brooding jealousy. The disagreement with Sally became so unpleasant that Molly left home and went to stay with a married sister. Synge, who was about to leave for Kerry, wrote her on August 20th: "I've written the letter to Kerry and I feel so lonesome at the thought of it. I hate the thought of leaving you for so long especially as you will have this tour with no one to look after your comfort. Please go home to your people as soon as you can after I am gone and make it up with Sally. She is your natural companion in the company, and it will be very unpleasant on tour if you are not on good terms. For the sake of my ease of mind do make it up if you can."

Synge left for Kerry on August 25th and went directly to Philly Harris's at Mountain Stage. For the first time his interest in the life around him had to compete with his loneliness for Molly. As a result, he stayed only eighteen days instead of the month he had planned, did not stir much from the Harris cottage and its environs, and ended up by spending more time writing letters to Molly than recording observations in his notebooks. He began a letter to her on Sunday, the day after his arrival, although he knew there was no post until Tuesday, and continued it on Monday. It was eleven o'clock in the morning, and as he wrote, sitting on the cliff in front of the cottage, he could look down on Dingle Bay at a seal sneezing and blowing and listen to the sea birds clapping their wings on the cliff below him.

An old man I know came into the kitchen last night and shook me by the hand. "A hundred thousand welcomes to you," he said, "and where is the missus?" "Oh," I said, "you'll have to wait till next year to see her!" There is an old tramper staying in the house who is eighty years old and remembers the famine and the Crimea war. He is one of the best story-tellers in the country and told us some last night in Irish. He says he used to be good at it, but he has lost his teeth and now he isn't able "to give them out like a ballad." This morning when I went into the kitchen he was sound asleep on the wooden settle in his bare feet with nothing over him but his coat.

Before he left for Kerry he had suggested that she look at a flat he was interested in which would be their home as soon as they got married. They were apparently thinking of living in the old part of Dublin near St. Patrick's Cathedral where rents were low and where they would not be likely to have Molly's married sister or any other friends from the theatre as neighbors. She wrote to him about their plans soon after he left Dublin, and he replied on August 28th, right after the post had come:

I am very glad to hear that your people are coming round. Sally shook me very cordially by the hand when I told her I was going away to Kerry for a month. I think she sees that she had been making rather a fool of herself, and I'm sure she'll be all right now. We are all fools at times so we cannot blame her, and you know I've a great respect for her in many ways. I am very glad you saw the flats, but you do not say a word as to how you like the place now you have seen it. Don't talk about it by the way or you'll have the Fays down there and then we could not go. It is too soon yet I think to take one. I would rather see them for myself first, and in any case I would not pay four or five months rent for nothing, and in the end perhaps see something else that would suit us better.

When he had finished the letter he put it in his pocket with his notebook and set off on his bicycle for the post office. Half an hour later, when he was sitting by the side of the road over the Windy Gap, he started another letter to her. He stopped several times on his way back to the Harris cottage to admire the scenery and get his wind, and each time he took out his notebook and added to his letter. "I have come out through the Gap and I am resting again. I have Carantual on my left—the highest mountain in Ireland and full of ragged peaks with white cloud twisted through them like a piece of lace." A few minutes later he resumed, "I'm resting again now, down among the woods. . . . It is good for anyone to be out in such beauty as this and it stirs me up to try and make my Irish plays as beautiful as Ireland—I wonder if you could act a beautiful part? If it was in your compass—as we say of singers—I think you could. We must try you!" Naturally, with all his letter writing he could write little else. "I haven't touched my play since I came down."

On Thursday the 30th he wrote to scold her for absent-mindedly putting her stamps on the backs of the envelopes and to tell her that he had gone to the fair at Killorglin and still had not done any work on the play. Two days later he wrote again to tell her that he was thinking of coming back to Dublin and had gone for a swim in the ocean for the first time in twenty-five years:

Last night when I was coming back from the cliffs, about seven o'clock, I came on the little girls belonging to the house and two or three others and I got them to dance and sing Irish songs to me in the moonlight for nearly an hour. They were in bare feet of course, and while they were dancing a little devil of a brother of theirs kept throwing in dried furze—thorns under their feet—so that every now and then one of them would go lame with a squeal. Remember in three little weeks there'll be another new moon, and then, with the help of God, we'll have some great walking and talking at the fall of night.

On the 3rd of September he wrote to say that he and Philly Harris had gone to the races on the stretch of sandy beach at Rossbeigh, the memory of which he drew on for Christy's race in *The Playboy*. "They—the races—were run on a flat strand when the tide was out. It was a brilliant day and the jockeys and crowd looked very gay against the blue sea. . . ." The next morning he wrote again to describe the people picking carrigeen moss. "Dozens of men and women are out in the sea up to their waist, in old clothes, poking about for it under the water. They only find it at the lowest spring tide, so the sea is far out and as smooth as a lake."

Molly wrote to say that she was still staying with her married sister instead of returning to her parents' home on Mary Street as she had promised. He was fearful that her married sister would not scrutinize her conduct, and suspicious of her relations with Dossie while he was away. He was furious:

You agreed not to stay there as I did not like it for you. Now at the last moment you tell me that you are going back on your definite word, and going to do what I asked you not. What does it all mean? Do you think—I had better not write what I think. I am too distressed. You seem determined that I am never to trust you. I do not so much mind your staying on as the way you seem utterly to disregard your word. If there is any reason for you to change your plans why do you not give it to me? I am very unwell and *now* very wretched. I am going home in a few days. Yours J. Surely you might have had the courtesy to consult me at least about your plans.

Molly must have decided to ignore him because when the post came again—there were only three a week—there was no letter from her. He wrote immediately, "I am very unwell—nothing at all serious but an ailment brought on by the damp, and unsuitable food that causes me intense pain at times. I nearly fainted yesterday, I was so bad. However I always get all right at once when I get back to civilization." But it seems to have been Molly's weakness, or strength, not to rush to him with sympathy when he complained about being ill.

Jack Yeats' sketches of jockey costumes for *The Playboy*, painted on brown paper and sent to Synge in a letter dated January 11th, 1907.

Maybe she realized that his pains were mostly imaginary, and was pleased that she had the power to make him cringe like a small boy asking for sympathy. She may also have been a little terrified of him when he talked this way. On the other hand, the asthma he complained of, which he had suffered with for years, was a very real source of discomfiture to him when he was staying in the little Harris cottage with its dirt floor, its sealed windows and its bad ventilation. Philly Harris's son Patrick, who was in his early twenties in 1906, remembers that Synge was always coughing and fighting for breath when he stayed at Mountain Stage.

If he had any doubts about an early return to Dublin they were dissolved by Molly's silence. When he did not hear from her after three days he left for Dublin. A few days later they both attended a dinner for the whole company given by an American woman named Agnes Tobin. Miss Tobin came from a wealthy banking family in San Francisco, had translated Racine's *Phèdre* and Petrarch's sonnets, and had just become acquainted with Yeats, who described her enthusiastically to Lady Gregory as the greatest American poet since Whitman.[113] But Miss Tobin's chief distinction seems to have been her generosity and her interest in the work of other writers. She befriended Arthur Symons, who described her as "bright, warm-hearted, very talkative, very amusing," and seems to have helped Joseph Conrad, who dedicated *Under Western Eyes* to her.

Synge may have told Miss Tobin at the dinner that he was betrothed to Molly or she may have guessed it. She wrote him two days later complimenting him on Molly's beauty and asking him if he would accompany her to Waterford, the birthplace of her ancestors. Although their friendship was slight—Synge saw her only twice again—they corresponded until his death. She interested him in the possibility of translating Petrarch by showing him her own translations of the poet, and she constantly urged him to write poetry, although she reported to him that Arthur Symons had reprimanded her for it —"No, no! He is the best dramatist of the lot."

Synge wrote to Molly to tell her of his trip to Waterford with Miss Tobin. "I was very pleased with you the other evening. You were so self-possessed and charming and got through very well, I think, considering your inexperience." What Molly's reaction was to the left-handed compliment and to his going to Waterford with an American woman more nearly his own age than she was can be imagined. He reassured her by expressing his impatience at their having to delay the open acknowledgement of their betrothal. "I am sick and tired of this sort of thing. I think in a week or two we had better make ourselves 'official' and then defy gossip. I may drop in to see your mother some day *unbeknownsted!*" When he came back from Waterford, and Miss Tobin had set off for London, he and Molly spent their usual Sunday together walking in the hills, and they quarrelled. He wrote her the next day, "You gave me an utterly hard hostile look, when I tried to put things right that is not pleasant to think of."

Molly must have begun to reveal doubts about their future. He wrote her a sermon: "I thought you had come altogether to like the sort of life you'll have with me best—the life I mean that we have out on the hills, and by the sea on Bray Head and in the art we both live for—but if you begin hankering after commonplace pleasures and riches and that sort of thing we shall both be made wretched. . . . I have often told you that I am sure with a little care we may have a beautiful life together, but that a little carelessness—especially with you as you are, so young and so quick and an actress—might easily ruin our happiness for ever. Forgive this preaching, my life, I daresay it is very absurd." She must have thought that he was paraphrasing one of his mother's admonitions.

The conference at Coole in July about the theatre was beginning to bear fruit. Henderson, the new business secretary, had relieved Synge of the practical work of managing the theatre, and a program had been drawn up for the coming season. Performances of new plays were scheduled for ten specified Saturdays between October and the end of January, and season tickets were issued for the whole series at a guinea apiece. A violinist named Arthur Darley had been playing Irish airs between the acts, but now a small orchestra conducted by G. R. Hillis was engaged to play at each performance. The demand for a cheaper admission was met by reducing the price of some seats to sixpence; October 20th was set as the date of the opening of the new season; and a reception for friends of the theatre was scheduled for October 13th. The directors also decided to publish periodically a new paper to be called *The Arrow*, edited by Yeats and devoted to explaining the theatre's objectives. The first number came out in October and the second a month later.

As the new season began, the directors were confident that Miss Horniman was satisfied and that all they needed now was some new plays to recapture the audiences they had lost in the spring. Yeats' new play *Deirdre*, with Miss Darragh in the leading role, was scheduled for November 24th, and he had revised *The Shadowy Waters* for her to act in later in December. Lady Gregory and William Boyle had new plays, and *The Playboy*, scheduled for December, was later postponed until the end of January. Yeats had plans too for developing a school of tragic acting, and in support of it William Magee—John Eglinton—was translating *Oedipus* and Robert Gregory, *Antigone*.

In late September the company was busy rehearsing for Lady Gregory's *The Gaol Gate* and Boyle's *The Mineral Workers*, which were to open the new season on October 20th. Molly had a good role in each play and was scheduled to play a minor part in Yeats' *Deirdre* in November. Her big opportunity was to come in January in *The Playboy*. After seeing her rehearse on September 29th, Synge wrote her to complain that his work on the new play and her rehearsals were keeping them apart. "This state of affairs can't last much longer, only I don't want to start making fusses till my play is off my hands. I had no notion that you had such a beautiful voice, at least it seemed beautiful to me. I liked your whole show of Mary* except one gesture that seemed forced. . . . I am not at all well, inside, I'm sorry to say. It is the worry of my play that is knocking me up I think, but I hope I'll be alright tomorrow. Please come down as usual by the quarter to eleven train."

Samuel Synge had left Dublin and was about to return to China. Synge wrote and told him of his marriage plans but insisted that the information be confidential. The mildness of Samuel's reaction surprised him and he wrote to Molly: "He seems quite pleased. I wish you could see him before he goes away. He is to be here I believe tomorrow morning and will stay about a week, then to China for seven years." But the meeting never took place, and one can imagine that Molly had little appetite for it.

The reception at the Abbey on October 13th was a *conversazione* consisting of a talk by Yeats, a program of songs by members of the company, and tea in the greenroom afterwards. Synge invited the two Stephens boys after convincing their grandmother that no play

* In *The Gaol Gate.*

would be performed. Edward Stephens remembered seeing Yeats greeting friends in the audience and speaking from the stage afterwards. Sara Allgood, without any accompaniment, sang a ballad. "Her voice was strangely clear and she sang with quiet confidence. There was a hush over the audience and at the end of her song a burst of applause." Frank Fay in costume recited Yeats' "The Death of Cuchullin," and there were other performances.

Synge and Molly were happy together again, and he was able to joke about her temper by calling her "Polly Popgun" after the young lady in a ballad which he sent her:

> Young Polly Popgun and her man went out one Autumn day
> When hips and haws and blackberries their millions did display.
> Then he and she did quarrel sore upon a mountain lane
> And first she swore and then she bit and then to ease her pain
> A black and bloody smudge she laid upon her lover's cheek,
> Who stood upon the pathway there in patience mild and meek.
> And then in passion and in pride she snivelled loud and long
> Till all her griefs he squeezed away upon his bosom strong.

Samuel had come back to Dublin for a final few days before sailing, but neither of them spoke of Molly. He wrote her on October 16th: "I have not had a word with my brother yet, the days seem to slip by and I never see him alone. I am very bothered with my play again now. The second act has got out of joint in some way, and now it's all in a mess. Don't be uneasy, Changeling, everything is going on all right, I think. I will go and see your mother soon. I don't much like the job so I keep putting it off. . . . I am sorry you are getting back into your bad ways. You want someone to look after you, eh?"

Molly's reaction was to write across the top of the letter, apparently for her own satisfaction, since she did not return any of his letters to him: "You may stop your letters if you like. I don't care if I never heard from you or saw you again, so there! And please don't let thoughts of me come into your head when you are writing your play. It would be dreadful if your speeches were upset. I don't care a rap for the theatre or anyone in it—the pantomime season is coming on and I can easily get 'a shop.' In fact I shall go out this afternoon and apply for one. M. Allgood."

On Wednesday evening, October 17th, they were both at the theatre and she complained to him about Willie Fay, who was driving her hard for the opening two days away. He wrote her the next morning, "You'll never get a perfect manager till you go to Heaven, and W.G. is a good fellow at bottom—you have often said so." That afternoon they went for their walk and quarrelled bitterly. The next day he was moody and unwell, and in the letter he wrote to her on Saturday he seemed scarcely aware of the fact that she had an opening that night:

My Own, I don't suppose I shall get a word with you tonight and I will not be well enough, I fear, to walk tomorrow, so I want to write you a line to thank you for your notes. Dearest, yesterday morning I sat down to write you a letter that would have made your hair stand on end, but fortunately when I got the pen in my hand I wrote to Germany instead.

I was greatly troubled all day—far more so than you imagine—by our quarrel on Thursday, and my first impulse was to give you a terrible scolding. But I'm going to drop my dignity and appeal to you instead. Don't you know, Changeling, that I am an exciteable over-strung fool— as all writers are, and *have to be*—and don't you love me enough to be a little considerate, and kindly with me even if you do not think that I am always reasonable in what I want you to do? Surely you wouldn't like to worry me into consumption or God knows what? And with the continual deadly strain of my writings I haven't much health [left] over to shake off the effects of these hideous little squabbles that harass me indescribably, because, my own darling, I love you indescribably. When you know how my whole heart has gone out to you, why do you speak to me as you did on Thursday, or break your word to me as you did a few days before? We may have a beautiful life together, but, if we are not careful, we may put ourselves into a very hell on earth. Do let us be careful, J. M. S.

The opening that night was a great success. Joseph Holloway noted in his diary that the house was crowded to overflowing and that the audience included Maud Gonne MacBride, Edward Martyn, George Russell—"with his long, untidy hair and reddish beard"—W. B. Yeats, "in his velvet coat, butterfly tie and pronounced stray lock," Lady Gregory and her son, J. B. Yeats and Jack Yeats, both with sketchbooks in hand. But Synge sat at home, brooding and ill. Molly's acting in *The Gaol Gate* attracted a great deal of attention, and the reviewers in Monday's papers paid her elaborate compliments. Synge was unaware of her personal success and wrote to her on Sunday morning. It was a wet day, so they would not have walked even if he had been feeling well. He was full of tenderness and had just conceived the idea of making a playwright out of Molly:

I've a new idea. Do you think you could write a little comedy to play in yourself, say about your life in the convent school? I could give you a scenario. Would not it be fun? And then you'd be able to patronize Miss Darragh, and Mrs. Bill Fay* and the lot of them. I'm sure you've as much humor as Lady Gregory, and humor is the only thing her little farces have. Or should you write a comedy about the woman at Kilmacanogue (that's how it's spelled) or about some incident of your early career? The one thing needful is to get hold of some little center of life that you know thoroughly, and that is not quite familiar to every one. I'm sure your old grandmother would be a lovely character in a play. Think about it, little heart, and when you're acting notice how the scenes *etc.* are worked out, one into the other. This is all a wild idea, but it would be fun to try; no one would know but ourselves and of course I'd help and advise you. You could write out your MS on the typewriter, so all is complete.

On Monday, when he read the newspaper accounts of her acting, he wired her congratulations and followed it up with a letter. "I am delighted to hear of the success of everything. When I read the compliments you got I had tears of pleasure in my eyes to the wonder of my family. Yes, you have a lovely voice I think. . . ."

He was fully recovered now. His brother Robert suggested a bicycle ride with Samuel, who was leaving in a few days. They headed out from Glenageary through the rocky ravine between the Dublin mountains, known as The Scalp, into Wicklow and were gone for three hours. As he rode along in the clear autumn air he wanted to talk to them about his marriage, but Samuel made no mention of his letter and he lost his nerve. On Thursday, the 25th, when Samuel was leaving, he pulled Molly's picture out of his pocket and showed it to him. In the afternoon he wrote Molly: "I showed my brother your photo today. He beamed at it most cordially and said with conviction 'That's a very nice face.' Also I heard people in the tearooms last night saying how good the 'younger girl' was in the G. *Gate*. Now are you buttered

* Brigit O'Dempsey.

up enough for one day? I've a crow to pluck with you all the same Miss P. P."

The next day he saw Samuel off for China and wrote to Molly: "He is one of the best fellows in the world, I think, though he is so religious we have not much in common. My old mother bore up wonderfully well, though she cried a good deal of course after he was gone." Molly's play was to close on Saturday night, October 27th, and he went in to see it. Holloway reported that the audience was a delight to behold and seemed to be a vote of confidence for the new policies of the theatre and for the ambitious program the directors had laid out for the coming season. The next day he and Molly went for their usual walk, and on Monday he saw her again when he came into the theatre in the evening. She was still keyed up about her success in her first important role. Willie Fay and one of the actresses in the company named Brigit O'Dempsey had gone off to Glasgow to get married. The atmosphere in the company was a happy one.

On Tuesday he returned grimly to his work on *The Playboy*, which was scheduled for a December production, and he wrote to Molly:

I had a dreadful turn of despair over the *Playboy* last night—it seemed hopeless—but I have come through the difficulty, more or less, that was in my way. I am feeling very much "done up" with it all and I fear I can't leave it for a walk this week. It is too bad, but I must get done with the thing or it will kill me. I am sorry to hear that you are having gloomy dreams. You must be done up too. I am too worn out to write much of anything to you now, but if you had seen my misery when the post passed last night without a letter from my little Changeling you would forgive me.

I don't know what will become of me if I don't get the *Playboy* off my hands soon. I nearly wrote to them last night to ask them to put on *The Well of the Saints* instead of it in December so that I might have a few months more to work at it, but I don't like the thought of having it hanging over me all this winter when I ought to be so happy! Parts of it are the best work, I think, that I have ever done, but parts of it are not structurally strong or good. I have been all this time trying to get over weak situations by strong writing, but now I find it won't do, and I'm at my wit's end.

She wrote words of encouragement, and he replied on Thursday, November 1st: "I like being lectured and I'll try and keep up my

spirits and work ahead. . . . I half hope I have got over the weakness
in my second act that has been worrying me so much." He did not
come into town that evening, although the company was holding a
party for the returning bride and bridegroom.

On Saturday he wrote to ask her to come the next day for their
walk. He had sent her *Aucassin and Nicolette* and she had written
that she liked it. On Sunday they went to Bray and walked out to
the Great Sugar Loaf mountain. After three or four hours on the
hills they walked back to the little village of Kilmacanogue in the
twilight. The next day he wrote:

I am just off to the post with the Aran book proofs, so I have only time
to write you a hurried line in spite of all your injunctions. I feel in great
form after yesterday and I have had a good morning's work. I hope you
aren't the worse. There was a very bad thunderstorm in Kingstown—
much worse than what we got—about five o'clock—the flashes we saw
I suppose in the Rocky Valley. We got off very well. Let me hear from
you soon.

My mother asked me again if I was alone, and I said I had "a friend"
with me. I must tell her soon. Do you really want more books? I will send
you as many as you like, but I don't want to plague you with books that
you have no time to read. Remember to get *Cuchulain of Muirthemne*
from the Abbey and read "The Sons of Usnach" in it. It is charming.
Now ten thousand blessing on you. I'll write soon—till next time, Your
Old Tramp.

The story in Lady Gregory's book which he wanted her to read was
to furnish him with the subject matter for his next play, *Deirdre of
the Sorrows.* It is the oldest and finest love story in the literature of
the early Celt. Lady Gregory's telling of it, in Anglo-Irish dialect, is
based upon translations of other versions, including the earliest extant
in *The Book of Leinster,* compiled in the twelfth century. The central
motif of a girl and her lover being pursued by an old man to whom
she is betrothed later became famous in the story of Tristan, which
is now believed to be a French adaptation of the Irish tradition. This
great romance from the Ulster cycle also had its influence within
Ireland because it obviously inspired the later, almost identical, story
of Diarmuid and Grania from the Fenian cycle.

Synge had been interested in the story from as early as 1901 when he took a version of it in modern Irish, published with glossary and translation, to Aran with him and proceeded to make his own translation of it.[114] He singled it out for comment in his article on Old Irish literature in *L'Européen* in 1902 and in his reviews of Lady Gregory's book in 1902 and of A. H. Leahy's *Heroic Romances of Ireland* in 1906. Lady Gregory had boldly written her stories from ancient Irish saga in the language of a modern English-speaking Irish peasant. Whatever Synge may have owed her for his mastery of the same medium, there is no doubt that she had shown him the possibility of making the personages of the past speak like peasants while still remaining heroes.

Deirdre of the Sorrows was a striking departure for him—a "springdayish, Cuchulainoid" drama of the type he had condemned in his letter to MacKenna. Instead of working directly from a folk tale he had heard or an incident of peasant life he had seen, he was attempting to breathe life into the "rare and royal names wormy sheepskin yet retains," as he phrased it in his poem "Queens," by visualizing them as the simple but passionate people he had known in the west of Ireland and in the hills of Wicklow. The problem was a linguistic one. His translations into dialect from a number of European poets were experiments which must have encouraged him to believe that a Deirdre speaking the language of a Pegeen Mike would have a vitality that would justify the linguistic incongruity. But he did not start work on the play until a year later.

He and Molly walked again on Sunday, November 4th, and he wrote to her on Tuesday that he was very busy reading proofs of his Aran book and writing a review of Stephen Gwynn's *The Fair Hills of Ireland* for *The Manchester Guardian*. "I want to read the P. B.* to the directors and Fay on Thursday or Friday so I don't know about a walk." He wrote again two days later: "*The Playboy* is very nearly ready. I am writing to Lady Gregory by this post to ask her to fix a time for me to read it to them. Then there will be the job of making a clean copy."

Molly had been complaining of a sore back, and she must have told him that she was thinking of going somewhere to recuperate. He wrote on Friday, the 9th:

* *The Playboy of the Western World.*

Of course you were right to tell me what was in your little scatterbrain, and I'd be much more hurt, profoundly hurt, if I thought you didn't tell me all you think of. I, and some other people of *genius* I have known, in my youth nearly always got a wild impulse to wander off and tramp the world in the spring and autumn, the time the birds migrate, so as you're a genius too it's right and proper that you should have the impulse. We're all wild geese, at bottom all we players, artists and writers, and there is no keeping us in a back yard like barndoor fowl. The one point is that when we fly it should be to the North Sea or the Islands of the Blessed, not to some sooty ornamental water in some filthy town.

He was displeased by Molly's reply and wrote two letters to her the next day. "I wish to God I could say something nice to you, but your letter and some things you have hinted (or seemed to hint) have frozen a little layer of ice round my old heart, which as you know very well is a mass of love for my little Changeling." His second letter was more conciliatory. He had gone on a bicycle ride to Enniskerry and was feeling better. "We are so fond of each other and we get on so beautifully when we like and still keep pulling each other's hair, and saying stupid things till we both get miserable. . . . This last tiffette, by the way, was your fault, wasn't it?" But they met the next day, walked and did not quarrel. He wrote her the next day that he was in "great form" and that the end of the week should see him finished with *The Playboy*.

His article "The Vagrants of Wicklow" which had been rejected by *The Cornhill* magazine in 1902, now appeared in Hone's magazine *The Shanachie*. He was to contribute another piece on Wicklow and three on Kerry during 1907. George Moore was delighted with it and wrote to him, on November 11th: "Form and substance alike are perfect, and I would I could convey to you some of the pleasure I experienced when I read anecdote after anecdote linked together finely as a rare chain of gold. The gathering of tramps on the hillside like swallows—I am thankful you did not use the simile—will never be forgotten by me—seven or eight lines, no more."

He went in to Dublin on Tuesday, November 13th, to dine with Yeats and Lady Gregory and read them the first two acts of his new play, the third not yet being finished. But he had a cold, was hoarse and had to ask one of the Fays—probably Frank—to read it for him. Lady Gregory wrote him three days later: "We are longing to have last act of *Playboy*. We were both immensely impressed and delighted with the play, but we were not a lively audience that night. Yeats has been quite pulled down with a cold, and I am struggling against one. We are tired out with rehearsals *etc.*—have done the *Arrow* today— no rows at the theatre. I am rather sad about *Deirdre* (as I don't like Miss D. in the part. But it can't be helped)."

Work on Yeats' *Deirdre* was under way, and Sally and Molly had parts in it. Holloway watched one of the rehearsals and described Miss Darragh "in a walking suit of tweed and a toreador hat with a pompadour plume in it. . . . The Miss Allgoods spoke in the measured tones dear to the heart of Yeats. . . . Miss Darragh's acting is of the soulful kind that is inclined to drop the voice into inaudible whispers." Synge was not present at rehearsals because he was working steadily at the third act of *The Playboy* and was still feeling his cold. On Sunday the 18th he was too ill to see Molly, but the next day he wrote to ask her to come to his house on Wednesday. He must have realized that if she came his mother would have little trouble in divining what their relationship was. His cousin Florence Ross, who had recently come back from South America and had been staying with the Stephenses, had moved into Glendalough House a few days before for a stay of nearly two months. She went openly to the theatre in defiance of her hostess and was continually uttering militantly liberal opinions. But Molly did not come, and Synge wrote her on Thursday, the 22nd: "I am afraid you must be ill again as you have not turned up. . . . I showed my mother your photo the other night and told her you were a great friend of mine. That is as far as I can go till I am stronger. I am thoroughly sick of this state of affairs. We must end it, and make ourselves public."

He had just posted this letter when Molly suddenly arrived. She did not explain whether her coming on the wrong day was deliberate or whether she had merely lost her nerve the day before. At any rate Mrs. Synge, who suspected that she had come as an actress with whom he had business, greeted her cordially and after a few words withdrew to leave the two of them alone in the dining room. In a short while she went out to a church missionary sale. When she returned some time later Edward Stephens and his sister came over, and he remembered that his grandmother "told us not to disturb John because one of his friends from the Abbey Theatre had called to see him. Soon we heard the hall door closing, and Mrs. Synge said that John's visitor had gone and that we should go into the other room for tea." Synge wrote to Molly the next day:

It was too bad that I had to let you trot off so soon, but it couldn't be helped. A whole pack of them were waiting to have tea in the room where we were. . . . It is curious what a little thing checks the flow of the emotions. Last evening because there was a sort of vague difficulty or uncertainty about our position in this house we were as stiff as strangers. I felt beforehand that it would be like that, so I was not disappointed, and I am delighted that you came. I do things gradually by nature and we have made a great step in the right direction. It is much better to let my mother get used to the idea by degrees than to spring it on her suddenly. I wish you could have seen your solemnity as you walked into the room yesterday with your long coat and glasses. You looked like a professor of Political Economy at the very least.

He wrote again the same day to tell her that he had been to see the doctor and that nothing serious was wrong with him. But he was still a bit feverish and had some congestion left in his lungs. The doctor had advised him to stop work on his play for a while and take a vacation. He was thinking of going to England to visit his cousin Edward Synge. The next day, which was Saturday the 24th, he wrote her two more letters, telling her that when he got to England he would write his mother from that safe distance and tell her all. "I am afraid I might say something too violent if we talked it over at first, as I lose my temper so easily." In his second letter he assured her that his mother was pleased with her. "She said you seemed very bright and she hoped I had asked you to come down again on Sunday and cheer me up."

That evening Yeats' *Deirdre* was given its première. Holloway remarked to D. J. O'Donoghue that there was "a touch of sensuality" in the play which annoyed him, and O'Donoghue replied that George Moore had been given all the credit for the sensual passages in *Diarmuid and Grania* but it was now apparent that his co-author Yeats had actually written them. Synge did not attend the opening and wrote to Lady Gregory next day to explain that he was still not entirely fit, that he had decided to take a fortnight's vacation in England, and asking if the production of *The Playboy* could be put back a few weeks. She agreed to a postponement to the third week in January. On Wednesday Synge went to town and read the third act to her and Yeats. Afterwards he went to the theatre and met Molly in the green room. But while he was busy she went out with some medical students. He waited, but when she did not return he went back to Dún Laoghaire in terrible distress. Since he was leaving for Surrey in the morning and would not see her until he returned, he was furious and wrote her before he went to bed. By the morning his anger had cooled, and he wrote a more temperate letter, slipping it into the first. The first post the next day brought a letter from her which made him happy, and he wrote a short note to her before he left for the boat to Holyhead.

Edward Synge was an etcher. He was unmarried, spent a good deal of his time travelling in Europe, and had a home in Byfleet, Surrey. Synge stayed with him for two weeks, until December 14th, and found his company congenial. They had known each other in Paris, were both artists and in that respect uniquely unrepresentative of the two branches of the same family. Synge had brought proof sheets of his Aran book with him and may also have put some final touches to *The Playboy* as a result of suggestions that came out of his reading to Yeats and Lady Gregory. He wrote to Molly almost daily. Her desertion of him in favor of the medical students still rankled. In one letter he cautioned her to "keep clear of the men who dangle after actresses. I know too well how medicals and their like think and speak of the women they run after. . . . I think you may turn out a very fine actress —if you can preserve your sincerity—and if the Abbey breaks up at any time I cannot of course ask you to give up your art. We shall have to live in London part of the year, and I think as my wife you will have more chance than you would have by yourself—I know so many writers *etc.* in London—of getting parts in the intellectual plays at the Court or elsewhere."

In another letter he describes his cousin's house, "full of cupboards and alcoves with bookshelves, and a lot of valuable etchings that he bought or had been given" in addition to his own. "My next play must be quite different from the P. Boy. I want to do something quiet and stately and restrained and I want you to act in it. I think I will work more easily when I have you at my elbow to advise me, and when we are in our own little abode." He wrote a day later to tell her that he was going to dine with Miss Tobin in London. "You needn't be jealous! no one will run away with me." But Molly apparently thought otherwise. She scribbled at the foot of his letter the word *frivolous* and waited for a few days before answering him. In another he told her that he hadn't yet written to his mother of their engagement, "but I will tell her in my next letter. I don't know whether it would be any use to write to your mother; I should think it would do as well to go and see her when I go over."

He continued to scold her because she had not written. "I dreamt last night that I introduced you to my brother and he began at once retrimming your hat!" On December 6th he wrote, "I am going to write to my mother tonight. About yours—is more difficult. I feel it hard somehow to write on such an important matter to a person I don't know. As soon as I speak to her I will *feel* how to put things, but my mind becomes a blank when I think of writing her now, and I am afraid my letter would be stiff and awkward. What do you think?"

That night he took his courage in his hands and wrote to his mother about himself and Molly. The next day he wrote to Molly:

I wonder what put it into your changeling's head that I want you to be "serious." The lighter your little heart is the better—the only thing I don't like is a certain cheap, commonplace merriment which is at times strongly felt among the company, but which you are naturally, thank God, quite free of. A kind of restraint in one's merriment—a restraint I mean not in the degree of it, so much as in the quality—gives style and distinction without taking any joyousness away. In a way I do perhaps want you to be serious, that is I want you to take serious things seriously, and to look where you are going so that you may not be a mere weather-cock, twisting about after every breeze that blows on you. This isn't a lecture, mind, but you mustn't get it into your head that I am a morose tyrant. Surely we are merry enough when we are out having walks and taking our little teas at Kilmacanogue, aren't we?

I have posted the letter to my mother today! So that is done. I will write yours also if you like. I spoke about it in my last letter, and I'll wait to hear what you say in answer.

I went up to London today and lunched with Miss Tobin. She was very nice and kind. There is not of course the remotest sign of flirtation about us, but I like her greatly and value her friendship. She has taken a great liking to you and Sally. She says she would hardly know me I have changed so much since the summer and I look so thin now and generally unwell. That is not very encouraging is it? Your last letter was the right kind of thing as it is possible to answer what you say. You say that I'll think you sentimental because of what you write about the verses. It is hard to define sentimentality, but you may be quite easy in your mind, you are not sentimental, and never will be in the sickly sense of the word. A full vigorous affection does not get sentimental. It is only sickly, inactive, half-and-half people who are really attacked. A true affection naturally occupies itself with the little things as well as the big things that concern it, but it does not grow any less healthy for that reason.

I am glad you were at *Don Giovanni*. We must hear a lot of good music together. There are so few ways of enjoying the arts in Dublin. I feel I have been foolish to neglect music so much. Is this letter too philosophical for you? If it is, tell me, and I'll write to you next time about "Jones," E. Synge's dog, and the "Encumbrance," as we call the housekeeper's baby.

His mother had known his secret for some time. She was a woman with a strong hold over all her children, and he was the one whose actions she scrutinized the most carefully. Her only reaction was to write in her diary, "I got a long letter from Johnnie telling me." She had obviously been expecting his confession.

A few days later he wrote, "I have not heard yet what my mother thinks. Why am I to put off telling Lady G? I thought you wished it? Dear Heart I am looking forward to fine walks during your holidays. Unfortunately the P. *Boy* is hanging over me still. I haven't been well enough to do much to him since I came over." In a postscript he noted that he had been "through Act 1" and it needed only a little more revision. "I wish I could say the same for Act 3." Her unwillingness to let Lady Gregory know of their engagement bothered him and he wrote again that night, "I keep wondering what you were going to say and why you do not want me to tell Lady G. when you have asked me so often to do so?" It was apparently Molly's turn to get cold feet.

Synge lunched with Miss Tobin in London once more on December 12th and took her to an exhibit of Edward Synge's etchings. He wrote to Molly to tell her that he was coming home on Friday the 14th and added in a postscript: "I heard from my mother. She says she thought 'the friend' I have been walking with was a man, but that my showing her the photo and the letters that came so often when I was ill made her think there was something. Then she says it would be a good thing if it made me happier, and to wind up she points out how poor we shall be with our £100 a year. Quite a nice letter for a first go off."

Back home on Saturday he had lunch with his mother and Florence Ross and went into town for the matinée and evening performances of *The Canavans* by Lady Gregory and Yeats' revised version of *The Shadowy Waters* with Miss Darragh as Dectora. Holloway noted in his diary that Synge was present at both performances, looking fit. "The audience was the smallest of any Saturday night this season. Yeats spells empty benches! Boyle full houses!! Synge cranks at home!!! Lady Gregory popularity!!! I hope Synge's presence means *The Playboy* soon. Heard he had been ordered away and his playwriting stopped for the time being. Perhaps it was only a rumor."

Synge walked with Molly on Sunday and on Tuesday and wrote to her on Wednesday:

Sweetest Heart, Do you remember what I told you once—in Liverpool, I think—that the love of a man of thirty-five was a very, or at least a rather different, thing from that of a man of twenty-five? I was making a mistake. Last night I felt all the flood of fullness and freshness and tenderness that I thought I had half left behind me. I can say now very truthfully that I have never loved anyone but you, and I am putting my whole life now into this love.

I have had no cold today after all, and I have had a good morning's work at the *Playboy*. I am going out now for a turn on my bicycle and then I am going to work again. I am sorry I did not arrange to see you sometime today. It is hard to be a whole day without you when you are so near, and your whole time is free.

My mother inquired quite pleasantly about our walk and where we had been. She is coming round to the idea very quickly, I think, but still it is better not to hurry things. Meet me tomorrow at the same time. . . .

The opening performance of *The Playboy* was now only a month away, and he was furiously rewriting the third act. He walked with Molly on Sunday, December 23rd, and wrote to her on Christmas night. He and his mother and Florence had had Christmas dinner with the Stephenses and he amused everyone after dinner with gymnastic tricks, picking up a bunch of keys with a hand that he had passed round one of his legs. He wrote again two days later:

I have had two hard days at P.B. and I am very tired again. In the evening now I am reading Petrarch's sonnets, with Miss Tobin's translations. I think I'll teach you Italian too so that you may be able to read the wonderful love poetry of these Italian poets Dante and Petrarch, and one or two others. . . . You feel as fully as anyone can feel all the poetry and mystery of the nights we are out in—like the night a week ago when we came down from Rockbrook with the pale light of Dublin shining behind the naked trees till we seemed almost to come out of ourselves with the wonder and beauty of it all. . . . I am growing sure of one thing and that is that we are not going to destroy the divine love that God has put between us by the wretched squabbles and fightings that seemed to threaten us at first. I wonder will that make you laugh?

The Abbey Theatre opened again on December 29th—the night originally scheduled for *The Playboy*—with revivals of *The Hour Glass* and *The Mineral Workers*, *The Playboy* went into rehearsal on January 8th, with Molly in the role of Pegeen Mike and a supporting cast that was never to forget the reception they got three weeks later. Yeats' *Deirdre* and *The Shadowy Waters* had been performed under duress because both the director and the company had resented Miss Darragh. The combination of two difficult, unpopular plays and a resentful supporting cast had once more emptied the theatre.

While Synge was in Surrey another crisis had developed over the management of the theatre. When it was finally settled, some feelings had been bruised, especially Miss Horniman's, and the foundations had been laid for the eventual departure of the Fays from the Abbey Theatre. What the main issues were can be seen from the sizable amount of correspondence which passed back and forth during December and January, Yeats being in London for the most of the period, Lady Gregory in Coole, Miss Horniman on the Continent and Synge, except for his two weeks in Surrey, in Dublin. A good many of the letters are not dated, and some important ones are missing. The confusion is further compounded by the fact that a number of Lady Gregory's letters remained unposted for some days while Synge and Yeats wondered why she had not written and misunderstanding developed.

The main issues are clear enough, however, and they go back to the discussions at Coole in July when the three directors decided to engage Miss Darragh to please Yeats, and to hire a business secretary. Miss Darragh's failure in Yeats' two plays and her inability to get along with Willie Fay and the company brought things to a head very quickly. She took her complaints directly to Miss Horniman, who was a friend of hers, and this was enough to alienate her from Lady Gregory, who had not been enthusiastic about her coming in the first place and was resentful of Miss Horniman's influence over Yeats.

Yeats on the other hand tried to justify his action in bringing in Miss Darragh, though he admitted that her acting had been a failure, and he defended her against Lady Gregory's charges that Miss Darragh had criticized her, abused the other members of the company and tried to assume control of the theatre itself. He was also beginning to side with Miss Horniman in her dissatisfaction with the Fays and felt that they could never develop the kind of tragic actors he needed for his own plays. Willie Fay, he wrote, "is not a romantic actor, he is not a tragic actor, he is a very clever man and can do not badly many things that are not his natural work, but the other side of the theatre . . . requires the entire time and thought of a different sort of actor or teacher." Frank Fay, Yeats argued, "is a born teacher of elocution up to a certain point, but people come from his hands certainly with great clearness of elocution, with a fine feeling for both line and passage as units of sound with a sufficient no less infallible sense of accent, but without passion, without expression, either in voice or gesture. William Fay has in comedy a most admirable understanding of gesture and of course of acting, but his ear for verse is very defective. Only experiment can say whether the two together can teach verse-speaking."

Miss Horniman went to her purse again with the offer of £500 to finance the hiring of a director from the professional theatre who would produce all the plays and leave only the directing of peasant plays to Willie Fay. Yeats immediately agreed, but both Lady Gregory and Synge opposed the demotion of Willie Fay and both were dubious about Miss Horniman's plans—which Yeats enunciated—of spending £25,000 on not only building up a tradition of tragic acting in the grand style by doing foreign masterpieces but of developing the Abbey Theatre along the lines of the continental municipal theatres. Lady Gregory did not want to oppose Yeats' wishes, but on the other hand she did not want to "be like Dillon and Co., giving up Parnell to please an English howl." She did not want the Fays "shoved out either by force or gentler means"; but if Yeats could convince the Fays to go along with the new plan she would not object. "I think as Yeats and Fay represent the extreme right and left," she wrote to Synge, "we who are the moderate centre are best out of it, leaving the arrangement to them." Synge stated his position in a long letter to Lady Gregory and Yeats, written from Surrey:

I think we should be mistaken in taking the continental municipal theatre as the pattern of what we wish to attain as a "final object" even in a fairly remote future. A dramatic movement is either (a) a creation of a new dramatic literature where the interest is in the novelty and power of the new work rather than in the quality of the execution, or (b) a highly organized executive undertaking where the interest lies in the more and more perfect interpretation of works that are already received as classics. A movement of this kind is chiefly useful in a country where there has been a successful creative movement.

So far our movement has been entirely creative—the only movement of the kind I think now existing—and it is for this reason that it has at-tracted so much attention. To turn this movement now—for what are to some extent extrinsic reasons—into an executive movement for the pro-duction of a great number of foreign plays of many types would be, I cannot but think, a disastrous policy. None of us are suited for such an undertaking—it will be done in good time by a dramatic Hugh Lane when Ireland is ripe for it. I think that Yeats' view that it would be a good thing for Irish audiences—*our* audiences—or young writers is mistaken. Goethe at the end of his life said that he and Schiller had failed to found a German drama at Weimar because they had confused the public mind by giving one day Shakespeare, one day Calderon, one day Sophocles and so on. Whether he is right or not we can see that none of the municipal theatres that are all over Europe are creating or helping to create a new stage literature. We are right to do work like the *Doctor** and *Oedipus* because they illuminate our work, but for that reason only. Our supply of native plays is very small, and we should go on I think for a long time with a very small company so that the native work may go a long way towards keeping it occupied.

As you [Lady Gregory] say, Miss Horniman's money—as far as I am aware—is quite insufficient for anything in the nature of a municipal

* Molière's *The Doctor in Spite of Himself.*

theatre. The Bohemian Theatre has £12,000 a year and all scenery. The interest on the £25,000 would be I suppose £800 or £900, so that for us all large schemes would mean a short life, and then a collapse as it has happened in so many English movements. If we are to have a grant from some Irish State fund, we are more likely to get one that will be of real use if we keep our movement local.

I do not see a possibility of any workable arrangement in which Miss Horniman would have control of some of the departments.

That is my feeling on the general questions raised by Yeats' statement. Now for practical matters. W. Fay must be freed; that I think is urgently necessary if he is to keep up the quality of his acting. An assistant stage manager as we agreed will do this if we can find the right man.

For verse plays—Yeats' plays—I am ready to agree to almost any experiment that he thinks desirable in order to ensure good performances. Mrs. Emery* as you suggest, might be of great use. At the same time I think he is possibly mistaken in looking on the English stage for the people that are needed. Looking back from here with the sort of perspective that distance gives, I greatly dislike the impression that *Deirdre,* or rather Miss Darragh has left on me. Emotion—if it cannot be given with some trace of distinction or nobility—is best left to the imagination of the audience. Did not Cleopatra and Lady Macbeth and Miranda make more impression when they were played by small boys than when they are done by Mrs. P. Campbell? I wonder how one of Dunn's kids† would be in Dectora!

I would rather go on trying our own people for ten years than bring in this ready-made style that is so likely to destroy the sort of distinction everyone recognizes in our own company. Still that is only my personal feeling and, as I said, I think it essential that Yeats should be able to try something that seems at all likely to help on his work, which requires so much skill.

To wind up, I am convinced that it would be our wisest policy to work on steadily and on our own lines for the term of the Patent. After that we may get a grant from our own Home Rule Government, or we may all have to go to the Workhouse—where I have no doubt W. G. F. would be exceedingly popular.

Since Yeats was in London, placating Willie Fay was left to Synge. Lady Gregory wrote: "All depends now upon you! Yeats writes that he hasn't seen Fay—so to you it is left to tell him of the proposal and

* Florence Farr.
† J. H. Dunne was a member of the company.

get his views—Yeats' letters and mine go round in a circle. I am in-clined, weighing all things, to try the £500 man, but I want to know Fay's point of view before urging it on him. Yeats says, 'If we are all three firm, Fay will give in,' but I say, 'If he doesn't give in, what?'" Willie Fay did not give in, whatever Synge said to him, and Lady Gregory wired to Yeats: "Fay refuses. Synge relieved. My instinct with them but most unwilling to go against you."

In the end, however, Willie Fay was forced to capitulate, and in a letter to Yeats written on January 11th, Synge stated the terms of the final agreement to which all hands finally agreed:

Dear Yeats, We accept the new man at the following terms:
1. £100 a year added to W. G. Fay's present wages.
2. We—the authors—to be free to withdraw all our plays at the end of six months—in other words that the agreement we signed as to the Irish rights to be cancelled at the end of six months.
3. You are if possible to talk out scheme of duties for new man with some one who knows and submit same to us.
4. We take it for granted that my—Synge's—suggestions have been agreed to or if not let us hear.
5. Fay must have a written contract defining his duties and giving him control of dialect work.
6. It is evident that new man will have more business than stage man-agement and it is essential that he should be thorough theatrical business man, if possible an Irishman.

Yeats and Miss Horniman had had their way. Fay's feelings were assuaged with an additional £100 in salary, and his work as director was henceforth to be limited to dialect work. Synge had won his point that they hold to their original objective of using a small company of native actors to perform native plays and not try to rival the state-endowed classical theatres on the Continent. At the same time Yeats was to be allowed whatever English actors he might feel were neces-sary to his work, and Lady Gregory had made a strategic withdrawal. As she wrote to Synge: "I would not for a moment think of accepting this 'fancy man' but that I think Yeats wants new excitement, a new impetus, or will tire of the theatre, and I feel myself very much bound to him, besides personal friendship, because we are the only survivors of the beginning of the movement. I think his work more

important than any other (you must not be offended at this) and I
think it our chief distinction."

When she wrote to Yeats and told him of what she had written to
Synge, he replied:

I don't suppose Synge sympathized with your telling him that you cared
most for my work. I really don't think him selfish or egotistical, but he
is so absorbed in his own vision of the world that he cares for nothing
else. But there is a passage somewhere in Nietzsche which describes this
kind of man as if he were the normal man of genius. A woman here the
other day told me that she said to Synge, "So and so thinks you the best
of the Irish dramatists," to which he replied, with a perfectly natural
voice as if he were saying something as a matter of course, "That isn't
saying much." In some ways he is as naive as Edward,* but Edward's
naiveté came not from absorption but stolidity of nerve.[115]

The new director, Ben Iden Payne, took up his duties at the end of
February but remained in the job less than four months, after which
Willie Fay once more took complete control. Fay probably knew all
along that he would win in the end. Yeats had compared him to "a
certain old Fenian" whose face brightened "when Mrs. MacBride's
Italian revolutionist wound up a detailed project for a rising in Connacht with the sentence, 'I see no chance of success before this
course.' "

One other result of the controversy was that Miss Horniman, whose
relations with Synge had been deteriorating since the trip to Glasgow
when he defended Fay, was infuriated by his letter condemning her
ambitious plan. She wrote to Lady Gregory from Algiers:

Mr. Synge's letter made me really angry. It carried this to my mind—
let us have a theatre where foreign classics and other plays may be used
to train actors to play Synge. Let other authors go hang! The lessee has
no vote, she is bound by her Saxon sense of honor, it is absurd that her
views or desires should be regarded except when she admires and pushes
Synge's plays. If he thinks honestly that Dublin was anything to me but
a mere geographical detail when I made my original offer he is making
a great mistake. Fay is necessary to Mr. Synge himself, but neither are
anything but extrinsic to my root idea.

* Edward Martyn.

Fortunately *The Playboy* went into rehearsal just as the crisis was passing, and absorbed everybody's energies. Molly was ill and in bed right up to the start of rehearsals, and Synge was fighting a cold which was to develop into influenza. But both were present when rehearsals began on the morning of January 8th.

Thirteen

THE PLAYBOY RIOTS

THE CURSE

TO A SISTER OF AN ENEMY OF THE AUTHOR'S
WHO DISAPPROVED OF *The Playboy*.

Lord, confound this surly sister,
Blight her brow with blotch and blister,
Cramp her larynx, lung, and liver,
In her guts a galling give her.

Let her live to earn her dinners
In Mountjoy with seedy sinners:
Lord, this judgment quickly bring,
And I'm your servant, J. M. Synge.

It is traditional at the Abbey Theatre to preserve a certain amount of secrecy about a new play before its opening. When Joseph Holloway, who was usually exempted from the ruling, dropped into the theatre on the morning of January 8, 1907, to satisfy his curiosity about Synge's new play, Frank Fay told him that he would have to leave. Holloway had suspected that special precautions were being taken over *The Playboy*, and his curiosity did not subside. Ten days later he wrote in his diary:

Had a chat with H. Young during the interval *re The Playboy* and pumped him on the subject. He candidly said he did not care for the piece and thought it had no plot. It was about a man who was supposed to have killed his father, and the people made much of him on that account and a girl worshipped him for the deed. It turns out that papa is not dead at all and he is left severely alone by his friends and the girl turns up her noble nose at him in scorn. "A play in praise of murder," I suggested, and he said he did not think so, but then he could not rightly tell me what it was all about, though taking part in it. He . . . added that he heard that there is an organized opposition present to hiss Synge's play and I pooh-poohed the idea and said it is all rot to think so.

Yeats, Lady Gregory and Fay had been apprehensive of *The Playboy*'s potentialities since the day Synge had read the first two acts to them. Willie Fay wanted Synge to take out the scene in the last act where a hot sod is applied to Christy's foot to quiet him when he is bound but still thrashing. Writing some years later, Lady Gregory recollected:

There were too many violent oaths, and the play itself was marred by this. I did not think it was fit to be put on the stage without cutting. It was agreed that it should be cut in rehearsal. A fortnight before its production, Mr. Yeats, thinking I had seen a rehearsal, wrote, "I would like to know how you thought *The Playboy* acted. . . . Have they cleared many of the objectionable sentences out of it?" I did not, however, see a rehearsal and did not hear the play again until the night of its production, and then I told Synge that the cuts were not enough, that many more should be made. He gave me leave to do this, and, in consultation with the players, I took out many phrases which, though in the printed book, have never since that first production been spoken on our stage. I am sorry that they were not taken out before it had been played at all, but that is just what happened.[116]

Some cuts were made by Synge himself, who was superintending the rehearsals, but—as Lady Gregory's recollection indicates—they must have been very few. Willie Fay wrote: "We might as well have tried to move the Hill of Howth as move Synge. That was his play, he said, and, barring one or two jots and tittles of 'bad language' that he grudgingly consented to excise, it was the play that with a great screwing up of courage we produced."[117] The jots and tittles included the lines in which Pegeen accuses the Widow Quin of having reared a black ram at her breast, "so that the Lord Bishop of Connaught felt the elements of a Christian, and he eating it after in a kidney stew," and Michael James' reference to "five men, aye, and six men, stretched out retching speechless on the holy stones" at Kate Cassidy's wake. But they did not, unfortunately, include Christy's boast, which finally ignited the opening night's audience—"It's Pegeen I'm seeking only, and what'd I care if you brought me a drift of chosen females, standing in their shifts itself, maybe, from this place to the eastern world?"

Synge was aware that his language was frequently robust and, at the urging of Lady Gregory perhaps, wrote the program note which was intended to turn away wrath but which only created it:

> In writing *The Playboy of the Western World*, as in my other plays, I have used few words that I have not heard among the country people, or spoken in my own childhood before I could read the newspapers. A certain number of the phrases I employ I have heard also from the fishermen of Kerry and Mayo, or from beggars nearer Dublin, and I am glad to acknowledge how much I owe, directly and indirectly to the folk-imagination of these people. Nearly always when some friendly or angry critic tells me that such or such a phrase could not have been spoken by a peasant, he singles out some expression that I have heard, word for word, from some old woman or child, and the same is true also, to some extent, of the actions and incidents I work with. The central incident of the *Playboy* was suggested by an actual occurrence in the west.

If he had offered no defence at all or used the preface which he had just sent off to the publisher, in which wording and tone were quite different, his audience might not have thought that they were being challenged by a man who had already been castigated as a slanderer of Ireland. The preface which is now considered an important contribution to the critical literature of the theatre is neither an apology nor a defence, but a statement of his theory of language for the stage.

Synge was at the theatre every day, although he was strained and weary. Holloway mentions seeing him two days before the opening, sitting in the gloom of the theatre, listening to the actors rehearsing on stage. On the same day J. B. Yeats made the drawing of him entitled "Synge at Rehearsal," as he sat with his arms folded, his black Stetson pushed back on his head. He wrote to Molly in the morning of Saturday, January 26th, that they would be unlikely to meet after the opening night and that they had better not try to meet the next day for their walk. He had a bad cough and was quite exhausted. "I am thinking more about my being without my little changeling tomorrow than I am thinking about the *P. B.* All the same I most fervently hope it will go off well and be a credit to both of us."

Despite the apprehensions Yeats and Lady Gregory had, and the rumour which Holloway recorded of an organized opposition, the directors had no real expectation of trouble. Yeats was in Scotland, and Lady Gregory would not have come up from Coole that night if Yeats had not wired asking her to see Synge about some proposals made in connection with hiring the new director.

The Abbey Theatre's usual audience consisted mostly of people who were Nationalist in outlook. Sometimes a party from the Viceregal Lodge was in the stalls, for the Viceroy's Liberal party advisers were anxious to show that the crown had no objection to purely artistic manifestations of Irish Nationalism. The Unionist minority, on the whole, ignored the Irish literary movement altogether. The audience on that opening night was a first-night audience and therefore probably attracted more distinguished Dublin people than an ordinary performance. Being for the most part Nationalist in their sympathies, they undoubtedly had opinions about Synge's work, and very likely knew of Arthur Griffith's attack even if they had not read *The United Irishman*. Synge's last play had been neither popular nor successful, even if his work had created more general interest than that of any other dramatist.

For the first two acts they were orderly and quiet but brooding. With the beginning of the third act the actors felt the air of restlessness in the audience, and by the end of the act the eruption had taken place. Holloway had noted that Willie Fay substituted the words "Mayo girls" for "chosen females" in Christy's "drifts of chosen females standing in their shifts" and that this speech more than any other set the audience to hissing. But there was applause, and the din was kept up until the curtain dropped. Holloway wrote:

On coming out Lady Gregory asked me what was the cause of the disturbance, and my monosyllabic answer was "Blackguardism"—to which she queried on which side? "The stage" came from me pat and then I passed and the incident was closed. Many gentlemen such as D. J. O'Donoghue and McNamara, the architect, said to me afterwards that they were delighted they had not taken their wives to the show. The latter said he never was so much taken aback in his life and hissed for all he was worth. What did Synge mean by such filth? Was there no one to supervise the plays? Synge met with his desserts from the audience and I hope he will take the lesson to heart. . . . Synge is the evil genius of the Abbey and Yeats his able lieutenant. Both dabble in the unhealthy.

Holloway was an unofficial member of the Abbey Theatre family, and his voluminous diary is a massive testimonial to his devotion to it over a period of many years. But he was not a man of much taste, and his dislike of Yeats made him unsympathetic to any plays that had pretentions to being more than mere entertainments. His angry reaction to *The Playboy,* however, was not very different from that of a number of Dublin literary men who can be blamed much more easily for what they said.

After the performance, Synge and Lady Gregory took counsel. Synge was exhausted, suffering from his cold, and shaken by the angry hostility to his play. To Yeats lecturing in Scotland that night Lady Gregory had sent a telegram after the second act reading, "Play great success." After the third act she and Synge sent another reading, "Audience broke up in disorder at the word shift." Whether they also asked him to return to Dublin immediately is not clear, but perhaps the telegram itself was enough, because Yeats returned by way of Belfast and arrived in Dublin on Tuesday morning. By that time Lady Gregory and Synge had already made the crucial decision to go on with *The Playboy.*

Synge's letter to Molly the next morning was restrained. He had been unable to sleep and had a splitting headache.

I wish I had you here to talk over the whole show last night. W. G. was pretty bluffy, and Power was very confused in places. Then the crowd was wretched and Mrs. W. G. missed the new cue we gave, though she can hardly be blamed for that. I think with a better Mahon and crowd and a few slight cuts the play would be thoroughly sound. I feel like old Maurya today. "It's four fine plays I have, though it was a hard birth I had with everyone of them and they coming to the world."

It is better any day to have the row we had last night, than to have your play fizzling out in half-hearted applause. Now we'll be talked about. We're an event in the history of the Irish stage. . . .

Dearest treasure you don't [know] how you have changed the world to me. Now that I have you I don't care twopence for what anyone else in the world may say or do. You are my whole world to me now, you that is, and the little shiny new moon and the flowers of the earth. My little love how I am wrapped up in you! It went to my heart to desert you last night, but I could not get away from Lady Gregory.

He went into Dublin at noontime, and over lunch he and Lady Gregory discussed the decision they had made the night before. When Lady Gregory suggested that they should call in the police for Monday's performance, he did not object. At home he had said very little about the performance on Saturday night; mostly he was accustomed to saying nothing about the theatre or his plays. Monday morning's *Irish Times*, which was less critical than the Nationalist papers, published a long account of the performance and the audience's reaction, and concluded that the dialogue was full of indiscretions which brought "what in other respects was a brilliant success to an inglorious conclusion." The other papers were not so restrained. *The Freeman's Journal* described the play as "unmitigated, protracted libel upon Irish peasant men and, worse still upon Irish peasant girlhood. The blood boils with indignation as one recalls the incidents, expressions, ideas of this squalid, offensive production, incongruously styled a comedy in three acts. . . . No adequate idea can be given of the barbarous jargon, the elaborate and incessant cursings of these repulsive creatures." *The Evening Mail* thought it might have been some kind of allegory—"the parricide represents some kind of nation-killer, whom Irish men and Irish women hasten to lionize. If it is an allegory it is too obscure for me. I cannot stalk this alligator on the banks of the Liffey. . . . If a man is stupid enough to suggest that the Irish people are cannibals or gorillas, my hand will not fumble for the sword-hilt." The other papers were scarcely less temperate.

The house was full again for Monday night's performance. Holloway was present at the conclusion and wrote:

Two stalwart police at the vestibule door suggested trouble and we found plenty and to spare when we went in. The performance was just concluding amid a terrific uproar (the piece had not been listened to we were told). The curtains were drawn aside and W. G. Fay stood forward amid the din. After some minutes in a lull, he said, "You who have hissed tonight will go away saying you have heard the play, but you haven't." "We heard it on Saturday," came from the back of the pit and the hissing and hooting was renewed. The scene which followed was indescribable. Those in the pit howled for the author, and he with Lady Gregory and others held animated conversation in the stalls. . . . Small knots of people argued the situation out anything but calmly and after about a quarter of an hour's clamour the audience dispersed hoarse.

What Holloway had not seen was the actors going through the motions of the play almost entirely in dumb show and then coming forward defiantly to bow to the audience at the end of each act. At one point in the middle of an act, when the shouting became too great, the curtain was rung down, the police clustered around what appeared to be the center of the disturbance, the curtain went up again and the play continued, once more with only an occasional line of dialogue spoken on the stage. At another point the action on the stage was stopped altogether, and the actors paused while Willie Fay came forward and asked the audience to withdraw and get their money back.

After the performance Synge, "excited and restless, the perspiration standing out in great beads over his forehead and cheeks," gave an interview to a reporter from *The Evening Mail* which he was later to regret. He had wisely kept aloof from the controversy over his first play and, as Yeats afterwards said, he was useless in such situations. He denied that his purpose in writing the play was "to represent Irish life as it is lived. . . . I wrote the play because it pleased me, and it just happens that I know Irish life best, so I made my methods Irish." His play, he insisted, was "a comedy, an extravaganza, made to amuse," and he didn't "care a rap how the people take it. I never bother whether my plots are typically Irish or not; but my methods are typical."

His excitement seemed to go on growing. . . . He went on talking to me at a rate which made me glad I was not taking him down in shorthand. . . . I was just able to catch him up at the end, to the effect that the speech used by his characters was the actual speech of the people and that in art a spade must be called spade. "But the complaint is, Mr. Synge, that you call it a bloody shovel. Of course I am not speaking from personal experience, for I have not heard a word at all from the stage, though I could not possibly be nearer it. And that reminds me, Mr. Synge, what do you propose to do for the rest of the week, in face of what has taken place tonight?" "We shall go on with the play to the very end, in spite of all," he answered, snapping his fingers, more excited than ever. "I don't care a rap."

On Tuesday morning Yeats arrived and took charge. He suspected, whether rightly or wrongly nobody knows, that the real centre of resistance had come not from the general public—since the opening-night audience could scarcely be called a cross section of the Dublin public—but from his old friends in the Nationalist movement. He knew that Edward Martyn, who had become president of Sinn Fein, the political party founded by Arthur Griffith, and who was also president of the Theatre of Ireland, made up of the seceders, was innocent, but his reservations stopped there. If there was any truth to the rumour that opposition to the play was organized—and it seemed to receive support from the newspaper accounts of the disturbances—he would deal with it as it deserved by offering counter-opposition. Tuesday night's audience would find even more police than on Monday night, and in addition there would be an organized claque. Diarmuid Coffey, the biographer of Douglas Hyde who was then an undergraduate at Trinity College, collected a few students, to whom Yeats gave free tickets, to give the play some support.

Yeats was full of fight when he and Synge, lunching in the Metropole Hotel, talked to a reporter from *The Freeman's Journal*. Yeats did most of the talking, but the report of the interview published next day was hardly more tactful than Synge's had been. Yeats said that "the people who formed the opposition had no books in their houses," and that their opinions were moulded not by leaders of ability but by societies, clubs and leagues headed by "commonplace and ignorant people who try to take on an appearance of strength by imposing some crude shibboleth on their own and others' necks. They do not persuade, for that is difficult; they do not expound, for that needs knowledge. . . . We will go on until the play has been heard sufficiently to be judged on its merits. We had only announced its production for one week. We have now decided to play all next week as well, if the opposition continue, with the exception of one night, when I shall lecture on the freedom of the theatre, and invite our opponents to speak on its slavery to the mob if they have a mind to."

Synge's rather mild contribution to the interview was a statement that the idea of the play had been suggested to him by an incident that had happened in the Aran Islands and also by the case of a man named James Lynchehaun who had assaulted a woman on Achill Island and managed to conceal himself from the police by the aid of peasant women. The Lynchehaun case was well known in Ireland—Lynchehaun is mentioned in Joyce's *Ulysses*—because he eventually escaped to America where the British secret service tracked him down in Indianapolis. Irish patriotic organizations, however, interested themselves in his case, and the American courts refused to extradite him on the grounds that he was a political prisoner. Not content with his freedom, Lynchehaun returned to Ireland, visited Achill disguised as a clergyman and got out of the country safely again before the police discovered his presence. Synge was telling the truth and not just bolstering his case, for in one of the earlier drafts of the play one of the minor characters was made to say, "If they did itself I'm thinking they'd be afeared to come after him. Sure they never laid a hand to Lynchehaun from the day they knew the kind he was."

Holloway was at the performance on Tuesday night, and his report of what happened is more revealing than any newspaper accounts because he knew all the principals on both sides of the footlights and knew in advance of the preparations made to deal with the disturbance. He stood in the back of the house with D. J. O'Donoghue and W. J. Lawrence, both of them literary men and in agreement with him over their dislike of the play. Holloway spotted the Trinity claque at once and noticed that some of them were drunk and apparently more interested in baiting the townees than in applauding the play:

This precious gang of noisy boys hailed from Trinity and soon after the *Playboy* commenced, one of their number . . . made himself objectionable and was forcibly removed by Synge and others after a free fight amongst the instruments of the orchestra. W. B. Yeats came before the curtain after *Riders to the Sea** and made a speech, inviting a free discussion on the play on Monday night next in the theatre. Shortly after the commencement of the police-protected play a remark from a pitite

* The curtain raiser.

Molly Allgood as Deirdre. Photograph by Chancellor, Dublin, taken early in January, 1910. *Deirdre of the Sorrows* opened on January 13.

set the college boys to their feet and for a moment they looked like going for those in the pit, but didn't. The uproar was deafening and it was here that Mr . . . got put out. One of the theatre bullies removed by the people who wanted him in struck me as a funny sight. This set the noise in motion and W. B. Yeats again came on the scene and with raised hand secured silence. He referred to the removal of one drunken man and hoped all that were sober would listen to the play.

The noise continued and shortly after a body of police led on by W. B. Yeats marched out of the side door from the scene dock and ranged along the walls of the pit. Hugh Lane now made himself very conspicuous by pointing out some men in the pit and demanding their arrest as disturbers of the peace. Yeats also was busy just now as a spy aiding the police in picking out persons disapproving of the glorification of murder on the stage. . . . At the end chaos seemed to have entered the Abbey and the college youths clambered on the seats and began the English national anthem, while those in the body of the hall sang something else of home growth.

Yeats actually shouted at the audience: "We have put this play before you to be heard and to be judged, as every play should be heard and judged. Every man has a right to hear it and condemn it if he pleases, but no man has a right to interfere with another man hearing a play and judging for himself. The country that condescends either to bully or to permit itself to be bullied soon ceases to have any fine qualities, and I promise you that if there is any small section in this theatre that wish to deny the right of others to hear what they themselves don't want to hear we will play on, and our patience shall last longer than their patience."

The next morning Yeats appeared in the Northern Police Court to testify against the rioters arrested the night before. Piaras Beaslai, who later became the biographer of Michael Collins, and Padraic Colum's father were among the defendants fined forty shillings. Padraic Colum came to his father's defence in a letter to the press, and refused Lady Gregory's offer to pay his father's fine.

When Holloway "sauntered down" to the theatre on Wednesday night he "saw an immense crowd awaiting the pit door to be opened and police everywhere." The audience seemed to be about equally divided between objectors and defenders, and it listened to the performances in patches. Fifty policemen in the aisles exercised "a somewhat restraining influence," as *The Irish Times'* reporter phrased it. Synge and Lady Gregory sat quietly in the stalls near the orchestra while Yeats prowled through the crowd, talking to the police. Willie Fay remonstrated with the audience once from the stage, and a fist fight got out of control in the pit. After the performance some of the audience paraded through the streets near the theatre. Court proceedings with Yeats again testifying took place next day before a magistrate who lectured the defendants and fined them ten shillings each. For the next three days he continued to lecture and fine the *Playboy* rioters brought before him, and the newspapers found him very good copy.

In a letter to *The Irish Times* on Thursday, Synge tried to dispel the impression he had himself created by his unfortunate interview in *The Evening Mail*, when he implied that his play was not to be taken seriously. "*The Playboy of the Western World*," he explained, "is not a play with 'a purpose' in the modern sense of the word, but although parts of it are, or are meant to be, extravagant comedy, still a great deal that is in it, and a great deal more that is behind it, is perfectly serious when looked at in a certain light. That is often the case, I think, with comedy, and no one is quite sure today whether Shylock and Alceste should be played seriously or not. There are, it may be hinted, several sides to *The Playboy*."

His cold had grown worse, and the strain of the riots was beginning to tell. Agnes Tobin wrote to him from London, "What a blessing you did not go on to version L* if version K has had such a disastrous effect." He went in to Thursday's performance, however, and wrote a short note to Molly, whom he had not been able to talk to very much during the week. It was a quiet evening—only two men were arrested from the audience. On Friday he wrote to Molly: "Cheer up, my little heart, the *P. B.* will soon be getting his rest, I hope, and then we'll be able to see a lot of each other till we get everything fixed up. . . . You don't know how much I admire the way you are playing P. Mike in spite of all the row."

Yeats told a reporter from *The Evening Mail* after Thursday's performance that he had decided not to continue the play for another week. "I think that gradually the audience are coming to understand what it means. We had tonight, for the first time I think, the majority

* Synge lettered the successive drafts of his plays.

of the pit on our side. We have always had the stalls." But it may have been the efficiency of the police that the audience was getting to understand, and Holloway's reaction to Thursday's performance was probably more representative: "The police-protected drama by the dramatist of the dung heap attached to the Abbey got a fair hearing tonight and was voted by those around me very poor dull dramatic stuff."

Friday's *Freeman's Journal* carried a letter from London by William Boyle, publicly dissociating himself from the Abbey Theatre and withdrawing his three plays from their repertoire. Despite Yeats' low opinion of Boyle's talents, his three plays had been popular and their loss at this time was a blow. Immediately after *The Playboy* had finished its run, Willie Fay went to London to reason with Boyle, but to no avail. It was a year and a half before Boyle came back to the fold and five years before he gave the Abbey a new play.

Friday night's audience was docile, if not friendly, and only one arrest was made. Saturday's papers printed a letter by Stephen Gwynn which deplored the rowdyism in the theatre, and blamed William Boyle for joining in the cry and "laying down the law to his own hurt." But at the same time Gwynn did "not in the least regret that the play was hissed at its first performance, for the very good reason that if it were played with acceptance, word would immediately go out that parricide is a popular exploit in Ireland." The sentiments were not unlike those expressed by some other literary men.

Synge's nemesis Arthur Griffith had not been inactive during the week; but his paper, which was now called *Sinn Fein* and was the official organ of a political party, was a weekly and he could only editorialize on the riots. He had been present at Tuesday's performance, and the account which appeared in his paper on Thursday described *The Playboy* as a "vile and inhuman story told in the foulest language we have ever listened to from a public platform." Griffith was sure that he had heard Old Mahon at one point in the play refer to his son as a "scuttering lout." *Scuttering* is a variant of *scuttling*, but in Dublin argot it has an indecent meaning. When Ambrose Power, the actor playing Old Mahon, insisted in a letter to the papers that he had said *stuttering*, as the script called for, Griffith was forced to accept his explanation in the next number. But he did not withdraw his charge of foul language notwithstanding.

Saturday's performances were relatively quiet, but not because the public opinion had changed noticeably. To Holloway the evening audience looked as though the music halls had "emptied themselves out into the pit and balcony to judge by the cut of the customers with patches over the eye, week-old mushroom beards, smelly pipes. I don't envy Mr. Synge his newly-found followers. . . . The police were as thick as blackberries in September and a row of them sat along the center of the pit as well as lining all the walls and filling the scene dock and laneway and streets outside." There was an atmosphere of brooding frustration over an audience forced to listen quietly to the first uninterrupted performance the play had had since the opening night. The most tumultuous event in Dublin theatrical history was over, though the debate over the man who had slain his *da* was to rage for weeks to come and the riots were to be repeated years later in places as remote from Dublin as New York and Montreal.

The Irishman's wars are always merry, even if his songs are always sad, as Chesterton once noted, and *The Playboy* riots were no exception. One amusing product of them was the pamphlet entitled *The Abbey Row*, the joint efforts of Page Dickenson, Frank Sparrow, Richard Caulfield Orpen, William Orpen and Joseph Hone. Dickenson wrote most of the prose selections in it, Sparrow the verse—though Susan Mitchell contributed at least one poem—the Orpen brothers designed and illustrated it and Joseph Hone published it through his firm of Maunsel and Company. It was made up to look like a copy of the Abbey Theatre's occasional publication *The Arrow*, but the figure of Eire on the cover was Mrs. Grundy carrying an umbrella instead of a quiver, and the wolf dog had the face of J. M. Synge. The humour of the whole pamphlet was good natured, only mildly satirical, and its effect was to remind Irishmen that they could at least laugh at themselves. Susan Mitchell's contribution was perhaps the most effective:

Oh, no, we never mention it, its name is never heard—
Now Ireland sets its face against the once familiar word.
They take me to the Gaelic League where men wear kilts, and yet
The simple word of childhood's days I'm bidden to forget!

They tell me no one says it now, but yet to give me ease—
If I must speak they bid me use a word that rhymes with "sneeze."
But, oh! their cold permission my spirits cannot lift—
I only want the dear old word, the one that ends in "ift."

Oh, cruel Gaelic Leaguers! cruel Sinn Feiners all!
Have you no little sisters, who once when very small,
Before they knew what sinfulness could lurk in one wee word—
Have you not from their artless lips its simple accents heard?

Then by those early memories, hearken to one who prays
The right to mention once again the word of other days,
Without police protection once more her voice to lift—
The right to tell (even to herself) that still she wears—a shift.

On Monday *The Freeman's Journal* carried the report of an interview with Yeats as well as letters from William Boyle, D. J.
O'Donoghue and Alice Milligan. Yeats did his best to pacify Boyle
by pointing out that his own plays had been attacked by the same opposition as Synge's and that the directors hoped he would reconsider
his withdrawal of them. Boyle replied to Gwynn; Alice Milligan objected to the play as well as the use of the police to force it down the
throats of the audiences. For O'Donoghue, "The continuous ferocity
of the language, the consistent shamelessness of all the characters
(without exception), and the persistent allusions to sacred things
make the play even more inexcusable as an extravaganza than as a
serious play. . . . To my mind the episode of the blessing by the
drunken publican is painfully gratuitous." Other papers were full of
letters attacking the play and gave accounts of Saturday's performances and of the court proceedings on Saturday morning.

Synge had gone home on Saturday night, wearied from the strain of
having sat through every performance of his play during the week. His
cold had got worse, and he went to bed with a fever. He was still
exhausted and feverish on Sunday but could not resist going to Bray
with Molly for a short walk. He returned home even more feverish,
stayed in bed throughout Monday and called the doctor. Padraic
Colum wrote him:

I've been to *The Playboy* again. I disliked the third act the first time
I saw it, and though it is still far from satisfying me, I did not dislike it

so much last night. There are several things wrong in it, I think. The crowd standing by and apparently watching a man being beaten with a log, the girl putting a red hot coal on Christy. The latter was cut last night and the other thing was so swiftly done that we did not realize it. Peggy is a creation distinctly and acted splendidly. Still I think she would have stood by her man when he was attacked by a crowd. The play does not satisfy me.

When the debate took place, as Yeats had promised, on Monday night, Synge was not present, but apparently everyone else in the Dublin literary world was. Mary Colum, who was then a student, wrote an eyewitness account of it, and the Dublin newspapers gave it full coverage. Yeats made what was certainly one of the most courageous utterances of his life to an audience almost entirely hostile and threatening. The riots and the bitter controversies that erupted out of them were to have a lasting effect on him—even more than upon Synge, "so absorbed in his own vision of the world that he cares for nothing else." But Yeats never weakened in his commitment to the ideals he had so belligerently expounded. As he stepped out on the stage that night his audience knew that he was as unruffled by their hostility as were the immaculate evening clothes he had put on as a further note of defiance. Mary Colum wrote that when they refused to listen to him he reminded them that he was the author of *Cathleen Ni Houlihan*. "The audience, remembering that passionately patriotic play, forgot its antagonism for a few moments and Yeats got his cheers. . . . I never witnessed a human being fight as Yeats fought that night, nor knew another with so many weapons in his armory."[118]

Lady Gregory sent Synge the next day a complete account of the whole affair:

. . . The theatre was crammed; all the stalls had been taken at Cramer's (we made £16). Before it began there was whistling *etc.* "Pat"* made a good chairman, didn't lose his temper and made himself heard, but no chairman could have done much. Yeats' first speech was fairly well listened to, though there were boos and cries. . . . No one came to support us. Russell was in the gallery we heard afterwards but did not come forward or speak. Colum "had a rehearsal" and didn't speak or come. T.

* Patrick Kenny, author of *Economics for Irishmen* and editor of a magazine called *The Irish Peasant*.

W. Russell didn't turn up. We had hardly anyone to speak on our side at all, but it didn't much matter for the disturbances were so great they wouldn't even let their own speakers be well heard. Lawrence* was first to attack us, a very poor speech, his point that we should have taken the play off because the audience and papers didn't like it, then a long rigmarole about a strike of the public against a rise of prices at Covent garden, and medal which was struck to commemorate their victory. But he bored the audience.

You will see the drift of the other speakers. Little Beaslai's was the only one with a policy, for he announced his intention of never entering the place again, and called upon others to do so. But the cheering grew very feeble at that point. A Dr. Ryan supported us fairly well, though it was hard to get speakers to come forward. At the thick of the riot Mrs. Duncan sent up her name to the platform offering to give an address! But Pat sent back word he would not like to see her insulted! A young man forced his way up and argued with Dossie till a whiskey bottle fell from his pocket and broke on the stage, at which Dossie flung him down the steps and there was great cheering and laughing, and Dossie flushed with honest pride.

Old Yeats made a very good speech and got at first a very good reception, though when he went up there were cries of "Kill your father," "Get the loy" *etc.* and at the end when he praised Synge he was booed. The last speakers could hardly be heard at all. There was a tipsy man in the pit crying, "I'm from Belfast! Ulster aboo!" Many of our opponents called for order and fair play, and I think must have been disgusted with their allies. The scene certainly justified us in having called in the police. The interruptions were very stupid and monotonous.

Yeats when he rose for the last speech was booed but got a hearing at last and got out all he wanted to say. He spoke very well, but his voice rather cracked once or twice from screaming and from his sore throat. I was sorry while there that we had ever let such a set inside the theatre, but I am glad today, and I think it was spirited and showed we were not repenting or apologizing. Pat came here afterwards, very indignant with the rowdies. It is a mercy today to think the whole thing is over.

I had a wire from Fay yesterday, "Tabby† completely upset Boyle. No use waiting here," and he came back this morning and has been here. He could do nothing with Boyle. Says it was temper roused by Miss Horniman's letter of cock-crows that roused him to write first, but now he won't withdraw unless Yeats will make a public declaration that we made

* W. J. Lawrence, author of *Pre-Restoration Stage Studies.*
† Apparently Miss Horniman.

a mistake in putting on *The Playboy*. Fay said of course that was impossible and Boyle won't give in. He seems to have no reason but Fay
thinks he had an uneasy feeling he didn't know where we might be
leading him. He refused to read the script. Fay would like to kick him,
which is healthy sign, and we have been arranging the programme for
the rest of the season without his work, which is rather a comfort. . . .

When a hoarse and weary Yeats walked off the stage, the controversy
over *The Playboy* was far from finished. It was to flare up again, less
violently, when the play was revived in 1909, two months after Synge's
death, and it was to follow the company on its first tour to the New
World in 1911 when Irish-American people in a dozen cities wrote
angry letters to the papers and came to the theatre to demonstrate
their patriotism by hissing *The Playboy*. In Washington the company
was attacked in sermons from the pulpit and in a pamphlet published
by "The Aloysius Truth Society." In Chicago they were attacked in
the city council, but the mayor turned down all demands that they be
denied the use of a theatre. In Philadelphia they were arrested for
producing "immoral and indecent" plays, but John Quinn rushed to
their rescue and demolished the charges of the witnesses who appeared
against them.

The Irish in this country were probably no more sensitive to the
fact of their emigrant origins and to the menial role they had played
in American life than other national groups. But unlike the others
they had no language barrier to overcome, and they were beginning
to assert themselves politically. *The Playboy* was an opportunity for
lusty, if not very dignified, self-expression. Their objections to Synge's
play were neither articulate nor informed, and one suspects that they
rose up in anger before they knew exactly what they were angry about.

In Ireland, however, the facts were somewhat different. The usual
explanation for the riots is that a resurgent Ireland would no longer
passively accept the caricature known to generations of theatregoers
as the stage Irishman, especially when it was offered to them on the
stage of a theatre they wanted to think of as a national theatre. But
the Abbey Theatre was not a national theatre. It was in fact the
personal property of an Englishwoman who was antipathetic to Irish
Nationalism and merely wanted to further the artistic career of W. B.
Yeats. Its dramatists, it is true, aimed at building a golden bridge be-

tween the present and the Celtic past by dramatizing the life of the peasant, but they insisted upon dealing with him as they saw him and not as they were expected to see him. Reduced to its essentials, the story of the riots is the story of a clash between two groups of dedicated people. Arthur Griffith and the other Nationalist leaders were not philistines, even if they did bear the chief responsibility for the opposition to Synge and Yeats. No doubt they attempted quite clearly to absorb every movement and organization in Ireland into their own orbit, because they believed that the effort to establish a free Ireland would be strengthened if every activity which touched the people could be drawn into the struggle. Like politicians everywhere, they were quite literal in demanding that if Irish writers could not be eulogistic of what was called the national character, they should at least not be critical.

The opposition to *The Playboy* may not have been organized deliberately, as Yeats suspected, but it could hardly have been called spontaneous. When one recalls the opposition to *The Countess Cathleen* in 1899, the attack on *In the Shadow of the Glen* in 1903, the actors' secession in 1906 and the setting up of a rival theatre more closely identified with the political movement, one can see that the Abbey Theatre needed only Synge's brilliant and mordant satire to ignite fires that were awaiting the torch anyway. Indeed, when one looks at the later history of the theatre and to the demonstrations which Sean O'Casey's scepticism towards Nationalist idealism aroused in the twenties, one can see that the battle would have been fought without *The Playboy*. Today the old hostility to Synge, Yeats and O'Casey has largely, but not entirely, disappeared, because the Nationalist dream has come true and Ireland has other battles to fight. The Abbey Theatre is now the property of the Irish government, and when *The Playboy* is revived Dubliners applaud it as a treasured classic.

But Irishmen know now, as they had suspected in 1907, that *The Playboy* was neither extravaganza nor the usual example of garrison-class humour caricaturing the wild Irish, but a satire whose thesis they chose not to acknowledge, much less challenge. The critic who suspected that *The Playboy* was an allegory in which the parricide represented some kind of nation-killer was right, and he would have found the alligator he tried to stalk on the banks of the Liffey if he had gone to the rural Ireland Synge was writing about. The point of Synge's play was that it glorified the lout who demolished the whole social structure of rural Irish life when he cleft his father from the gullet to the navel for trying to force him into marrying a woman "did suckle me for six weeks when I came into the world." It also ridiculed the people of Mayo, who could be delighted with the father-murderer as long as he was the hero of a "gallous story" but would not accept him when he committed the "dirty deed" under their very noses. The Playboy's self-liberation from parental tyranny and from the loveless marriage imposed on him by peasant custom was a symbol of their own deep-seated urge to reject the tyranny in their own lives exemplified by Pegeen's forthcoming marriage to an oafish and spineless kinsman, dictated by her father and with the endorsement of Father Reilly's dispensation. The villagers in that Mayo *shebeen* could applaud Christy for his desperate act of emancipation because it was an embodiment of their own subconscious desires. But when it became a reality—suddenly and violently—and they were asked to stand up and be counted, they had only the courage of their dreams. Pegeen deceives nobody more than herself when she says that a strange man is a marvel with his mighty talk but that a squabble in your back yard is an apple off another tree. For when Christy walks out at the end, driving his father before him "like a gallant captain with his heathen slave," her momentary dream of liberation departs with him. It is he, and not she, who is "master of all fights from now." There is more truth and more tragedy in her final lament than most Irishmen of 1907 were able, or willing, to see.

The Playboy is a strikingly original play, but its brilliance and vitality were the result of conscious and deliberate workmanship over a long period of time. How Synge first conceived the play can be seen from a short sketch in an early notebook called "The Murderer":

Act I (a potato garden). Old Flaherty describes his son's life and exasperates him so much that in the end he takes the loy and hits his father on the head with it, then runs across the stage and out on left.

Act II (public house, bar, or shebeen). Christy bossing the show, tells his story three times of how he killed his father. Police are afraid to follow him and other bombast, love affairs, *etc.* At the slightest provocation he starts off again with his story.

Act III He is being elected county councilor. Old man comes in first and shows his head to everybody. He is as proud of it as his son is, as he is going round the crowd. His son comes out the elected member. He is put on a table to make a speech. He gets to the point where he is telling how he killed his father when the old man walks out. "You're a bloody liar, that's what you are."

As Synge developed his idea, modified the action and filled out his conception of the characters, he abandoned the election, substituted the romance with Pegeen as the central incident, and developed Shawn Keogh as a rival for Christy. Next he decided to rehabilitate the character of Christy after his father exposes him as an imposter. In the earlier versions of the play Christy is dismissed as a coward and walks off tamely, with a ballad singer already at work on the incident:

> Young Christopher, the daddy man,
> Came walking from Tralee.
> And his father's ghost the while
> Did keep him company.

When Shawn Keogh tells him to stop singing, that the murderer was an imposter, the ballad singer rings down the curtain. "Oh, God help me, and I after spending the half of me day making of his deed. But it's a lovely song, Well I'll sing it other roads where he's not known at all. It's a lovely song surely."

For more than two weeks after the riots Synge stayed in bed fighting his influenza. He wrote to Molly that he was glad he had not been present at the debate because "I would have got into a towering rage." Meanwhile Griffith's paper *Sinn Fein* and *An Claidheamh Soluis* [The Sword of Light], edited by Padraic Pearse for the Gaelic League, both announced in editorials that the *Playboy* riots had finished off the "Anglo-Irish" dramatic movement and that the need for a truly Irish National theatre had been demonstrated. On Saturday when the Abbey opened with *The Pot of Broth, Cathleen Ni Houlihan* and *The Doctor in Spite of Himself,* the audience was large and responsive, even if many old faces were missing.

The riots were having their repercussions outside Ireland. Word came from Liverpool that a resolution had been passed by delegates of the United Irish League, the Gaelic League, the Irish National

Foresters, Cumann na nGaedheal and the Gaelic Athletic Association affirming their appreciation "of the gallant stand by the Irish men and Irish women of Dublin in their defence of the pure, honest, and noble characteristics of their people at home" and belligerently vowing to "prevent any such production being given in the Liverpool District." Not the last had been heard of *The Playboy*, it seemed, especially for future tours of the company to the English provinces.

Synge was still in bed, though his letters to Molly were cheerful and he complained only about his influenza. Miss Horniman wrote to him on the 12th—her first letter since her bitter denunciation of him in December—to say that *The Playboy* was splendid. "I feel myself a worm having not come over, but the directors took notice of my offers to come and join the fray." Meanwhile a good many people had written him complimentary letters, but he had learned the lesson of not being drawn into any more pronouncements about its meaning. He wrote to one of his correspondents: "Whether or not I agree with your final interpretation of the whole play is my secret. I follow Goethe's rule, to tell no one what one means in one's writings. I am sure that you will agree that the rule is a good one!"

As soon as he had recovered sufficiently to get up, his mother became ill, apparently with the same infection. He decided to stay at home and finish the Wicklow pieces he had promised Joseph Hone for *The Shanachie*. Molly came out frequently, and in the intervals between their visits they wrote to each other almost daily. When she complained about the parts she was being assigned, he scolded her. "I would not bother about your parts. You have played lead in the biggest play of the season, so that ought to satisfy you for the time being. . . . You have made your place in the peasant plays, and you may, I dare say, do the same in verse. But you will never reach the very top in either unless you read plenty of what is best and train your natural instincts. There is a sermon!"

On March 1st he had a relapse and went back to bed for a few days. When Molly wrote that she was going on a picnic with members of the company, he replied:

I would be a brute indeed if I objected to your going. I know you wont let them walk arm-in-arm with you or anything of that kind, and I hope when you are coming back you will keep with the crowd. It would give me pain to think of you walking through *our roads* in the twilight with anyone else. . . . When I came to the part in your letter when you spoke about our last walk up there, and the beauty of the mountains yesterday, a wave of anguish came over me. I got a lump in my throat, and the next thing I had tears streaming down like a baby. There in my bed I cannot even see a bit of sky or a cloud. That's what comes when you are as weak as I am, and as wretched. I can't live any longer without you.

The Playboy meanwhile was published and had sold two hundred copies during the first week. Willie Fay had been to Clare and Kerry and reported that all the county councils were passing resolutions condemning it. George Moore wrote to him on March 6th:

My Dear Synge, I have just returned from France, and the first thing I did was to read your play which I admire very much. Oscar Wilde or somebody before him said, "the majority is always wrong." I wish he had added as a corollary "but the majority is never wholly wrong." If what I hear is true, [that] the audience accepted your play gleefully up to the last five minutes of the third act, I confess to sympathizing with the audience. Your play does not end, to my thinking, satisfactorily. Your end is not comedy, it ends on a disagreeable note, and that is always a danger, especially when one chooses parricide as the subject of a jest. The comedy end and the end which would make it acceptable to an audience seems to me to be that at some moment the old man Mahon discovers that his son is about to marry a very rich girl; the peasant's instinct for money overtakes him, causes him to forget his wounds, and he begins to boast like his son: "No one has ever overthrown him in this world, and no man ever will except his own son." To the peasant anything is preferable rather than money should pass out of the family; and with his boasting about himself and his son he induces Pegeen's father to accept Christy as his son-in-law. This end would be in keeping with the facts.

Your end is not only not a comedy end but it is a little out of keeping with the facts. Christy has distinguished himself in the "lepping" and his horsemanship in the male race (forgive the bull!!); he is clearly not such a dolt as his father represents him. I suppose you want the play revived, and I am sure that the last few pages will always prejudice it whether the audience be an Irish, an English or a French one. Forgive me for speaking so candidly. I do so because I sincerely admire the play. . . . The burning of Christy's legs with the coal is quite intolerable and wouldn't be acceptable to any audience—French, German or Russian. The audience doesn't mind what is said, but what is done—the father coming in with his head bandaged was a dangerous make up.*

Synge acknowledged Moore's letter, but he wrote Frank Fay, "I have had a letter from George Moore approving highly of [my] play but as usual wanting me to rewrite some of it according to an idea of his—one by the way which I tried myself a year ago and rejected as too commonplace."[119] But criticism of the third act had reminded him of his dissatisfaction with it, and a few days later he wrote to Molly, "I fully agree that the third act wants pulling together." In the end, however, he left it as it was.

He wrote to Molly on March 9th: "My mother was talking the other day about our marriage and how we intended to get on. She is still rather frightened at our poverty, but she is much more rational about it than she was. You must have charmed her!" But he was annoyed that she continued to go on picnics, and when he wrote on the 11th complaining about her neglect of him she wrote the word *appalling* twice across the bottom of it. His health was still uncertain, and in his letter of March 16th he described himself as "a poor fellow shut up here looking out back and front at wet roofs and dark drizzling rain." The next afternoon she came out to visit with him, and as soon as she had left, Willie Fay and his wife arrived to tell him that the New York producer Charles Frohman was coming to Dublin to arrange an American tour for the company and to select the plays he wanted done. What Fay told him angered him, and he wrote to Molly the next day:

Dearest, You were not five minutes gone last [evening] when W. G. and Mrs. F. turned up. We had a long chat and I heard all the inner news which does not definitely reach you. Nothing is settled!—as I

* ". . . the letter I sent to Synge was superficial. I hope he destroyed it. He was glad that his play had pleased me, but he could not alter the third act. It had been written again and again thirteen times. That is all I remember of his letter, interesting on account of the circumstances in which it was written and the rarity of Synge's correspondence. It is a pity his letter was destroyed and no copy kept; our letters would illuminate the page that I am now writing, exhibiting us both in our weakness and our strength—Synge in his strength, for if the play had been altered we should have all been disgraced, and it was Yeats' courage that saved us in Dublin." George Moore, *Hail and Farewell: Vale* (New York, 1922), p. 165.

thought—about the tours. I hear however that they are showing Frohman *one* play of mine—*Riders*—five or six of L. G.'s and several of Yeats! I am raging about it, though of course you must not breathe a word about it. I suppose after the *P. B.* fun they are afraid of stirring up the Irish Americans if they take me. However I am going to find out what is at the bottom of it, and, if I am not getting fair play, I'll withdraw my plays from both tours, English and American together. It is getting past a joke the way they are treating me. I am going to write to "my dear friend"* again to tell her how I am getting on and let her know incidentally what is going on here. I don't think she will be pleased. She, I imagine, does not worship Lady G.

By the next day, however, his anger had cooled a great deal and he wrote again to Molly, "If Frohman is genuinely afraid of taking my work for fear of making a row with the Irish Americans then of course I have no cause to be annoyed with the directors, but if, as I understand, the tour is going largely for the cultivated university audiences in America it is a very different matter." In two days he wrote again. He had been to the doctor, but still felt wretched and lopsided from deafness in one ear:

I have written to F. J. F. for a list of how many times *Spreading the News, The Shadow, Cathleen* and *Riders* and *Baile's Strand* have been played in the Abbey since we opened. I expect their pieces have been done at least three times as often as mine. If that is so there'll be a row. I am tied to the company now by your own good self, otherwise I would be inclined to clear away to Paris and let them make it a Yeats-Gregory show in name as well as in deed. However it is best not to do anything rash. They have both been very kind to me at times and I owe them a great deal. . . . My mother was inquiring about your temper today. She says my temper is so bad, it would be a terrible thing to marry a bad-tempered wife! If she only knew!

Frank Fay's response to his request effectively reminded him that he had been away from the firing line for a long while:

I send you on the dates of performance of the plays you name from which I think you can make out the number of shows given of each piece. Of course the answer will be, we have staged *Riders to the Sea* very

* Apparently Agnes Tobin.

frequently and when you write uncontroversial pieces you will get plenty of show. When we actors made a trade of our work, we more or less gave up our power of playing anything we liked, because our livelihood in the future depends on our power, during the next two years, of making an audience that will support us for the rest of our lives.

Those who write have always the reading public; but those who act are useless without an audience. I am quite willing at any time to go back and typewrite, but I am only one. There is a strong feeling in the company against *The Playboy*, and I doubt if they will agree to take it to the other side; but I may be wrong here and they may raise no objection. One thing is certain, no crowd of professional actors would have gone through what the company went through during *The Playboy* week, and if we go to London there will probably be a storm. I will face that storm and *all* its consequences; so will the brother. But will the others? I think that having done the play here, it must be done everywhere. It is no more a libel on Ireland than a French play about a husband, lover and mistress is a libel on France.

I absolutely agree with you that a Yeats-Gregory theatre would not benefit anybody. Boyle's action unfortunately has put us in that predicament, but Fitzmaurice and Norreys Connell* may get us out of it.

You have doubtless thought the thing out well, but so long as you write plays like *The Playboy* the other directors will always have an excellent answer. I have no ties and am not likely now ever to have any, so it doesn't matter whether I live in the gutter or as I am doing. I shall not shirk playing in any play that I think good, but how many others can do so now?

I am deliberately arguing against you. Quite likely the London Irish will only boycott the season or with their broader views—if they have such—may like the play, but the whole thing is problematic.

Synge was chastened, and wrote to Molly: "I have not come off so badly—largely no doubt because I was always there to fight my own battle and did so—as I thought, and I have decided to make no row for the present at least. This American tour is of course very important, and I don't want anyone to be able to say I wrecked it by forcing on my unpopular plays. I don't think it is wise to leave me out the way they have done, but let them take the responsibility, my plays will get their chance in the long run."

He was already beginning to turn over in his mind the possibility of

---

* George Fitzmaurice and Norreys Connell, two new dramatists.

getting away from contemporary subject matter—perhaps because it would be less controversial but more likely because he was beginning to wonder if he had gone as far as he could with the particular medium he had developed. He thought about writing a play on an Irish saint, possibly St. Kevin, about whom he had once sketched a rough scenario. But on March 18th he jotted in his notebook some observations which show the reservations he had about the language difficulties in adapting historical subject matter to the stage. Modern prose was impossible, and verse was likely to be just as ineffective.

The moment the sense of historical truth awoke in Europe historical fiction became impossible. For a time it seemed otherwise—antiquarian writers, fools now exploded, old writers (Elizabethan, Louis XIV) saw historical personnages as living contemporaries. Now it is impossible to use our own language or feelings with perfect sincerity for personnages we know to have been different from ourselves. Hence historical fiction insincere. It is possible to use a national tradition a century or more old which is still alive in the soul of the people. See Walter Scott. But anyone who is familiar with Elizabethan writers will not tolerate *Kenilworth* or *Westward Ho! Promessi Sposi*. To us now *as readers* the old literature itself is so precious we look with disgust at imitations of it. As creators? It is possible to use a legend like Faust, which from the outset defies historical reality in the making of an absolutely modern work, but is only to be done possibly in verse, as our modern spoken prose cannot be put into the mouths of antique persons. On stage this is so most of all. In thinking over the poems of the last century that one reads with most pleasure how many are historical? Browning, Rossetti. For my own part I only care for personal, lyrical, modern poetry, and little of that. I am possibly exceptional. That is why lyrical poetry is now the only poetry.

The real world is mostly unpoetical; fiction even in poetry is not totally sincere, hence failure of modern poetry. This is to be taken with all reserve—there is always the poet's dream which makes itself a sort of world, where it is kept a dream. Is this possible on the stage? I think not. Maeterlinck, *Pelléas and Mélisande?* Is the drama as a beautiful thing a lost art? The drama of swords is. Few of us except soldiers have seen swords in use; to drag them out on the stage is babyish. They are so rusted for us with the associations of pseudo-antique fiction and drama. For the present the only possible beauty in drama is peasant drama. For the future we must await the making of life beautiful again before we can have beautiful drama. You cannot gather grapes [out] of chimney pots.

He and Molly walked at Bray on Sunday, March 24th, and he wrote the next day, "I have written a lovely curse on the 'flighty one' but I'm half afraid to send it to you. . . . I thought a lot more over my play last night, and got some new ideas. I think I'll make the old woman be the mother of the man the saint killed, instead of his own mother. She might be a heathen and keep up a sort of jeering chorus through it all." The "flighty" one was Molly's sister Mrs. Callender, who had expressed her dislike of *The Playboy*. The text which he later sent to Molly was eventually rewritten and appears among his published poems as "The Curse," but at this time it read:

> Lord curse this female's fickle head.
> With gripes and colic grace her bed.
> With corns and bunions cramp her toes.
> Deck with pimples brow and nose.
> Contort her liver, lungs and brain.
> For all her parts contrive a pain,
> Till devils, though she wake or sleep,
> Through her flesh with horror creep.
> May her supper, breakfast, dinner,
> Choke with wind this flighty sinner.
> Lord these torments quickly bring,
> And I'm your servant, J. M. Synge.

He sent her another poem the next day:

> May one sorrow every day
> Your festivity waylay.
> May seven tears in every week
> From your well of pleasure leak
> That I—signed with such a dew—
> May for my full pittance sue
> Of the Love forever curled
> Round the maypole of the world.
>
> Heavy riddles lie in this,
> Sorrow's sauce for every kiss.[120]

Molly's picnicking continued to annoy him. He wrote to her on March 29th to scold her about a proposed trip to Glendalough with

some of her fellow actors. "It is of course impossible that you should
go off that way with those four oafs. . . . It is a disgusting excursion
on Sunday as everyone gets drunk. Surely you must have known that I
would not be able to tolerate the idea of your going off that way with
four men!" His remarks were followed by his usual complaints about
his health and having to go see the doctor again.

The next day, which was Friday, Molly came out to Glendalough
House and apparently assured him she wouldn't go. But when she
got back home she dropped him a note telling him she had changed
her mind. He wrote immediately: "I cannot decide whether you are
to go or not! If you think you promised to go, and they want you to
go, and you want to go, you had better go, though you are not bound
to go and you can so badly afford it. I won't be hurt. . . . Dear Heart,
you are utterly mistaken in thinking that I do not trust you. I trust
your little heart and soul utterly. But I do not trust your judgement
and your knowledge of the world, that is all, and that is not your
fault. . . . I feel a queer sad feeling that you are going to see the
Wicklow lakes for the first time without me. That is selfish and foolish
I suppose. Your Old Tramp." Molly went to Glendalough just the
same, and the only visitor Synge had the next day was Yeats, who
came out to see him for the first time since the riots and was obviously worried about Synge's health.

Charles Frohman had arrived in Dublin, and for Easter Week Yeats
and Lady Gregory scheduled for his benefit—as well as the holiday
theatregoers—a program made up of the plays he would be most
likely to select. Included were six of Lady Gregory's, Yeats' *Deirdre*
and *Cathleen Ni Houlihan* and Synge's *Riders to the Sea*. It was not a
representative list, but the directors could hardly be blamed for selecting so many of Lady Gregory's popular plays and avoiding another
demonstration over Synge's work which might discourage Frohman
altogether. Moreover, William Boyle decided to draw Frohman's attention to his plays by announcing again the reasons for his action in
withdrawing them from the Abbey Theatre. The article he wrote for
The Catholic Herald of London was reprinted in *The Evening Tele-
graph* in Dublin during the week when Yeats and Lady Gregory were
apparently trying to quiet Frohman's apprehensions. After citing the
popular approval of his own three plays, Boyle devoted the rest of his
article to an attack on *The Playboy*, which he called "gross in con-

ception, coarse beyond possibility of quotation, and false to the verge
of absurdity."

Synge wrote to Molly: "I would like to wring Boyle's neck. The
last time I saw him he was all cordiality, inviting me to stay with him,
and Heaven knows what, and now he turns on me and attacks me
scurrilously in the papers. I'll roast him yet." But he ignored Boyle
and turned instead upon his tormentors in the Gaelic League by
writing a letter to the newspapers. He never sent it, however, either
because Yeats advised him not to or because his own instincts saved
him from a controversy which would certainly have finished him
forever in Dublin. It was entitled "Can We Go Back Into Our
Mother's Womb? A Letter to the Gaelic League by a Hedge Schoolmaster":

Much of the writing that has appeared recently in the papers takes it
for granted that Irish is gaining the day in Ireland and that this country
will soon speak Gaelic. No supposition is more false. The Gaelic League
is founded on a doctrine that is made up of ignorance, fraud and hypocrisy. Irish as a living language is dying out year by year—the day the
last old man, or woman who can speak Irish only dies in Connacht or
Munster—a day that is coming near—will mark a station in the Irish
decline which will be final a few years later. As long as these old people
who speak Irish only are in the cabins the children speak Irish to them—
a child will learn as many languages as it has need of in its daily life—
but when they die the supreme good sense of childhood will not cumber
itself with two languages where one is enough. It will play, quarrel, say
its prayers and make jokes of good and evil, make love when it's old
enough, write if it has wit enough, in this language which is its mother
tongue. This result is what could be expected beforehand and it is what
is taking [place] in Ireland in every Irish-speaking district.

I believe in Ireland. I believe in the nation that has made a place in
history by seventeen centuries of manhood, a nation that has begotten
Grattan and Emmet and Parnell will not be brought to complete insanity
in these last days by what is senile and slobbering in the doctrine of the
Gaelic League. There was never till this time a movement in Ireland
that was gushing, cowardly and maudlin, yet now we are passing England
in the hysteria of old woman's talk. A hundred years ago Irishmen could
face a dark existence in Kilmainham [Jail], or lurch on the halter before
a grinning mob, but now they fear any gleam of truth. How are the
mighty fallen! Was there ever a sight so piteous as an old and respectable

people setting up the idea of Fee-Gee because, with their eyes glued on John Bull's navel, they dare not be European for fear the huckster across the street might call them English.

This delirium will not last always. It will not be long—we will make it our first hope—till some young man with blood in his veins, logic in his wits and courage in his heart, will sweep over the backside of the world to the uttermost limbo this credo of mouthing gibberish. (I speak here not of the old and magnificent language of our manuscripts, or of the two or three dialects still spoken, though with many barbarisms, in the west and south, but of the incoherent twaddle that is passed off as Irish in the Gaelic League.) This young man will teach Ireland again that she is part of Europe, and teach Irishmen that they have wits to think, imaginations to work miracles, and souls to possess with sanity. He will teach them that there is more in heaven and earth than the weekly bellow of the Brazen Bull-calf and all his sweaty gods, or the snivelling booklets that are going through Ireland like the scab on sheep.

Synge's illness dragged on for weeks, but the doctor continued to find nothing basically wrong with his lungs or with his constitution. Recently, however, the glands in his neck had begun to enlarge again, but they did not give him any pain and he never realized the dread implications they held. His doctor merely told him that he ought to have them removed before his marriage. Meanwhile his marriage plans were held in abeyance. He wrote to Molly on April 13th, "You must not mind if I seem a little distant at the theatre; everyone is watching us, and even when we are publicly engaged I do not care to let outsiders see anything." Four days later he had decided definitely to have the operation. "It seems hard to have to put off our wedding again, but it will only be I hope till autumn or early winter. I will take a 'digs,' our digs! when I come home from my summer outings, and then it will be ready for us as soon as we are ready for it."

He wrote to MacKenna in Paris:

Forgive an unfortunate poor devil who has been ill for two months—four weeks not even downstairs—for not answering your letter long ago, and for not thanking you for your invitation which my poor bowels—they've had dysentery—yearned to accept. I am much better now, but I'm to have an operation on my neck in about a month so there is no chance of getting to Paris at present. Have you heard of the *Playboy* row? I am sending you a copy and a few cuttings. They are too great a nuisance.

Did you hear that we had to have fifty-seven peelers* in to keep the stage from being rushed, and that for four nights not a word could be heard for booing? A number of young men, however, were on our side, and on the whole I think—we all think—we have gained ground in Dublin. But in the country and in America (where one side only can be heard) we have come off badly. Lady Gregory and Yeats thus suffer more than I do. I wonder did you hear that Dublin and the *Freeman* were chiefly outraged because I used the word *shift* instead of *chemise* for an article of fine linen, or perhaps named it at all. Lady G. asked our charwoman—the theatre charwoman—what she thought of it. The charwoman said she wouldn't mention the garment at all if it could be helped, but if she did she hoped she would always say *chemise*, even if she was alone! Then she went down on the stage and met the stage carpenter, "Ah," says she, "Isn't Mr. Synge a bloody old snot to write such a play?" There's Dublin delicacy!

I sometimes wish I had never left my garret in the Rue d'Assas—it seems funny to write the words again—the scurrility and ignorance and treachery of some of the attacks upon me have rather disgusted me with the middle class Irish Catholic. As you know I have the wildest admiration for the Irish peasants, and for Irish men of known or unknown genius— do you bow? But between the two there's an ungodly ruck of fat-faced sweaty-headed swine. They are in Dublin and Kingstown and also in all the country towns. Do you know that the B[oards] of Guardians all over the west and south have been passing resolutions condemning me and the French government? Irish humour is dead, MacKenna, and I've got influenza.

MacKenna's reply was six and half pages long. He had just read *The Playboy* and was lyrical in his praise. "I think your poet-weakling-braggart-frightened-murderer that didn't murder a wonderful being you have made. . . ." But he was able nevertheless to see the offence it had given Dublin audiences:

My Dear Man, I followed all that history from Dublin: I see the *Freeman*. I agreed on the whole with the *Freeman*, though I need not, I hope, tell you not with the *Freeman*'s tone in the matter. I even began your play with a prejudice against the parricide hero idea. The play itself did not take that away at the start—rather it drove it deeper in. I was shocked, though you'd be a fool to fail to see that even from the beginning I was delighted with everything but the main thing. But as I read, all the

* Policemen.

griefs shrivelled away from me. The thing is too great for such reserves and doubts and little problems of propaganda. It is the kind of thing a man, once he has conceived it, has to write even though he went to hell immediately, which I sincerely hope you will not. But I, ever the unhappy, half-way-house man, quite understand Dublin's mind in the matter. Probably if Dublin had read the play in its back parlor before going to Abbey Street, it would have heard you with tears mingled of joy and reprobation but heard you in the end and crowned you with a double crown of roses and of thorns. . . .

Synge replied:

Of course *Playboy* is serious. Extravaganza theory is partly my fault. An interviewer—whom the devil hang by his own guts—ran up and downstairs after me for two hours on Monday night when there was the first riot and I was in charge as Yeats was away. He—the interviewer—got in my way—may the devil bung a cesspool with his skull—and said, "Do you really think, Mr. Synge, that if a man did this in Mayo, girls would bring him a pullet?" The next time it was, "Do you think Mr. Synge, they'd bring him eggs?" I lost my poor temper (God forgive me that I didn't wring his neck) and I said, "Oh well, if you like, it's impossible, it's extravagant, it's extravgance (how's it spelt?). So is *Don Quixote!*" He hashed up what I said a great [deal] worse than I expected, but I wrote next day politely backing out of all that was in the interview. That's the whole myth. It isn't quite accurate to say, I think, that the thing is a generalization from a single case. If the idea had occurred to me I could and would just as readily have written the thing as it stands without the Lynchehaun case or the Aran case. The story—in its essence —is probable, given the psychic state of the locality. I used the cases afterwards to controvert critics who said it was impossible.

Lady Gregory, her son Robert and Yeats were getting ready for a trip to Italy from which they would not return until May 22nd. Synge's health was better and he was to take charge of the theatre while they were gone. He bought a new suit to celebrate his return to action and wrote Molly on the 25th that he had received the first copies of *The Aran Islands* from his publisher. He was cheerful and optimistic about the future. He met W. J. Lawrence on the street in Dublin and had it out with him over *The Playboy*, but the bitterness had been diluted and they parted with a handshake. Masefield wrote, thanking him for the complimentary copy of the new book: "I meant to write to you at the time of your trouble at the theatre, as I feared that the bitterness of the fools who attacked you might have discouraged you; but Yeats made the uproar so much of a comedy that I did not send the letter. There are a damned lot of fools in the world. As a rule we can ignore them. But when they try to impose their cockold laws upon the artist they need a strong jolt. I am glad that they got it at the Abbey Theatre."

The company left Dublin during the second week of May for what was to be their longest and most important tour, which included Glasgow, Cambridge, Birmingham, Oxford and London. Synge decided to stay in Dublin, leaving the company under Payne's authority. He planned to go to Devon on the 28th to visit Jack Yeats and then be present at the London performances. He wrote to Molly in Glasgow on the 12th: "I got your two little notes yesterday, and they brought tears into my gizzard! I have been going about since yesterday morning feeling as if I had one of those iron balls we saw in the convict ship tied to each of my legs and another hanging to my heart. . . . I am going to the doctor tomorrow and then I'll either have the operation or go away to Jack Yeats. I cannot stick on here doing nothing in particular for a long weary month. I wrote to Oxford yesterday to say I would not go there. If my neck is as bad as it is now I would not care to go and stay with strangers—I mean I feel rather queer with this unsightly lump in my lug." He wrote the next day to tell her about the International Exhibition currently being held in Dublin and that he had visited the Somali village and heard some of the natives singing "exactly like some of the keens on Aran." In his letter of the 16th he wrote to her that he had been working a good deal on his Wicklow articles:

I have written in all about 1300 words today, that is, typing out stuff from my notes taken on the spot. That is a good day's work isn't it? Do you know what? I've got an idea! Go out when you get this and buy a good thick square note-book with a strong cover and begin to keep a journal of your tour, writing down everything as it comes helter-skelter, especially the small things. Say what sort of a landlady you have and what she says to you, if it is funny, what you have for dinner, what your dressing rooms are like and your journeys *etc*. Will you do it? At the least you will find it intensely interesting and amusing reading ten years hence

—and later (if not now) when you are touring in Ireland and you have caught the knack, you will write stuff about places like the Wexford Theatre that, with my help, you will be able to sell. . . . I have been working all the morning at a ballad for two voices for you and F. F. to recite if it comes off.

In arranging the tour Yeats and Lady Gregory had convinced a reluctant company to take their courage in their hands and do *The Playboy* again. Their strategy was to play it only in Cambridge, Oxford, and London and omit it in Glasgow and Birmingham, where there were large numbers of Irish people likely to react as the Dublin audiences had. They were not afraid of more demonstrations—in fact they had an eye on the publicity—but they preferred to fight the next battle in an atmosphere more congenial to victory. While the company was still in Glasgow, Miss Horniman wrote Synge from London that she had been in touch with the Lord Chamberlain's reader, Mr. Redford, and was having trouble getting a license to perform *The Playboy* in England. Mr. Redford's apprehensions persisted, and she wrote to say that he was consulting the Home Office and the Lord Chamberlain about it. "He sent me a polite letter and asked me to give an account of the rows [in Dublin]. . . . Fancy the Lord Chamberlain and the Home Office following the behests of Arthur Griffith!"

The license was eventually granted. But Yeats and Lady Gregory, who arrived in London from Italy on May 22nd, were surprised to learn that their careful strategy had been upset. Either Synge, Payne or Willie Fay had taken *The Playboy* off the bill for Cambridge and scheduled it for Birmingham. Yeats decided that Redford's apprehensions about Birmingham were well founded, that *The Playboy* should be performed only at Oxford and London, and directed Payne and Willie Fay accordingly. Meanwhile the players, who had been told nothing of the licensing difficulties, had become suspicious; and when Molly wrote to ask about rumours she had heard, Synge replied:

I do not think the story you heard about *Playboy* in Birmingham was quite true. It was withdrawn for political reasons I believe. I am not satisfied with the way things are going in the company—(Miss H. is at me again, so far in a friendly way, about some "fit up"* that was to

* A stage set.

have been made last summer, and that I know nothing of)—and I wrote to Yeats yesterday proposing to resign my directorship. It does not do me or anyone else any good, that I can see, and it is an endless worry to me. I will not do anything in a hurry, however, and please don't speak of this to anyone. I do not think things can go on much longer as they are, and I think I would have a freer hand to ask for what arrangements I want made for the working of the company if I was outside it. I will not desert W. G. F. if he wants me to stay on, so I must consult him.[121]

Yeats was angry at Synge's protest, and replied:

My Dear Synge, The reason for taking off *Playboy* from Birmingham bill was that we believed after the correspondence with censor that if there was a row at Birmingham the censor would take back the license, and we considered it being brought to Oxford and London of the utmost importance. There are enough slum Irish in Birmingham to stir up a row, and we are not sure of any friendly audience there to help us. We have just had evidence of organization against us. The decision had to be made quickly. As a matter of courtesy, I think Lady Gregory and I, who induced the company to promise to play the play in London, Oxford and Cambridge as intellectual centres, should have been consulted before it was put on the Birmingham bill. It was also arranged with the players at their request that the cast should be exactly the same as in Dublin, and I now learn with surprise that three or four have been changed. When we proposed to take the play off the Birmingham bill we asked Fay if there was any reason against it and he said "none whatever." As he is responsible, that seemed to us sufficient. As to the £50 I understand from Miss Horniman that the check was made payable to me, and with no more financial knowledge than you have I am quite prepared for investigations. While we are fighting your battles is hardly the moment to talk of resignation.

Yeats' next step was to have reprints made of his speech at *The Playboy* debates to sell to the audiences in Oxford and London, along with a new number of *The Arrow*, for which he wrote a fresh defence of *The Playboy*. "The failure of our audience to understand this powerful and strange work," he wrote, "has been the one serious failure of our movement, and it could not have happened but that the greater number of those who came to shout down the play were no regular part of our audience at all but members of parties and societies whose main interests are political."

The entire cast was jumpy when the curtain went up at the New Theatre, Oxford, on the evening of June 5th for the first performance of *The Playboy* since that nerve-racking week in Dublin. They could not realize that their audience, mostly undergraduates, would not threaten to erupt at any moment or start shouting at them. *The Oxford Times* reported that they were received "with a warmth and enthusiasm that appeared to surprise the company." Synge had left Dublin on May 30th to spend a week with Jack Yeats before coming up to London on June 8th, the day before the company were to open their week's run at the Great Queen Street Theatre. Yeats had shrewdly scheduled *The Playboy* for the opening night so that the box office for the rest of the week might profit by the publicity from any demonstrations that might develop. Synge was standing in the foyer of the theatre the next night when his friend Masefield came in. They chatted for a while, but Synge was tense and soon went to the box reserved for himself, Lady Gregory and Yeats next to the stage. Masefield later wrote that Synge sat still all during the performance, "watching with the singular grave intensity with which he watched life. It struck me then that he was the only person there sufficiently simple to be really interested in living people, and that it was this simplicity which gave him his charm." The play was a great success, and at the end of the performance Masefield noticed him "standing in his box gravely watching the actors as the curtain rose and again rose during the applause."

Yeats had been right in thinking that if *The Playboy* could be brought intact to London it would make its way. It was from this London success that Synge's reputation dates, but it was due as much to the little company of actors who had already attracted critical attention by the freshness of their style as it was to Yeats' courage in standing between Synge and his enemies. The London publisher, A. H. Bullen,[122] who had just taken over Yeats' books, was annoyed that Synge, and not Yeats, had become the talk of literary London. Some years later when he was trying to explain to Yeats why his books did not sell he argued that "certain people (both in the press and public) were exalting Synge at your expense. The older critics were not gulled; nor those young men who kept their fine enthusiasm. But the unbaked and doughy youth, semi-educated people who had no standard of comparison, proclaimed Synge to be the master-spirit of the Irish movement." Yeats was a great man as well as a great poet.

He had seen his own work assaulted by the same forces that had nearly destroyed Synge, and he knew that the battle was for himself and for his own theatre as much as it was for Synge. He had written to Horace Plunkett as early as 1904 that he believed Synge "to be a great writer, the beginning it may be of a European figure," and that conviction lasted a lifetime.

Synge wrote to Molly the next morning: "You were capital last night in almost all of it, and everyone is speaking well of you, Yeats especially. He says also that you are excellent in *The Shadow of the Glen* and that he withdraws all his former criticisms of you. My poor pet I am sick of being shut away from you like this, and I fear it will get worse as the week goes on, as I am being asked to go to all sorts of teas and things." Both authors and players were being fêted, and though it kept him from seeing Molly, Synge must have been pleased to contrast the teas and receptions where he was lionized to the lonely weeks he had spent in bed following the first performances of *The Playboy* in Dublin. He had "supper with Miss Meakin and Lord Dunraven and his daughter," was invited to the House of Commons by Stephen Gwynn, had dinner with Masefield and met important people whose names impressed but had little meaning for him. His health, which was always affected more by a tiff with Molly than by trouble in general, was never better. Masefield was romanticizing long after the fact when he described Synge during that week telling the story which had inspired his ballad "Danny." "His relish of the savagery made me feel that he was a dying man clutching at life, and clutching most wildly at violent life, as the sick man does." But he and Synge talked "of the great times we should have and of the jolly times we had had. None of our many talks together was happier than the last."

After the London performances Synge and the company went back to Dublin, but in London where Lady Gregory and Miss Horniman were tussling over Yeats another drama was being enacted. Miss Horniman had decided to pour no more money into the Abbey Theatre, except for the subsidy, and was about to found another theatre in Manchester, make Payne the manager, and offer it to Yeats if he would desert Dublin and bring his plays with him. Maud Gonne, who was amused by the spectacle of Yeats being fought over by the two women, attributed Lady Gregory's victory to the Italian trip. "Miss Horniman's money converted the old city morgue into the

Abbey Theatre, but it was Lady Gregory's plays that were acted there. Miss Horniman brought back Italian plaques to decorate it but Lady Gregory carried off Willie to visit the Italian towns where they were made. . . ."[123] But Yeats—Lady Gregory wrote to Synge—told Miss Horniman that he was too old to change his nationality and in addition that he could not assign her the plays. Miss Horniman's interest in her Irish toy was never the same again, but the subsidy was good until 1910. Meanwhile, both Yeats and the Abbey Theatre as well had been saved for Ireland.

Fourteen

THE DEPARTURE OF THE FAYS. AN ILL MAN.
GERMANY. FINAL ILLNESS

But Death had his grudge against me, and he got up in the way, like an armed robber, with a pike in his hand.

Synge had decided that he would have the operation on his neck performed in September. Meanwhile, he did not accompany his mother to Tomrilands House for the summer, where his asthma always bothered him, but decided instead to take a month's vacation beginning on June 28th at Mrs. McGuirk's cottage in Glencree in the Wicklow mountains and then return to Glendalough House where he would be alone except for a servant or two. Mrs. McGuirk's is a pretty little whitewashed cottage which had been the gate lodge on the summer estate of Lady Powerscourt. From its doorway Synge could look down the wide valley of Glencree and could hear the stream from Lough Bray behind the cottage, running down among boulders to the glen below. Molly and Sally were also in need of rest, and they decided to stay in a cottage in Enniskerry, a little more than half a mile down the Featherbed Road from Mrs. McGuirk's.

It was the happiest two weeks of his life. Molly and he had come from the greatest triumphs of their careers, and they could walk the hills and make love without discretion or concern for anyone but themselves. When the girls went back to Dublin on July 11th, Frank Fay came out for a night and Synge was saved from the loneliness of Molly's departure. He wrote to Molly: "The purple grapes are ripe now. I got a lot of them last night on our nook road. The nightjar is singing every night also in the heather. I took F. J. to hear it last night, but he was so busy talking about pronunciation that he would hardly listen to it."

On July 23rd Molly came back for another two weeks, alone this time, and they both found it difficult to leave on August 4th. But the theatre was to open again for five days before the company left on the 11th for a tour which would take them to Waterford, Cork, Kilkenny and back to Cork again, until the 26th when they were due back in Dublin for performances during Horse Show week. Yeats wrote to Synge from Coole on August 14th to try to explain why only *Riders to the Sea* among Synge's plays had been considered for the tour:

> . . . We thought it best to let Fay have a free hand in the tours as none of us could go running after him. You know of old that I don't believe that Fay is a very competent man to run a theatre, that in fact I think him particularly unfitted for it, but Miss Horniman has definitely announced that she will do nothing more for us at the end of two years. In all probability Fay may survive us, and at the end of that time may carry on some sort of touring company with our good will and what he wants of our plays. I wanted somebody in control over Fay, but now that [that] plan has failed and that we have lost Miss Horniman I think we must give Fay every opportunity to acquire experience and amend his faults. . . . The theatre is now a desperate enterprise and we must take desperate measures. . . .

For Synge the exhilaration of his weeks with Molly at Glencree had evaporated; he was unhappy about the decision to omit his plays from the tour and he began immediately to complain to Molly about not feeling well again. "I met Dr. Gogarty the other day, and he says I ought to get the glands out as soon as ever I can and that I will be all right then.* So there is a good hope that I may shake off the delicate condition I have got into the last couple of years. I know I haven't been always like this. One thing is certain—I'm not going to kill myself anymore for the Theatre. I get no thanks for it, on any

---

* In a letter of Sept. 20, 1956, Dr. Oliver St. John Gogarty wrote, "I did not think from their position (back of the neck) that they were tubercular but Hodgkins, and I said to have them out."

side, and I do no good—at least as things are going now." The
weather was wet and he was afraid of cycling or walking. He found
that he could not work either, so he wandered about the empty house
and broke the monotony by an occasional trip to Dublin to see the
elder Yeats. "I wrote to Lady G. the other day about various matters,
and got an answer from Yeats—and I fancy rather a stiff one." He
had, in fact, become almost as much of a problem to Yeats as Willie
Fay, and his friendship with Fay did not help matters very much.

His old suspicions about Molly's conduct had been revived. Almost
everything she wrote of her doings made him uneasy. "I don't want
my wife to be mixing with music-hall artists. Now won't you be
good? I wish you would tell me more that you are doing." But the
more she told him, the unhappier he became. "Oh God this cough
is a fearful worry, and I am not getting on very well I am afraid; at
least there is no change from day to day." But his letters are not those
of a man who had any pain or discomfiture beyond what was produced
in his own imagination.

He had thought of taking a short trip to Brittany during Molly's
absence and had written to tell MacKenna that he would see him as
he passed through London. But he wrote to Molly on the 21st that
his cough was too bad and that he had better stay home. He was
now unable to do anything for himself, and his mother, who would
at least have sympathized with him, was still in Wicklow. The only
thing that gave him any comfort was that six hundred copies of *The
Aran Islands* had been sold and the book was being discussed widely
in Dublin. He wrote to Molly on the 22nd: "I met a youth this morning who has just been in Aran. He says the people are deeply offended
by my story about the tea being kept hot for three hours."

A cheerful letter from MacKenna encouraging him to get to work
again was of slight comfort. Being an experienced journalist Mac-
Kenna could never quite believe that a man who could write *The
Playboy* could also write the lifeless prose of Synge's early articles for
The Speaker. He urged Synge to write a book, or some essays, in which
the personality of the author of *The Playboy* and the other plays
would be revealed. "I am horribly practical and I wish Shakespeare,
after or between the plays, had written something in his own person
—attacking life directly so that my creeping wit would know him
better." He thought Synge's preface to *The Playboy* was "Yeatsy" and

Pastel drawing in color by James Paterson, late June, 1906.

"quite unworthy of the splendid virility of *The Playboy* itself." He
could not realize that the only way Synge could really express himself
was with the freedom that only the dramatist has. Writing a play was
like playing in the student orchestra—he could hide among the characters he created and parcel out to each one as much or as little of
his own personal vision as he liked without any commitment on his
part. He could be Christy Mahon, and at the same time Shawn
Keogh. He could be the young hero of his last play loving under a
shadow of death and at the same time the old king hopelessly striving
for the love of a young girl whose thoughts are of other things.

The London success of *The Playboy* was beginning to have its influence meanwhile. John Quinn, who had protected the American
copyrights on *In the Shadow of the Glen*, *The Well of the Saints* and
The Playboy by privately printing them, wrote suggesting an American edition of the plays with an introduction by Yeats' father. He
also offered to buy the manuscript of *The Playboy* for £20 and enclosed a letter from an Irish-American friend who had found the play
"unduly grotesque" and "superfluously coarse." Synge agreed to any
plan Quinn could arrange, and commented tactfully on his friend's
remarks:

When he blames the "coarseness" however, I don't think he sees that
the romantic note and a Rabelaisian note are working to a climax through
a great part of the play and that the Rabelaisian note, the "gross note,"
if you will, must have its climax no matter who may be shocked.

As to my manuscript, I work always with a typewriter—typing myself
—so I suppose it has no value? I make a rough draft first and then work
over it with a pen till it is nearly unreadable; then I make a clean draft
again, adding whatever seems wanting, and so on. My final drafts—I
letter them as I go along—were "G" for the first act, "I" for the
second, and "K" for the third. I really wrote parts of the last act more
than eleven times, as I often took out individual scenes and worked at
them separately. The MS as it now stands is a good deal written over,
and some of it is in slips or strips only, cut from the earlier versions. . . .[124]

No date had been set for the operation, but on the 12th of September his doctor examined him and set it for the following Saturday.
The doctors must have known for some time that he had a malig-
nancy which would soon destroy him, but they did not tell him. He

wrote to Molly, trying to cheer her up about the prospects. "I got a qualm when I left you today and sat down in the doctor's waiting room, but as soon as I saw him and started off for the surgeon's I felt as gay as if I was going to order a pair of boots. When I had seen [Dr.] Ball I went off to the hospital and engaged a room. Then I got some tea in O'Brien's and went off and saw old Yeats and came home by the quarter to six. . . . Ball says the glands will come out 'beautifully' and that I will be much the better for it, so cheer up now and don't dream of being uneasy." The next day he continued to assure her with a long letter:

I feel perfectly hard, and fearless and defiant now, but if I saw your little sweet face looking mournfully at me I'd get sentimental and qualmish at once. . . . I'm going in there to be cured, I hope, and it isn't at all as if I was going to the wars. How would you like it if I was a "gaudy officer" getting potted at by the Boers or some one. . . . I feel wonderfully gay! I'm going in by the quarter past eight this evening, so I haven't much longer to wait. The worst time will be tomorrow morning waiting about without any breakfast till 12 o'clock at the hospital. I don't believe you'd like me a bit if I was a kind of cast-iron man who didn't know what it was to be ill. . . . Meanwhile try and keep philosophical and cheerful—a certain amount of wretchedness is good for people when they're young. I wouldn't be half as nice as I am if I hadn't been through fire and water!!!

My spirits are going up, and up, and up. They always do when I get into a good tight corner. The only weight on me now is the thought that you are unhappy. Of course I'll have qualms tomorrow, but after all it's an interesting experience to break the monotony of one's daily. I believe if I was a woman I'd have a big family just for fun! I wish you could see me grinning over this letter and you'd get as cheerful too. By this time tomorrow of course I'll be pretty flat. Now Goodbye for a few days my own pet, treasure, life, love, light and all that's good. Your T.[125]

On Sunday morning his brother Robert went to the hospital and reported that the operation had been successful. It was four days, however, before Synge was well enough to write to Molly and ask her to come to see him with Frank Fay. On the Monday following the operation the stitches were removed; he sat in the garden for a while and Molly and Frank Fay visited him the next day. He was dismissed and came home on the 25th feeling weak but in good spirits. Edward Stephens went in to see him. "I found John still looking rather pale and haggard but in good spirits. He told me that as he was coming out of the anaesthetic the first thing he shouted out was 'Damn the bloody Anglo-Saxon language that a man can't swear in without being vulgar."

During his convalescence he was happy because he and Molly were thinking in concrete terms of their marriage. In between comments about her buying table linen for them he still lectured her about her reading. He wanted her to get a notebook and begin writing down the titles of books she was reading. "I have a wheelbarrowful of such notebooks (everyone who reads seriously keeps them) and you will find it no trouble, and the greatest use. . . . In a few years you'll be the best educated actress in Europe, and I want you to take a pride and pleasure in your progress."

He was also eager to get to work again on his next play and told Edward Stephens that he was going to write a play about Deirdre and the sons of Usna. "I said, 'Won't you be accused of copying George Russell and Yeats? Haven't they written plays about Deirdre?' He said, 'Oh, no—there isn't any danger of that. People are entitled to use those old stories in any way they wish. My treatment of the story of Deirdre wouldn't be like either of theirs!' " Meanwhile the Abbey Theatre had discovered a new young dramatist named George Fitzmaurice, and Synge went into Dublin on October 4th to see his first play, *The Country Dressmaker*. Fitzmaurice has been described as the first Irish dramatist to come under Synge's influence. Holloway noted in his diary that Fitzmaurice, whom he met at the theatre, was "a nice unassuming fellow with, I am sorry to say, a hankering after Synge and his methods of presenting the Irish character on the boards. We had a long argument over the matter, but he was of the same opinion at the end I fear."

Synge, feeling better than he had felt in years, decided that he was up to another trip to Kerry. Getting to work on a new play seemed to necessitate a return to the west of Ireland. He left Dublin for Ventry on Saturday, October 12th, and began writing in his notebook the moment the train left Tralee. He wrote to Molly from the cottage of a man named Thady Kevane in Ventry on Saturday night:

I did not get here till ten o'clock last night, the trains were so late. Then at Dingle I found they had only sent a little flat cart with a jennet

for me and my luggage and bike so I had to ride four miles in the dark*
on very wet muddy roads. However I got here in great spirits and I wasn't
anything the worse. Today I've been walking nearly six hours on the
mountains in heavy showers of rain—like the ones we had at Glencree—
and I feel very well except that I am a little inclined to have asthma. . . .

The new burst of enthusiasm was short lived, because Thady
Kevane's cottage turned out to be impossible for his asthma. Out on
the hills during the day he had no trouble but at night he wheezed and
felt suffocated. His good spirits rapidly evaporated, and in discourage-
ment he returned to Dublin on the 16th. At home the asthma disappeared and he got to work immediately on his new play. A week later
he had written the first ten pages of dialogue "in great spirits and joy,"
as he wrote to Molly. "But alas, I know that that is only the go off.
There'll be great anguish still before I get her done if I ever do." He
continued to write her about his progress. On November 9th: "I've
been working at *Deirdre* till my head is going round. I was too taken
up with her yesterday to write to you—I got her into such a mess I
think I'd have put her into the fire. . . . Since yesterday I have pulled
two acts into one, so that if I can work it the play will have three acts
instead of four, and that has of course given me many problems to
think about." Later the same day: "I finished a second rough draft of
the sons of Usna today. So I have the whole thing now under my
hand to work at next week." A week later he was sketching out the
second act: "I did a good [deal] of work on Deirdre, not on the MS
but just notes for a new scene in it."

He drove himself steadily and by December 1st wrote: "I finished
the (G) i.e. the 7th division, or rewriting of the III Act yesterday.
It goes now all through—the III Act I mean—but it wants a good
deal of strengthening—of 'making personal' still, before it will satisfy
me."† The pace was beginning to tell, and he complained about not
being able to sleep with the excitement and worry of the work. The
next day he went to the city to see the other directors. "Lady Gregory
went out to call on Mrs. Russell in the afternoon, and Yeats set to to
find out my stars. He says there is very big event coming off in my life
in the next month—a good one on the whole, though with unusual

* On his bicycle.
† He wrote five more versions of the third act in the next thirteen months.

circumstances and some breaking of ties. . . . At the end he said, 'If you were a different sort of man I'd say it was a wild imprudent love affair.'" But Yeats was "very much pleased" with the account of his new play.

Molly and the company had gone on tour to Manchester, Glasgow and Edinburgh on November 24th. None of Synge's plays was to be offered at Glasgow; Manchester was to see only the two one-act plays and Edinburgh only *In the Shadow of the Glen*. The tour was to prove Willie Fay's Waterloo. It was impossible for him to maintain discipline among the company. The only solution, he thought, was that the players should all be put under contract to him—"that the power of dismissing those under my contracts shall rest with me after due consultation with the directors in the case of principals," and "that there shall be no appeal to any other authority than mine by people engaged by me on all matters dealt with in their contracts."[126]

This was the opportunity that Yeats had been waiting for, because he knew that with the company in revolt against Fay's authority Fay would have to stand alone in a fight with the directors. Fay's situation was most difficult because he could hardly be expected to control the actors when they knew that they could appeal over his head to Yeats. He can not be blamed for trying to put a final stop to the same conditions which had brought Miss Horniman down on his head before and led to his demotion under Ben Iden Payne. On the other hand he was asking for an authority which even a sympathetic directorate would hardly have given. He had also lost the support of Synge, which he had always had up to now. Why Synge, who had written to Molly six months before that he would not desert Fay, suddenly deserted him is not clear. Molly was one of the members of the company about whom Fay had complained to Yeats—she had been late for rehearsals—and she may have been responsible for Synge's change in attitude. She had complained to him of Fay before. But there is no evidence that she did.

The directors met in Dublin on December 4th. Action had to wait until the company returned to Dublin, but meanwhile they decided to refuse Fay's demands and drew up a plan whereby the company would be asked to elect a committee of three "to consult with the Stage Manager and Directors as to the rules of discipline," and that the rules should then be submitted to the whole company for ap-

proval. It was Yeats' effective method of guaranteeing that in the
showdown Willie would have nobody but his wife and his brother
on his side. On December 6th Synge wrote to Molly, asking her to
use her influence with one of the actors who had given in his notice
in protest over Fay's actions:

I have had long talks with the directors, and we have to come to some
important decisions which you will hear of in good time. Meanwhile, you
are to stop Kerrigan* leaving the company—if he is taking his notice
seriously—just tell him to stay on till he has seen the directors—this
privately from me. If he is not really meaning to leave don't say anything
about it. You know, I suppose, that we are to have Miss H.'s subsidy for
three full years more, if nothing unforeseen happens—that is great news
for us two, as by three years I ought to have a much better position than
I have now and I think we'll come through all right, so that it is really
worth while to fight the battle on. And we the directors are going to do
it at all risks. We have just got a really excellent play from a new young
man†—in many ways really clever and good, so that we won't run short
of work this season.

I was at the new Arts Club debate with Yeats the other night, and I
was delighted to find him the favorite and star of the evening with a
crowd of young men hanging on his words—new, clever young men who
have nothing to do with all the worn-out cliques. Trinity College is also
becoming vehemently interested in Irish things, so that if we can only
get good plays we may strike a new audience any day. . . . I remember
I spoke gloomily about the Abbey a few days ago, but somehow the new
play and the new sympathetic people at the Arts Club have given me
new hope. Long may it last. . . .

I think the directors must know that we are getting married. They
probably have no idea that it is so close. We talk about you and the com-
munications I have with you, quite frankly of course. Now be discreet
and don't let Kerrigan or anyone else leave. This is very private—it is
likely that on any further tours one of the directors will go also, so perhaps you and I will be on the road again together before too long. . . .

I went to Parsons the other day. He thinks I am "grand," my neck and
chest are very satisfactory. I had not been quite well this week with queer
pains in a portion of my inside, but he couldn't find anything the matter,
so I hope it is nothing.

* J. M. Kerrigan.
† *The Man Who Missed the Tide* by W. F. Casey.

The ominous pain inside did not go away, however, and he wrote again on December 8th complaining of it. "It seems years since you went away. I feel like a blind man, a deaf man, or something queer and horrible ever since. I can't live now without you." A week later he returned from a bicycle ride. The pain had increased. "I hope it is only fancy, but I think I'll have to go to Parsons again."

The directors had not yet communicated their decision to the company or to Willie Fay, and meanwhile the morale was getting worse. Sara Allgood had handed in her notice and was awaiting some action from Dublin. Yeats had gone to London, but Lady Gregory wrote to Synge from Coole on December 14th that a "dry rot" was setting into the company. "There is no use in fighting Fay on behalf of Miss Allgood if she is anxious to leave us—but she may only have applied when her temper was up. I still hope that if Yeats puts the case before the company, they will decide to go on or drop off, and we shall have more hearty work." But she thought it was better to wait. "I think you will be able to find out how things are as soon as the company returns, and you ought to see Fay and judge whether he really hopes for dismissal of the company,* or has given it up. You could then let us know what you think best." She wrote again a few days later to say that she was summoning Yeats to Dublin for a meeting when the company returned.

Yeats meanwhile had begun to see the danger in setting up a committee for the actors which might later provide them with a means for voting against performing in unpopular plays like *The Playboy*. He was willing to revert to democratic principles only for as long as it took to defeat Willie Fay:

I have written to Lady Gregory that it may be better for the Allgoods, Kerrigan *etc.* to meet and formulate their complaints in writing—better for us as I mean this would put us outside the dispute and make us arbitrators, and make it impossible for Fay if we decide against him, to raise a popular cry against us. It is important that we should not seem to be the aggressors. But wait till you hear from Lady Gregory. It is impossible for us to put the company, as Fay wishes, into the power of one we know to be unjust and untruthful. I too think that compromise is out of the question or drifting on—but I won't act without Lady Gregory

* That is, formal dismissal before being rehired under new contracts to him personally.

as the loss of Fay affects her work chiefly. She knows what I think. If he
is to stay it should be as a defeated man. I believe him to be unfit to
manage a company.

Poor Willie Fay, who had literally created the company and nur-
tured its raw talents, had made the mistake of turning virtually everybody against him and was completely unable to match either wits or
political tactics with Yeats. As a matter of fact, when the end came
a few weeks later, his old enemy Miss Horniman, who had shown no
interest in the theatre since June, joined in the kill. Many years later
Fay wrote: "What agitated confabulations the directors held I know
not. All I know is that after a few days Lady Gregory came to me to
say that they were not disposed to make any changes, and what was
I going to do about it? I did the only thing that was left to me—I
resigned on the spot."[127] Holloway, who talked with him after he returned from the tour in December, gives an impression of his attitude
at the time: "He was most despondent. . . . Even the company are
getting out of control and come and go when they like. . . . Yeats
and Lady Gregory as dramatists are played out. Synge might not be,
but he appeals to a very limited audience. The company, when they
were rehearsing *The Well of the Saints* used to say the play made
them sick. Synge had the black drop in him, but was a kindly fellow
to speak to." Fay had obviously come to the conclusion that the
theatre's achievement was behind it, and one can hardly blame the
directors for feeling that his association with them was no longer practical, even if their methods of ending it strike one as being ruthless.
The directors held their hearing on January 11, 1908, and two days
later the Fays resigned.

While the latest crisis in the theatre was still unresolved, the company went to Galway city for three nights beginning January 6, 1908.
Synge wrote to Molly and told her he had resumed work on *Deirdre
of the Sorrows*: "I have changed the first half of the first act a good
deal." He was also looking for a flat for them, which he would occupy
until their marriage, and had looked at one in Upper Rathmines. She
returned from Galway on Sunday, January 12th, and they spent the
afternoon discussing their marriage plans. She was patient, even
though family pressure had made her unhappy at home. He suggested
in a letter the next day that she take a room with her married sister—

making sure that it was a business arrangement and that she paid rent. "It would simplify matters in several ways—I feel so strongly so —and it would be convenient as we would then, I think, be in range of St. Peter's Church where the curate is an old friend of mine." He finally found a flat at 47 York Road, Rathmines, and wrote to Molly on the 17th that it had three rooms—one with a place for a gas cooker —with attendance and cooking for thirteen shillings sixpence a week. He knew the neighbourhood well because he had lived in lodgings there in 1904. It was much nearer to the theatre than Dún Laoghaire was, and he would be able to see Molly more easily and more freely. He moved into it on Sunday, February 2nd, and it was to be his home until the end of May, when his belongings were removed while he was in Elpis again.

After the departure of the Fays a controversy ensued in one of the Dublin newspapers in which Yeats argued by letter with an anonymous opponent who seemed to know a good deal about the theatre's affairs. But the directors were beginning to adjust to the new state of things. Two new dramatists had appeared—W. F. Casey, who later became editor of *The Times*, and Norreys Connell, who was to succeed Synge as director. When there were demonstrations at the performance of Connell's play *The Piper* on February 13th and Yeats had to make a curtain speech to a hissing audience, the attention of the public was diverted from the war within the ranks. In March, when *The Gaol Gate*, *In the Shadow of the Glen*, *The Hour Glass* and *The Rising of the Moon* were revived, the audiences were enthusiastic and seemed unaware of the fact that the Fays were gone. Even Holloway had to admit to himself that the company had the resources to survive without the Fays.

Synge was playing a more active role in the management than he had ever done before, even though Yeats was with him. He wrote to MacKenna on February 23rd. "Yeats and I have been running the show, *i.e.* Yeats looks after the stars, and I do the rest. Everything luckily has gone well and I think we have pulled through the crisis, but it might have meant any time the breaking up of our whole movement." He also began to direct plays other than his own— Sudermann's *Teja*, in March, and Molière's *The Rogueries of Scapin*, in April, both in Lady Gregory's translations. He wrote to Joseph Paterson, the Scottish artist he had sat to when he was in Edinburgh in the spring of 1906, to thank him for the portrait which had just arrived: "I dare say you have heard that the Fays have left us, and that Yeats and I are looking after everything now. The Fays are a great loss in some ways, yet in other ways we get on better without them as we have more direct control. I am sending you a little play which I wrote some years ago but did not publish till the other day— *The Tinker's Wedding*—as you will understand we think it too dangerous to put on in the Abbey. It is founded on a real incident that happened in Wicklow a few years ago."

He and Molly were beginning to think of a definite date for their wedding. He had a long talk about it with his mother, and she wrote to his brother Robert on April 14th:

As he is determined to marry it is no use opposing him any more, and we must only trust that he may get on. I hope you will give him a wedding present. You can afford it, and he has so little furniture for his sitting room he ought to buy a few little things. I am going to give them some money as soon as they are married as a wedding gift. I have not much to give at present, I have had so much to pay. Johnnie said he thought they would be married in St. Mary's Parish Church as she lives in the parish. I was very glad to hear that as it is so much nicer than the Registry, and I hope it may be a good sign that his mind has become more enlightened. I asked no questions, but I gave him some information and advice—he has been so busy with the theatre work he had left himself very little time to make arrangements. The company has a few days holiday at Easter so he wants to avail himself of that, but I doubt very much that he can manage it so quickly, because he did not begin in time. Annie* has no sympathy in the matter so I don't talk to her. The boys† are kind and sympathetic. Ned‡ is kind but he has such a horror of Johnnie marrying on such small means I am afraid to say anything to him.

But time was not his greatest worry—the pain in his side had returned. He wrote to Yeats, who was in London, on April 28th, "I have just been with my doctor again and he has found a lump in my side so that it is necessary for me to go into a private hospital again —first of all to let them diagnose me, and then probably for an operation." He went out to Dún Laoghaire to tell his mother that

* Mrs. Stephens, Synge's sister.
† Edward and Frank Stephens.
‡ Synge's brother Edward.

the wedding would have to be postponed, and she was shocked by his pallor. The pain in his stomach and back had been growing more intense and he had been unable to sleep. The next day—April 30th— he entered Elpis nursing home for the second time, and on May 4th was operated on. He wrote to Molly, "My dearest love—this is a mere line for you my poor child, in case anything goes wrong with me tomorrow, to bid you good-bye and ask you to be brave and good, and not to forget the good times we've had and the beautiful things we've seen together. Your Old Friend." He put it in a sealed envelope and marked it, "To be sent in cover in case of death to Miss M. Allgood."

After making a bundle of his salvageable manuscripts, he also wrote a letter to Yeats, similarly marked, asking him to get MacKenna "to go through them for you and do whatever you and Lady Gregory think desirable. It is rather a hard thing to ask you, but I do not want my good things destroyed or my bad things printed rashly—especially a morbid thing about a mad fiddler in Paris which I hate."[128]

Two days after the operation the doctors wrote to Mrs. Synge giving her the dreaded news, which she sent to Robert immediately. "Sir C. Ball found the tumor was adherent and considered it would not have been desirable to attempt its removal. . . . This is sorrowful tidings, my dear Robert, and I have been weeping over it; but God *must* be going to answer my prayers by this terrible sorrow, and I lean on Him." On Saturday, May 9th, news reached the Abbey Theatre that there was little hope of Synge's life, but he rallied and on Tuesday Mrs. Synge reported to Robert, "Ball had no hope of our dear boy's life . . . [but] the tumor or abscess is still there as it cannot be removed, and I wonder what it will do. . . . He has no idea he was in danger—the Drs. hid it from him completely; when he said he would like to see Harry* he thought J. knew and wanted to make a will, but he found he had no idea of such a thing." By June 11th he was sufficiently recovered to write to Molly, who had gone to Balbriggan with Sally for a rest, his first letter since the operation. Meanwhile she had gone to York Road and packed his personal things for the movers, and they were taken back to Glendalough House on May 25th. It was not a happy omen, but she had no idea that his death was less than a year away.

While he was at Elpis, Molly and other members of the company

*Harry Stephens.

visited him, and John Quinn cheered him up with a letter containing a check for *The Playboy* MS, an offer to buy the MS of *Deirdre,* and the news that plans for an American edition of his plays were progressing. Synge replied: "I am glad to be able to answer your letter myself, sitting in an armchair—the stage I have reached now. I hope to move out of this place somewhere into the country in a week or so, and then gradually to pick up my strength. . . . I was greatly obliged for your kind invitation to New York, but I'm afraid it would be hardly the thing for me. I am not always a good sailor; and, with this recent and deep wound in my stomach, the strain of being sick might do me harm."[129] Yeats was in Paris, but Lady Gregory was keeping in touch with the hospital from Coole.

His illness had one good effect. Harry Stephens and his wife had been horrified at the prospect of Molly becoming a member of the family circle and had never hesitated to express their dislike of her to Mrs. Synge. But Molly had already succeeded in breaking down some of Mrs. Synge's antipathy to her, and when Harry Stephens met her at the hospital, dressed simply in white and looking her best—as he confessed to Mrs. Synge—he was surprised to find himself amusing her with an account of his experiences arranging for land purchases on the Aran Islands and telling the islanders stories about *The Playboy* riots. "This illness has brought a kindlier feeling in H. and A. towards J. and M. which I am thankful for," Mrs. Synge wrote Robert.

Meanwhile Synge's recovery was rapid—his mother noted on June 24th that he was "quite fat and looks very well and weighs 12 stone 8."* He began to write a poem to celebrate his illness—on the back of a postcard.

> I'll write a masque of liver, kidneys and the spleen.
> My hero'll be the Major, gut the less my heroine.
> And in my torn stomach I'll lay my tragic scene.
> A dark and lurid tone of red'll be my color scheme.
> And I'll untwine the hidden seeds of them that deeply dream.
> And what has sent the blessed saints to bay the passing stream.

He left the hospital on July 6th and went to the Stephens' house for his convalescence, since his mother had gone for the summer to

* 176 pounds.

Tomrilands House. He had made a great impression on the nurses in the hospital. Four of them wrote to him several times after his discharge and came out to Dún Laoghaire to see him. MacKenna, who had come back to Dublin to live, wrote to him of the difficulties he was having finding a flat for himself and his wife, who was still on the Continent:

Synge, tell it not, but don't get married. Your wife will write to you one day from Paris and tell you to lay in by Friday evening a pound of tea, a gas-stove, a loaf of bread and a lemon. I know—it has just happened to me. I forgot to congratulate you on your health. I read this yesterday, and thought of you: "O health, unto thine ordinance, wealeful Lord, meekly submit I me! I am contrite and of full repentance that ever I swimmed in such nicety as was displeasant to thy diety. Now kythe on* me thy mercy and thy grace. It fits a god to be of his grace free. Forgive and never aft will I trespass." See that you swimme in no niceties, but have your health. I welcome you back to the land of the living with a sincere bravo and *failte*.†

Since the departure of the Fays there had been nobody to train the actors. William Poel, the founder of the Elizabethan Stage Society, had agreed to come to Dublin during his summer vacation and rehearse the company for the opening of the coming season. Lady Gregory, meanwhile, had taken a cottage in the Burren—that barren expanse of stone in County Clare—and was entertaining Yeats, her son Robert and his wife. She wrote to Synge, inviting him to join them: "Robert is painting cottages and sea. Yeats is dictating a scenario of his *Player Queen* and writing more discoveries. Lobsters and crabs and bars [sic] are landed living on our doorstep. . . . I am glad we are so far from Poel and the Abbey. Yeats' stars mean a row on the 14th! But he is not sure where it will fall." She wrote again from Coole on August 1st about her plans for taking the company to Galway and about a new play entitled *The Clancy Name* by a young Cork man named Lennox Robinson, which they had decided to produce in the fall.

Synge was walking again—though only for short distances—and he began to think of going to Lough Bray for a few weeks, or to Kerry

* *Manifest to.*
† Ir. *welcome.*

again. He saw his doctor on July 23rd and wrote to Molly: "He seems to think I am all right now, and says I may do what I like—only I am not to go to the Blaskets! He told me about the operation, but I'm not much the wiser." He wrote again the next day, "My God if we could only be well again and out in the hills for a long summer day and evening, what Heaven it would be! I feel ready to cry, I am getting better so slowly." On Saturday, August 1st, he saw Molly at Bray and the next day wrote that he had had a slight relapse. "I cannot let things go on like this. I don't know what is going to become of me. I wouldn't be surprised if they send me back to Elpis for a while." But Molly, who was accustomed to his fits of depression, especially after one of her visits, was probably not alarmed. When he did not recover he went to see the doctor again but was not much better for it. When Yeats came out to see him on August 5th, Synge was too uncomfortable to talk much about the affairs of the theatre. A week later he was still depressed, and wrote to MacKenna:

I've been pining for the sight of your face all these weeks, but somehow from the uncertainty of my inside I've never had the decision necessary to say "tomorrow I'll have MacKenna" and then write to you to fix a time. In fact I've not been very well, and I've been sitting quaking in the garden like a sear and yellow leaf. The doctors say I'm a very interesting case and generally patronise my belly. To think that I used once to write Playboys, MacKenna, and now I'm a bunch of interesting bowels! My mother has come home unwell from the country so I return to Glendalough House tomorrow. Then forthwith I'll write and beseech you to come and see me. I am a little in dread of your ten minutes walk just yet.

MacKenna replied, his good spirits for the first time shaken by the tone of Synge's letter: "Many thanks for your letter, though it made my wife weep. . . . My dear friend, you must not think there will be no let-up from this state of interesting bowelhood. This is a rest, a living of another kind. You will write more Playboys out of yet another kind or set of experiences."

Moving back to his mother's house did not help, however, because she was at least as ill as he was. Looking at the furniture which had been moved from 47 York Road, he wrote to Molly: "My poor mother is not at all well and is in bed still. This illness seems to have aged her in some way, and she seems quite a little old woman with an old woman's voice. It makes me sad. It is sad also to see all our little furniture stowed away in these rooms. It is a sad queer time for us all, dear Heart. I sometimes feel inclined to sit down and wail. . . . Oh Mother of Moses I wish I could get well. I have less pain at night, I think, than I had; but I'm all queer inside still." Three days later he was still "as flat as a mangled pancake." But he forced himself to start work again on *Deirdre* for the first time since the operation. He wrote to Molly on August 24th, "I've decided to cut off the second act—you remember Jesus Christ says if the second act offend thee pluck it out; but I forget you're a heathen, and there's no use quoting Holy Scriptures to you." Five days later he wrote to Lady Gregory: "I think I'll have to cut it down to two longish acts. The middle act in Scotland is impossible."

He was beginning to live with his queer insides at least, and his doctor told him that he could ride his bicycle again. George Roberts came out to discuss the American edition of his plays, and Synge read some of his verse to him. On Sunday the 30th he went to the MacKennas' in Donnybrook for lunch. He wrote to Molly the next day, "I'm a bit bellysome today—isn't that a fine word?—as I ate a whole dish of cabbage yesterday." On Saturday, September 5th, he went in to town to see Yeats and Lady Gregory. The next day Molly was unable to come out, so he walked alone by Bray Head and amused himself by jotting down the words of some ballads he heard a street singer entertaining a crowd with.

Because Roberts wanted to publish some of his verse, Synge wrote to Yeats and sent a collection of them to him for advice. "I do not feel very sure of them; yet enough of myself has gone into them to make me sorry to destroy them, and I feel at times it would be better to print them while I am alive, than to leave them after me to go God knows where."[130] On Sunday, September 6th, he went in to town to meet Yeats, and the next day he wrote Molly that they had had a long talk about the poems. "He is thinking of putting them with Dun Emer* after all." Yeats wrote him in a few days to ask him to come to Dublin again for another talk about the poems, some of which he thought were "very fine." Synge wrote to MacKenna immediately about Yeats' reaction, and MacKenna replied, "I was sure the poems would stand the test, though why you should test 'em I know not."

* The Cuala Press, founded by Yeats' sister.

But showing them to Yeats had indeed been a test for him. He had written to Molly, "I don't know how I'll ever face showing them to Yeats, but it will have to be done, God help me."

However modest their achievement may be, the poems assembled by Yeats from Synge's papers after his death gave, as Masefield wrote of them, a direct impression of the man speaking. Most of them were written during the last three years of his life. Elizabeth Yeats suggested including the translations from European writers, which were essentially only experiments with dialect, to fill out the volume. Of the twenty-two poems seven were inspired by Molly, six dealt with incidents of Kerry peasant life and two others were written in the early nineties and are not the work of the mature writer. He argued in his preface that "before verse can be human it must learn to be brutal," and it might be said of his best poems that they embody not only humanity and brutality but also the sensitivity to death and physical decay that found expression in his plays and in his letters to Molly.

With their "unpoetic" language, their naïveté of form, Synge's poems resemble the work of an uneducated man and thus reveal their origin in his observations of Irish peasant life rather than in literary sources. They make an unusual contrast to the delicate lyrics of Joyce's *Chamber Music*, James Stephens' *Insurrections* and Yeats' *The Green Helmet*, all written in the same period. One is inclined to feel that they are at least uniquely different from the work of his contemporaries. The peculiar combination of the tragic and the grotesque in such a passage as

> Yet these are rotten—I ask their pardon—
> And we've the sun on rock and garden;
> These are rotten, so you're the Queen
> Of all are living, or have been

or

> Yet knew no more than knew those merry sins
> Had built this stack of thigh-bones, jaws and shins

has been attributed to the influence of Baudelaire. But Synge repudiated Baudelaire's morbidity in his preface to *The Tinker's Wedding*— he preferred a brand of morbidity all his own:

And so when all my little work is done
They'll say I came in eighteen-seventy-one,
And died in Dublin . . . what year will they write
For my poor passage to the stall of night?

His mother's health was steadily failing, and the suspicion that she was actually dying did not help him to forget the dull ache that reminded him of his own mortality. Molly came out on Sunday, September 27th, and they talked about the poems he was preparing for publication and about the possibilities of resuming their wedding plans. But the fear of death, which had motivated the showing of his verses to Yeats, hung over him. He asked Molly jokingly if she would come to his funeral, and her answer evoked a short poem entitled "A Question":

I asked if I got sick and died, would you
With my black funeral go walking too,
If you'd stand close to hear them talk or pray
While I'm let down in that steep bank of clay.

And, No, you said, for if you saw a crew
Of living idiots pressing round that new
Oak coffin—they alive, I dead beneath
That board—you'd rave and rend them with your teeth.

On October 2nd he handed Yeats the poems he thought finished enough for publication and wrote to Molly the next day that Yeats thought "A Question" *magnificent*. Three days later he signed a contract with Roberts. The plan was for the Cuala Press to publish a limited edition and Maunsel and Company a trade edition.

Molly was busy in a new play—*The Suburban Groove* by W. F. Casey—and getting flattering notices from all the Dublin critics. She was unable to come out to see him as often as he wished, and the prospects of staying alone with his dying mother had begun to unsettle him. Quite suddenly he made up his mind to go to Germany, and wrote to the von Eikens at Oberwerth to ask if they could take him for a few weeks. His doctor had prevented him from going to Kerry—where he would be subject to asthma again—but apparently felt that a trip to Germany would be all right. On Monday, October

5th, George Roberts came out to see him and, in the evening, Padraic Colum. The next morning he left by boat from Dún Laoghaire and arrived in London late Tuesday night, was turned away from three hotels and had to stay in a "sort of boarding house," as he described it to Molly.

The next day he had to wait until evening for a boat which would take him to Holland, and spent the afternoon sitting on a chair in Hyde Park. He wrote to Molly: "I hope this trip will set me up. I am only beginning to realize what a wreck this business has left me." He got to Coblenz the next day and wrote to Molly almost at once, saying nothing about the von Eikens or the reception he had got from his old friends. "This place is a good deal changed but very pleasant still. I have been out by the Rhine till six o'clock—it was very clear and beautiful. I hope this will make a man of me again. As soon as ever I got into the train last night I felt better, and I got on as well as possible on the journey."[131]

The next day he began a long letter to her in a small notebook and continued adding to it during the next four days, before tearing the pages out and mailing them to her. He spent most of Friday, the 9th, on the bank of the river, watching the steamers pass in the morning fog and jotting an occasional observation down. The next day he got a letter from her and wrote:

Yesterday at dinner one of the Von Eikens plumped out that Mrs. Vanston had told them I was engaged to an actress—and then they popped out their eight heads to see what I'd say. So I told them the story and now they know all about you. Of course I'd have told them in any case. The married sister and her daughter have been here for the last couple of days and when they were going away the good lady made me a long speech of congratulations and good wishes for my marriage and so on, so on, so on! So you see you aren't forgotten. All the Von Eikens are very kind —by the way it's *fraulein*, not *frau*—but, poor things, they are most of them getting old. My friend is nice still, but you needn't be uneasy. I am beginning to count the days till I can get back to you.[132]

The next day he added only a few lines to his letter, but on Monday he received a letter from Molly which "nearly wrung my poor guts out with delight," and he wrote a running account of his walk in the woods for her:

I have been wandering on for an hour, squatting down on every seat I came to (every quarter of a mile or so) to rest my poor ripped belly. The weather couldn't be better. Now I've come out of the trees into the sun on a big cliff over the Rhine and I'm sitting in front of a restaurant with a bottle of beer. . . . I think this knocking about in the woods may help me with *Deirdre* in a way. I have written no more verses since I came here. I am not alone enough for one thing and for another the confusion of images one gets travelling about does not help one to write. . . . On Saturday night a friend of the Von E's sent in a present of a great dish of oysters. They wanted me to have some, but like a wise man I didn't, glory be to God, for the family began to puke yesterday and nearly split themselves![133]

On Tuesday he went in to Coblenz to buy some books, and when he came back he sat on the bank of the river watching the people wave to him from the passing boats. "Yesterday there was woman beating a cushion, and when she saw me lying on the stones she held it up and patted it as much as to say would you like that to put under yourself? Another girl waved a bowl of soup at me."

He wrote on Friday the 16th to scold her for not having written. The next day he wrote again, furious that he had still received no letter from her. "If I do not hear by return post I will go home." He had also received a letter from some member of his family with discouraging news about his mother. He wrote to Molly: "I am very sad tonight as I have just got very bad news of my poor old mother. She is much worse I am afraid—if she does not soon get better I shall have no one in the world but you. . . . I have a lump in my throat as I am writing—she is in bed again now, too weak to read or write. Her life is little happiness to her now, and yet one cannot bear the idea of not having her with us any more. If she gets worse I will go home, perhaps, very soon. I do not like to think of her all by herself in the house."[134] But another letter from home quieted his fears about his mother, and his only problem was Molly's faithfulness in writing.

He was reading Walther von der Vogelweide, and turned a bit of him into dialect because it reminded him of himself and Molly:

I never set my two eyes on a head was so fine as your head, but I'd no way to be looking down into your heart. It's for that I was tricked out and out—that was the thanks I got for being so steady in my love. I tell you, if

I could have laid my hands on the whole set of the stars, the moon and the
sun along with it, by Christ I'd have given the lot to her. No place have
I set eyes on the like of her; she's bad to her friends, and gay and playful
to those she'd have a right to hate. I ask you can that behavior have a
good end come to it?

He also began a poem about the Minnesinger:

> Oaks and beeches, jays and thrushes
> Live as gayly by the Rhine
> Since Walter Von der Wogelweide
> Sang from Coblenz to the Main.

> But the great-great-great-great bastards
> Of high queens that Walter knew,
> Wear pot-bellies in their breeches,
> And bald heads are potted too.

He wrote to Molly on Sunday, October 25th:

I am sitting up in my little room reading Walter Von der Wogelweide
and waiting for supper. I wonder what you're at! This has been a diabolical
day—cold, raw and wet, with snow in the morning—the first bad day since
I left home. It reminded me of the speech in *The Well of the Saints*
about the Almighty God looking out on the world, bad days *etc.* I'm lonesome. It is absolutely silent up here except for an odd whiff of piano. The
man who is playing is the landlord of Oberwerth—a baron—and lives in
a big house stuck onto this one.

He was married a long time ago and had one daughter; then he got tired
of his wife, and when I was here last she was a faded poor creature who
used to go streeling about by herself. The next thing was he fell in love
with one of his farm girls and "kept" her in Coblenz. The wife heard of
it and went off to Vienna and sent for the Baron. He went to her, and
she asked him would he break off this connection. He said divel a bit and
came back here. The next day he got a telegram to say his wife had
poisoned herself. He put the girl into a convent for six months and then
married her. Now the lady baroness is going about in furs and furbelous,
and the men she used to make hay with are still working in the yard. The
baron is cut by everyone and shuts himself up and plays the piano and
composes all day. He is gray-haired now, but a fine musician. They have
three children—fine ones too.

The next day Robert Synge wired to him that his mother had died. He decided that he could not face a funeral in his present state of health and wired immediately that he could not get back in time for the funeral. He wrote to Molly: "I am trying to be cheerful again, and to think happily of my poor old mother as I know she would have wished. . . . My going home now will be very sad—I can hardly bear to think of going to Glendalough House. She was always so delighted to see me when I came back from a journey—I can't go on." Three days later his mother was buried beside her husband in Mount Jerome Cemetery. That evening the Abbey Theatre revived *The Well of the Saints* for a three-day run. Very few Dubliners realized that the dead woman mentioned in the obituary columns had never seen one of her son's plays performed in the theatre.

When Synge arrived in Dublin on Saturday, November 7th, Robert met him at the boat and went with him to Glendalough House, where Mrs. Stephens awaited them. Edward Stephens saw him the next day and noted that he looked ill and tired. Because the lease on Glendalough House still had some time to run, Synge decided to stay on alone in it except for his mother's two maids until he could make more definite plans. He bought a mourning suit and wrote to Molly:

My sister told me all about the money affairs today. I am to have £1500 share (at 5%) out of the property. That with what I have will make £110 a year, so if only my health holds we will be able to get on now. My sister says that apart from my share of things I can have all the little things I need for a house, if I take one—carpets, saucepans, linens *etc.* I will not get any money for six months. You need not repeat these particulars. The £1500 is, I think, really mine, not for my life only, so I will have that to leave you. Otherwise I should have had to save closely. If the Abbey breaks now we will have enough to live quite comfortably in Dundrum or somewhere in the country.

He wrote again the same day:

As you are not here I feel as if I ought to keep writing to you all the time, though tonight I cannot write all that I am feeling. People like Yeats who sneer at old fashioned goodness and steadiness in women seem to want to rob the world of what is most sacred in it. I cannot tell you how unspeakably sacred her memory seems to me. There is nothing in the world better or nobler than a single-hearted wife and mother. I wish you had known her better. . . . It makes me rage when I think of the people who go on as if art and literature and writing were the first things in the world. There is nothing so great and sacred as what is most simple in life.

Under the loneliness of his loss he was beginning to feel some regrets for the differences he had had with his mother and for the sorrow his career as a writer had brought to her. Identifying himself with the stern and unyielding ethic which she had preached and he had rejected made him feel that he was being a good son, if somewhat belatedly.

When Molly came out to Glendalough House they were alone except for the two servants. He wanted desperately to finish *Deirdre* now, but often during the next two months, as his health gradually waned, he had to give up work on it in despair. Molly read passages aloud for him in the dining room of the house, but the legend that she acted out scenes in his hospital room later is not true. The Stephenses did not forget him living alone next door and had him in for meals frequently. The two Stephens boys visited him often. Edward, who was then an undergraduate at Trinity College, sometimes "found him in the little front room upstairs, sometimes in the dining room, where he had hung his portrait by Paterson over the chimney piece. He had begun to talk to me more about literature than he used in earlier years." They discussed Yeats' poems, and Synge told of hearing Frank Fay recite "The Ballad of Father Gilligan" to an audience of Irish workers in Manchester, many of whom wept upon hearing it.

He also worked at his poems and was thinking of a preface to be published with them. He jotted down critical notes in his notebook, and at the end of November began to draft the preface which was published with the poems after his death. One of the poems written now which was not included in the published selection shows the frame of mind he was in:

> I read about the Blaskets and Dunquin,
> The Wicklow towns and fair days I've been in.
> I read of Galway, Mayo, Aranmore,
> And men with kelp along a wintry shore.
> Then I remembered that "I" was I,
> And I'd a filthy job—to waste and die.

But he was not always gloomy. He began a little skit in which his old enemies were to be lampooned. It was called "Lucifer and the Lost Soul," and begins:

Lucifer. You were a fine lad one time.
Lost Soul. I was, your reverence.
Lucifer. And what brought you to this place?
Lost Soul. The way of the world, your reverence.
Lucifer. Bad company?
Lost Soul. The worst. In Maynooth* I was with all nice little priests, talking ever and always of the deadly merits. I run from that.
Lucifer. It was drink then maybe?
Lost Soul. It was, your reverence—a pint of warmed milk I got every night from my mother. I run from that too.
Lucifer. And from that you went racing?
Lost Soul. I did not, your reverence. I went writing pages for *The Catholic Young Man.*
Lucifer. What kind were your pages?
Lost Soul. They were mighty flat, your reverence.
Lucifer. That's a sin [writes] putting out pages could make men swear oaths. Go on.

But the dull ache in his stomach never ceased, and MacKenna wrote to him:

Please don't say anything more about "guts." I begin to see you as a long twisty bowel, slimy and gray with a sort of hideous flaming eye jutting out of one end of it. I would rather think of you as a sort of Stevenson sick man in a velvet coat with long languid face and a winning sad smile such as grows in little girls story books. And there's the tip— why not be a Stevenson? Be sick to your heart's content but make your books and jokes and mock at the devil. You have your brain back now, that you tell me sat grinning at you from a distance on the bedpost at Elpis. I feel very sure that, accomodating yourself to your iller health, you will do *Playboys* and *Deirdres* and other things galore for us. Of course I see the weary worry of it all as regards your marriage, and for herself too it must be tragic, the doubt, the not-knowing what is to be.

He gave MacKenna's advice a try. He wrote to Molly on November 24th, "I have very nearly got a full version now of the second act of *Deirdre.*" His book of poems also was in his mind. Elizabeth Yeats

* The leading Roman Catholic seminary in Ireland.

wrote to him that she planned to begin setting up the volume in a week or so, but she preferred not to include "Danny" and "The Curse" because one was too violent and the other too coarse. He did not object—he had sent some of them to *The Nation* and they had come back as "not quite suitable," so he was prepared to make some concessions.

On November 29th Molly left with the company for a week's performances in Belfast. When she wrote to him that she planned to stop off in Balbriggan on her way back to Dublin with Dossie Wright's people, he was unhappy, but his protest had lost some of its bite. When she returned they went to visit the MacKennas. They were happy together but no longer spoke of the marriage which had been interrupted by his operation. They had delayed so long that it seemed normal to go on as in the days when his mother had to be reckoned with.

He continued to drive himself to work on his play. He decided to call it *Deirdre of the Sorrows,* and wrote to Molly on December 22nd: "I've pretty nearly gone on to the end of *Deirdre* and cut it down a little. It is delicate work—a scene is so easily spoiled. I am anxious to hear you read it to me." But it was hard work, and he complained constantly about his pain. She must have become very angry about his complaints, because he wrote to her the day before Christmas: "I feel humiliated that I showed you so much of my weakness and emotion yesterday. I will not trouble you any more with complaints about my health—you have taught me that I should not—but I think I owe it to myself to let you know that if I am so 'self-pitiful' I have some reason to be so, as Dr. Parsons's report of my health, though uncertain, was much more unsatisfactory than I thought it well to tell you. I only tell you now because I am unable to bear the thought that you should think of me with the contempt I saw in your face yesterday."[135] She forgave him, and they went to the Christmas Eve carol services in St. Patrick's Cathedral.

The stomach ache got worse. Dr. Parsons sent him to the surgeon again, who recommended that he take castor oil. He wrote to Molly on January 12th: "I'm not cured yet, so I'll have to give myself more doses. God help me. However, if that will set me right, then may Heaven's eternal fragrance fall on castor oil. I wonder if you can follow all this. I've been thinking about you a great deal with your little socks for me, and all your little attentions and I'm ready to go down on my knees to your shadow if I met it in a dry place. I think I'm drunk with castor oil." A few days later he was given a new medicine called Fermolactive. Edward Stephens found him "sitting in the big arm chair by the fire with an earthenware vessel near him in the fender. He explained that it contained a concoction made from sour milk and that he had been advised by Sir Charles Ball to take this regularly, because it contained organisms that would tend to fight the poison in what remained of the tumor and assist in its drying up. The organisms, he said, developed best when the vessel was warm and that was why he kept it in the fender."

But in addition to the stomach pains his general health was also beginning to decline. His brother Robert noted that his nights were disturbed and feverish. The Stephenses as well as Molly were worried about him alone in the house except for the servants, and they were all aware by this time that his energy was slowly seeping out of his sturdy body. Dr. Parsons called to see him on January 30th and made the decision to put him back into Elpis again for observation. The end was in sight, but whether Robert and the Stephenses who knew the truth ever told him or Molly is very unlikely. He wrote Molly a short note on February 1st telling her he was entering Elpis the next morning and asking her to get him *The Mill on the Floss* or *Silas Marner*. Edward Stephens helped him get ready for the trip to the hospital.

I found him in the dining room where there was a fire. If I remember rightly he was stuffing books into the lower part of his book case, which stood between the window and the chimney piece. He arranged things about the room silently, then he said that he would like to show me where he had left his papers. We went up to his bedroom. He opened the old painted wardrobe and showed me where he kept his manuscripts and letters. Every thing we went through under the shadow of his unspoken belief that he would not handle them again. I went about with an awed feeling, which I failed to interpret in the conscious knowledge that he could not recover.

Robert Synge, who accompanied him to Elpis the next morning and who saw him on Wednesday and on Friday, wrote in his diary on

Saturday that the doctors had decided not to operate. Molly came to
see him every day, and Harry Stephens came to make out his will on
Saturday, February 13th. To Molly he left a lifetime annuity of £80,
to be reduced to £52 if she married. The rest of his property and the
income from his plays and books he left to his nephews Edward
Stephens and Hutchinson Synge "for their books, education and advancement." His spirit was still strong, and he had even brought the
MS of *Deirdre* with him in the hope that he would feel well enough to
work on it. But his strength continued to ebb, and when Molly left
with the company on February 14th for a week's engagement in Manchester he was so weak that he knew he would not be able to write
her and asked his sister to keep her informed of his condition. Mrs.
Stephens wrote to Molly on the 17th and again on the 19th, "I went
in to see John today and found him a little better. He was allowed to
sit by the fire for a short time yesterday evening."

When Molly returned with the company on the 22nd and went to
see him immediately, she could see that his grip on things was weaker.
Nobody had told her that it was only a matter of a short time now,
and she had continued to act every night. The strain of her daily
visits to the hospital was beginning to tell on her health as well as
on her performances, and everyone in the company could see what
she was going through. On the 25th Yeats visited him and wrote in
his diary the next day: "If he dies it will set me wondering whether
he could have lived if he had not had his long bitter misunderstanding
with the wreckage of young Ireland. . . . In one thing he and Lady
Gregory are the strongest souls I have ever known. He and she alike
have never for even an instant spoken to me the thoughts of their in-
feriors as their own thoughts. . . . Both Synge and Lady Gregory
isolate themselves, Synge instinctively and Lady Gregory consciously,
from all contagious opinions of poorer minds."[136]

Meanwhile Robert Synge had entered Elpis, under Sir Charles
Ball's care, for some minor surgery. When he was released on March
15th, he brought home with him the manuscripts of *Deirdre of the
Sorrows* which Synge had not been able to touch.* On March 21st
Robert was able to go and see him again and noted in his diary that

---

* *Deirdre of the Sorrows*, with Molly playing the leading role, was performed
at the Abbey Theatre on January 13, 1910. The acting text was assembled from
Synge's MSS by Yeats, Lady Gregory and Molly.

John was rather worse. Molly told Edward Stephens afterwards that she had gone in a frenzy of despair to more than one priest seeking to have a mass offered for Synge's recovery. "The priests, she said, had asked how she was seeking to have a mass offered for a Protestant. She had been distraught and incoherent. Nothing had come of her mission."

Edward Stephens went to see him on the 23rd and took a bottle of champagne with him that Robert had bought the day before, apparently at Synge's request. Edward wrote:

A nurse on the landing at Elpis, when she saw me going to the room where John had been, said, "Mr. Synge is in here," and took me into a sunny back room from which there was a view across house tops to the hills. . . . At first he was too weak to talk, but the nurse screwed the tap into the cork of the bottle I had brought and gave him some champagne, and then he seemed a little brighter. He asked me whether I had heard any blackbirds singing yet. I said that I had heard thrushes, but had not heard any blackbirds. For a few minutes I chatted with him about home and college interests and left without understanding that I would not see him again.

The next morning the Stephenses were notified by a telegram from one of the nurses reading "All is over." He had died at five-thirty in the morning. The next day Yeats and Henderson came out to Glena-geary to ask permission to have a death mask made, but Robert Synge refused them. Burial was to be in the family plot in Mount Jerome, and the only service was to be held in the cemetery. Only the family and close friends of the family rode behind the coffin from Dún Laoghaire. When the cortege reached the gate of the cemetery they were met by members of the company and others who joined the procession that followed the coffin up the main avenue to the chapel and, after a short service, to the open grave. Edward Stephens wrote: "As the words of commitment were said, I noticed there the people John had known, divided as they had always been in his life time, into separate groups. His relations were together in black, carrying bowler hats and, a little apart, the people among whom he had worked. I knew few of them even by appearance, but I can remember seeing Sara Allgood and watching Padraic Colum's hair blowing in the wind."

Synge once wrote in his notebook that originality was not enough unless it had the characteristic of a particular time and locality and the life that was in it. He had had the good fortune to live in an Ireland where even men of mediocre talent were fired by the enthusiasms of the day to write better than they were able to. But the particular life Synge was born into did not fire anyone's enthusiasm. Like others of their class, the Synges could only look with alarm at the new Ireland coming to life. Instead of meeting it halfway, they withdrew even further into the garrison and sent sons like Robert and Samuel Synge to the colonies to make up for the fortunes lost at home or to labour among the heathen. The sons who remained, like Edward Synge, clung to what was left of the heritage. There were Big Houses still and tenants to evict. Still other sons who chose to go it alone could expend their energies in the study of music, natural history, antiquities or theosophy. Those with an urge for self-expression had the arts. For some young men of the Ascendancy, like Percy French who wrote entertainments for his own class in Irish peasant dialect and said, "I was born a boy and remained one," this was harmless enough. But others did not remain boys. Life led them outside the stockade. It led Synge to a fisherman's cottage in the Aran Islands.

To some Irish people he was—and still is—a suspicious visitor bearing dubious gifts from the Big House, and this explains why his short career was so tempestuous. Yeats wrote, "Synge is invaluable to us because he has that kind of intense, narrow personality which necessarily raises the whole issue." Which is to say that his work more than that of any of his contemporaries comes closer to achieving the assimilation of the Gaelic past which the Irish Renaissance stood for. Whether he was dramatizing a tragic fact or incident of violence in contemporary Irish life, exploring the applications of ancient folk tale or heroic myth, or merely describing in unpretentious language the daily life of the tinker, the farmer or the fisherman, he was interpreting the traditional life of Ireland. It is to him more than to any other Irishman writing in English that we go for an insight into this life.

Notes

Unless otherwise identified, all quotations in the text are from unpublished papers in the possession of the Synge estate.

[1] W. E. H. Lecky, *A History of England in the Eighteenth Century* (New York, 1879), II, 333-334.

[2] "Letters Patent (34 George III) were issued under the Great Seal, which enacted that Roman Catholics can enter Trinity College and take the degree of the University." The Dublin University Calendar 1912–1913.

[3] "What Is Popular Poetry," *Essays* (London, 1924), p. 3.

[4] *The Works of John M. Synge* (Dublin, 1910), IV, 53. Hereafter referred to as *Works*.

[5] "The Old and New in Ireland," *The Academy and Literature*, Sept. 6, 1902, p. 238.

[6] Donal O'Sullivan, *Irish Folk Music and Song*, Irish Life and Culture Series (Dublin, 1952), pp. 25 ff.

[7] *The Life and Labours in Art and Archaeology of George Petrie* (London, 1868), p. 49.

[8] *Ibid.*, p. 58.

[9] "What Is Popular Poetry," *Essays*, p. 3.

[10] *Works*, IV, 53.

[11] *Ibid.*, p. 19.

[12] C. H. H., "John Synge as I Knew Him," *The Irish Statesman*, July 5, 1924, p. 534.

[13] *Ibid.*, p. 532.

[14] *Ibid.*

[15] *Ibid.*, p. 534.

[16] Philadelphia, 1879, p. 12.

[17] "John M. Synge," *The Contemporary Review*, April, 1911, p. 471.

[18] *The Well of the Saints* (London, 1905), p. v-vii.

[19] *A Servant of the Queen* (London, 1938), p. 170.

[20] "J. M. Synge and the Ireland of His Time," *Essays*, p. 395.

[21] "Anatole Le Braz. A Breton Writer," *The Daily Express* (Dublin), January 28, 1899, p. 3.

[22] *Journal and Letters of Stephen MacKenna*, edited with a memoir by E. R. Dodds (London, 1936), p. 14.

[23] *Ibid.*, pp. 84-85.

[24] Letter to *The Irish Statesman*, Nov. 3, 1928, p. 169. Quoted in *Journal and Letters of Stephen MacKenna*, p. 11.

[25] *Works*, IV, 27.

[26] Letter to Maurice Bourgeois, *John Millington Synge and the Irish Theatre* (London, 1913), p. 34, fn. 3.

[27] Note in Yeats' hand in the possession of Mr. J. A. Healy.

[28] *The Letters of W. B. Yeats*, ed. Allan Wade (New York, 1955), p. 268.

[29] *Cities and Sea-Coasts and Islands* (London, 1918), p. 307.

[30] Unpublished letter to Mr. Leon Brodzky (Mr. Spencer Brodney), Dec. 12, 1907, now in the library of Trinity College, Dublin.

[31] A. G. Van Hamel, "On Anglo-Irish Syntax," *Englische Studien*, XLV (1912), 274.

[32] *Our Irish Theatre* (New York, 1913), p. 120.

[33] *Works*, III, 88.

[34] *Ibid.*

[35] "Geography of an Irish Oath," *Traits and Stories of the Irish Peasantry* (London, 1869), II, 1.

[36] *An Gaoth Aniar* (Dublin, 1920), p. 93-98.

[37] W. B. Yeats, *Autobiographies* (New York, 1927), p. 425, and Arthur Symons, *Cities and Sea-Coasts and Islands*, pp. 307 ff.

[38] "In a cell, in the walls of this fort [Dún Conor], a man named Mailly, who had accidentally killed his father in a fit of passion, hid for two months. He was captured by the police, but escaped and hid in the fort again, and at last was taken out of the isle by night, and escaped to America." *Illustrated Guide to the Northern, Western, and Southern Islands and Coast of Ireland*, Antiquarian Handbook Series, No. VI (Dublin, 1905), p. 87.

[39] "A View of the State of Ireland," *Ireland Under Elizabeth and James the First*, ed. Henry Morley (London, 1890), p. 94.

[40] *Works*, III, 52.

[41] *W. B. Yeats* (New York, 1943), p. 144.

[42] *Inishfallen, Fare Thee Well* (London, 1949), p. 154.

[43] Quoted in Lady Gregory's *Our Irish Theatre*, pp. 8-9.

[44] *Official Guide, Dublin* (Dublin, n.d.), p. 96.

[45] *Hail and Farewell: Ave* (New York, 1923), p. 169.

[46] Sister Marie-Thérèse Courtney, *Edward Martyn and the Irish Theatre* (New York, 1956), p. 41.

[47] *Works*, IV, 6.

[48] *Hail and Farewell: Vale* (New York, 1923), p. 156.

[49] *The Letters of W. B. Yeats*, ed. Allan Wade, p. 314.

[50] *Dramatis Personae*, Dublin, 1935. Quoted in Joseph Hone's *W. B. Yeats*, p. 170.

[51] *The Saturday Review*, May 13, 1899.

[52] *The Letters of W. B. Yeats*, ed. Allan Wade, p. 279-280.

[53] *Works*, III, 101, 102, 116, 143, 144.

[54] *Aid to the Immortality of Certain Persons in Ireland, Charitably Administered by Susan L. Mitchell*, Dublin, 1908.

[55] Letter to *The Freeman's Journal*, March 20, 1900, *The Letters of W. B. Yeats*, ed. Allan Wade, p. 336.

[56] Letter to *The Daily Express*, April 3, 1900, *The Letters of W. B. Yeats*, ed. Allan Wade, p. 338.

[57] *The Letters of W. B. Yeats*, ed. Allan Wade, p. 338.

[58] *Prose, Poems and Parodies of Percy French*, ed. Mrs. De Burgh Daly (Dublin, 1941), p. 55.

[59] *Works*, III, 147.

[60] *Ibid.*, p. 151.

[61] *Ibid.*, p. 166.

[62] *The History of Ireland by Geoffrey Keating D.D.* (London, Irish Texts Society, 1902), I, 141.

[63] *Synge and the Ireland of His Time* (Dublin, 1911), p. 11.

[64] *Our Irish Theatre*, p. 125.

[65] *Works*, III, 199.

[66] *Ibid.*, p. 222.

[67] *Ave*, pp. 264 ff.

[68] XXVI (April-June, 1951), 1-41.

[69] *Hail and Farewell: Salve* (New York, 1923), p. 93.

[70] Letter to *The Academy and Literature*, May 16, 1903.

[71] Maurice Bourgeois, *John Millington Synge and the Irish Theatre*, p. 35.

[72] *Hail and Farewell: Vale*, p. 167.

[73] Preface to *The Playboy of the Western World*, *Works*, II, 4-5.

[74] "The Oppression of the Hills," *The Manchester Guardian*, Feb. 15, 1905, p. 12, and "The Vagrants of Wicklow," *The Shanachie*, Autumn, 1906, pp. 93-99.

[75] *Samhain*, October, 1902, p. 4.

[76] An interview reported in *The Sun* (New York), Dec. 10, 1911, and quoted by Bourgeois, *op. cit.*, p. 225, fn. 2. See also *Our Irish Theatre*, p. 124. "When my *Cuchulain of Muirthemne* came out, he said to Mr. Yeats he had been amazed to find in it the dialect he had been trying to master. He wrote to me: 'Your *Cuchulain* is part of my daily bread.'"

[77] *The Academy and Literature*, Sept. 6, 1902, p. 239.

[78] *The Letters of W. B. Yeats*, ed. Allan Wade, p. 379.

[79] W. G. Fay and Catherine Carswell, *The Fays of the Abbey Theatre* (New York, 1935), p. 125.

[80] *Our Irish Theatre*, p. 125.

[81] "John M. Synge," *The Contemporary Review*, April, 1911, pp. 470-471.

[82] Letter to Harriet Weaver, Nov. 8, 1916, *James Joyce. Letters*, ed. Stuart Gilbert (New York, 1957), p. 98.

[83] *The Splendid Years* (Dublin, 1955), pp. 40-41.

[84] *Works*, IV, 110 ff.

[85] See Bourgeois, p. 193, fn. 1.

[86] *Annals of the Kingdom of Ireland by the Four Masters*, ed. John O'Donovan (Dublin, 1856), pp. 593-597. The reference is to Nial Glundubh, High King of Ireland 916–919. I am grateful to Mr. Pádraig O'Broin for this reference and translation and to Professor Charles Dunn for citations of numerous other uses of the phrase in early Irish texts.

[87] *Synge and the Ireland of His Time* (Dublin, 1911), p. 11.

[88] See Stith Thompson, *Motif-Index of Folk Literature* (Bloomington and Helsinki, 1932).

[89] See David H. Greene, "The Shadow of the Glen and the Widow of Ephesus," *Publications of the Modern Language Association*, LXII (March, 1947), 233-238.

[90] The author of *The Midnight Court* is Brian Merriman. For Frank O'Connor's English translation see David H. Greene, ed., *An Anthology of Irish Literature* (New York, The Modern Library, 1954), pp. 252 ff. The author of "The Great Hunger" is Patrick Kavanagh. See *A Soul for Sale and Other Poems* (London, 1947), pp. 31 ff.

[91] "Some months before his death Mr. Synge got the idea that it was consumption he had and he would not see Molly. This was, of course, the greatest pain to her, but he was at last convinced by the doctors that there was no danger to her." Unpublished letter to John Quinn, May 31, 1909, in the New York Public Library.

[92] *The Letters of W. B. Yeats*, ed. Allan Wade, pp. 437-438.

[93] *Ibid.*, p. 436.

[94] *Ireland's Literary Renaissance* (New York, 1916), p. 214.

[95] Unpublished letter to W. G. Fay, undated, in the possession of Mr. Gerard Fay.

[96] *The Fays of the Abbey Theatre*, pp. 167-168.

[97] *The Letters of W. B. Yeats*, ed. Allan Wade, p. 448.

[98] *Ibid.*, pp. 447-448.

[99] *Ibid.*, p. 447.

[100] *The Fays of the Abbey Theatre*, p. 168.

[101] London, 1906, II, 311.

[102] "Letters of John Millington Synge," *The Yale Review* XIII (July, 1924), 690-709.

[103] *The Letters of W. B. Yeats*, ed. Allan Wade, p. 461.

[104] *Ibid.*

[105] Unpublished letter, dated Sept. 27, 1905, in the possession of Mrs. W. B. Yeats.

[106] Unpublished letter, dated Sept. 26, 1905, in the possession of Mrs. W. B. Yeats.

[107] Unpublished letter, dated Sept. 25, 1905, in the possession of Mrs. W. B. Yeats.

[108] Maire Nic Shiublaigh, *The Splendid Years*, pp. 72-73.

[109] *Ibid.*, p. 77.

[110] *Dialogues of Alfred North Whitehead, as Recorded by Lucien Price* (Boston, 1954), p. 107.

[111] Holloway's diary is in the National Library, Dublin.

[112] Unpublished letter in the possession of Miss Pegeen Mair.

[113] Unpublished letter, dated July 3, 1906, in the possession of Mrs. W. B. Yeats.

[114] *Fate of the Children of Uisneach*, published for the society for the Preservation of the Irish Language, Dublin, 1898, from a manuscript written by Andrew MacCurtin of Corcomroe, Co. Clare, in 1740.

[115] Unpublished letter, dated Jan. 21, 1907, in the possession of Mrs. W. B. Yeats.

[116] *Our Irish Theatre*, p. 133.

[117] *The Fays of the Abbey Theatre*, p. 213.

[118] "Memories of Yeats," *The Saturday Review of Literature*, XIX (Feb. 25, 1939), 4.

[119] Unpublished letter, dated March 8, 1907, in the possession of Mr. Gerard Fay.

[120] Unpublished manuscript in the possession of Miss Pegeen Mair.

[121] Unpublished letter, dated May 26, 1907, in the possession of Miss Pegeen Mair.

[122] Quoted in Joseph Hone's *W. B. Yeats*, pp. 235-236.

[123] *A Servant of the Queen*, p. 333.

[124] Unpublished letter, dated Sept. 5, 1907, in the New York Public Library.

[125] Unpublished letter, dated Sept. 13, 1907, in the possession of Miss Pegeen Mair.

[126] Unpublished manuscript in the possession of Mr. Gerard Fay.

[127] *The Fays of the Abbey Theatre*, p. 231.

[128] Yeats published this letter in *Synge and the Ireland of His Time*. It was dated May 4, 1907, but it was not actually delivered to Yeats until after Synge's death a year later, when it was discovered among Synge's papers.

[129] Unpublished letter, dated June 16, 1908, in the New York Public Library.

[130] Yeats published this letter in his introduction to *Poems and Translations by John M. Synge*, Dublin, Cuala Press, 1909.

[131] Unpublished letter, dated Oct. 8, 1908, in the possession of Miss Pegeen Mair.

[132] Unpublished letter in the possession of Miss Pegeen Mair.

[133] Unpublished letter in the possession of Miss Pegeen Mair.

[134] Unpublished letter, dated Oct. 20, 1908, in the possession of Miss Pegeen Mair.

[135] Unpublished letter in the possession of Miss Pegeen Mair.

[136] Joseph Hone, *W. B. Yeats*, pp. 243-244.

A List of the Published Writings of J. M. Synge

BOOKS

In the Shadow of the Glen, New York, 1904. A limited edition published by John Quinn simultaneously with the publication of the play in *Samhain*. See below.

The Shadow of the Glen and Riders to the Sea, London, Elkin Mathews, 1905. *Riders to the Sea* had previously appeared in *Samhain*. See below.

The Well of the Saints, London, A. H. Bullen, 1905. A limited edition was published simultaneously in New York by John Quinn.

The Playboy of the Western World, Dublin, Maunsel and Co., 1907. A theatre edition, which omitted Synge's preface and certain passages from the text of the play, was issued immediately after the appearance of the first edition. A limited number of copies of the second act only was published simultaneously in New York for copyright purposes by John Quinn.

The Aran Islands, London, Elkin Mathews, and Dublin, Maunsel and Co., 1907. Illustrated by Jack Yeats. A large-paper edition was issued simultaneously.

The Tinker's Wedding, Dublin, Maunsel and Co., 1908.

Poems and Translations, Dublin, Cuala Press, 1909. A limited edition was published simultaneously in New York by John Quinn.

Deirdre of the Sorrows, Dublin, Cuala Press, 1910. A limited edition was published simultaneously in New York by John Quinn.

The Works of John M. Synge, Dublin, Maunsel and Co., 1910.

Volume I In the Shadow of the Glen, Riders to the Sea, The Tinker's Wedding, The Well of the Saints.

    II The Playboy of the Western World, Deirdre of the Sorrows, Poems, Translations from Petrarch, Translations from Villon and Others.

    III The Aran Islands.

    IV In Wicklow (The Vagrants of Wicklow, The Oppression of the Hills, On the Road, The People of the Glens, At a Wicklow Fair, A Landlord's Garden in County Wicklow, Glencree), In West Kerry, In the Congested Districts, Under Ether.

This is the most satisfactory edition of Synge's collected works. *Plays by John M. Synge*, London, Allen and Unwin, 1932, contains extracts from Synge's notebooks and one of his letters which have not been published elsewhere.

CONTRIBUTIONS TO PERIODICALS

The Academy and Literature (London)

"The Old and New in Ireland," September 6, 1902, pp. 238-239.

"The Winged Destiny," November 12, 1904, p. 455. A review of Fiona Macleod's *The Winged Destiny.*

The Daily Express (Dublin)

"La Sagesse et la Destinée," December 17, 1898, p. 3. A review of Maurice Maeterlinck's *La Sagesse et la Destinée.*

"Anatole Le Braz. A Breton Writer," January 28, 1899, p. 3.

L'Européen (Paris)

"La Vieille Littérature Irlandaise," March 15, 1902, p. 11.

"Le Mouvement Intellectuel Irlandais," May 31, 1902, p. 12.

The Freeman's Journal (Dublin)

"A Celtic Theatre," March 22, 1900, p. 4.

The Gael (New York)

"The Last Fortress of the Celt," April, 1901, p. 109.

"An Autumn Night in the Hills," April, 1903, p. 117.

"A Dream of Inishmaan," March, 1904, p. 97. Reprinted from *The Green Sheaf.* See below.

The Green Sheaf (London)

"A Dream on Inishmaan," No. 2, 1903, pp. 8-9. Reprinted in *The Gael* under the title "A Dream of Inishmaan." See above.

The Irish Times (Dublin)

A letter on the subject of *The Playboy of the Western World,* January 31, 1907.

Kottabos (Trinity College, Dublin)

"Glen Cullen," Hilary Term, 1893, p. 103. A sonnet.

The Manchester Guardian

"An Impression of Aran," January 24, 1905, p. 12.

"The Oppression of the Hills," February 15, 1905, p. 12.

"In the Congested Districts." This was a series of twelve articles, illustrated by Jack Yeats, describing the living conditions of Irish peasants in the impoverished districts of County Galway and County Mayo.

"From Galway to Gorumna," June 10, 1905.

"Between the Bays of Carraroe," June 14, 1905.

"Among the Relief Workers," June 17, 1905.

"The Ferryman of Dinish Island," June 21, 1905.

"The Kelp Makers," June 24, 1905.

"The Boat Builders," June 28, 1905.

"The Homes of the Harvestmen," July 1, 1905.

"The Smaller Peasant Proprietors," July 5, 1905.

"Erris," July 8, 1905.

"The Inner Lands of Mayo," July 19, 1905.

"The Small Town," July 22, 1905.

"Possible Remedies," July 26, 1905.

The Manchester Guardian (continued)

"A Translation of Irish Romance," March 6, 1906, p. 5. A review of A. H. Leahy's *Heroic Romances of Ireland*.

"The Fair Hills of Ireland," November 16, 1906, p. 5. A review of Stephen Gwynn's *The Fair Hills of Ireland*.

"At a Wicklow Fair. The Place and the People," May 9, 1907, p. 12.

"A Landlord's Garden in County Wicklow," July 1, 1907, p. 12.

"Good Pictures in Dublin. The New Municipal Gallery," January 24, 1908, p. 12.

"In Wicklow. On the Road," December 10, 1908, p. 14.

The New Ireland Review (Dublin)

"A Story from Inishmaan," X (November, 1898), 153-156.

Samhain (Dublin)

"Riders to the Sea," October, 1903, pp. 25-33. The full text of the play.

"In the Shadow of the Glen," December, 1904, pp. 34-44. The full text of the play.

The Shanachie (Dublin)

"The Vagrants of Wicklow," No. 2, Autumn, 1906, pp. 93-98.

"The People of the Glens," No. 3, Spring, 1907, pp. 39-47.

"In West Kerry," No. 4, Summer, 1907, pp. 61-70.

"In West Kerry. The Blasket Islands," No. 5, Autumn, 1907, pp. 138-150.

"In West Kerry. To Puck Fair," No. 6, Winter, 1907, pp. 233-243.

The Speaker (London)

"The Poems of Geoffrey Keating," December 8, 1900, p. 245. A review of *Danta Amhrain is Caointe Sheathruin Ceitinn*, ed. Rev. J. C. MacErlean, S.J.

"An Epic of Ulster," June 7, 1902, pp. 284-285. A review of Lady Gregory's *Cuchulain of Muirthemne*.

"Irish Fairy Stories," June 21, 1902, p. 340. A review of Seumas MacManus' *Donegal Fairy Stories*.

"An Irish Historian," September 6, 1902, pp. 605-606. A review of *Foras Feasa Ar Eirinn. The History of Ireland* by Geoffrey Keating, ed. David Comyn.

"Loti and Huysmans," April 18, 1903, pp. 57-58. A review of Pierre Loti's *L'Inde* (*sans les Anglais*), Anatole France's *Monsieur Bergeret à Paris* and J. K. Huysmans' *L'Oblat*.

"Celtic Mythology," April 2, 1904, pp. 17-18. A review of H. D'Arbois de Jubainville's *The Irish Mythological Cycle and Celtic Mythology*, translated by R. I. Best.

The United Irishman (Dublin)

A letter on the subject of *In the Shadow of the Glen*, February 11, 1905, p. 1.

Index